Certification Study Companion Series

The Apress Certification Study Companion Series offers guidance and hands-on practice to support technical and business professionals who are studying for an exam in the pursuit of an industry certification. Professionals worldwide seek to achieve certifications in order to advance in a career role, reinforce knowledge in a specific discipline, or to apply for or change jobs. This series focuses on the most widely taken certification exams in a given field. It is designed to be user friendly, tracking to topics as they appear in a given exam. Authors for this series are experts and instructors who not only possess a deep understanding of the content, but also have experience teaching the key concepts that support readers in the practical application of the skills learned in their day-to-day roles.

More information about this series at https://link.springer.com/bookseries/17100

Microsoft Power BI Data Analyst Certification Companion

Preparation for Exam PL-300

Jessica Jolly

Apress®

Microsoft Power BI Data Analyst Certification Companion: Preparation for Exam PL-300

Jessica Jolly
Evanston, IL, USA

ISBN-13 (pbk): 978-1-4842-9012-5   ISBN-13 (electronic): 978-1-4842-9013-2
https://doi.org/10.1007/978-1-4842-9013-2

Managing Director, Apress Media LLC: Welmoed Spahr
Acquisitions Editor: Jonathan Gennick
Development Editor: Laura Berendson
Coordinating Editor: Jill Balzano

Cover designed by eStudioCalamar

Distributed to the book trade worldwide by Springer Science+Business Media New York, 1 New York Plaza, Suite 4600, New York, NY 10004-1562, USA. Phone 1-800-SPRINGER, fax (201) 348-4505, e-mail orders-ny@springer-sbm.com, or visit www.springeronline.com. Apress Media, LLC is a California LLC and the sole member (owner) is Springer Science + Business Media Finance Inc (SSBM Finance Inc). SSBM Finance Inc is a **Delaware** corporation.

For information on translations, please e-mail booktranslations@springernature.com; for reprint, paperback, or audio rights, please e-mail bookpermissions@springernature.com.

Apress titles may be purchased in bulk for academic, corporate, or promotional use. eBook versions and licenses are also available for most titles. For more information, reference our Print and eBook Bulk Sales web page at http://www.apress.com/bulk-sales.

Any source code or other supplementary material referenced by the author in this book is available to readers on GitHub via the book's product page, located at www.apress.com/. For more detailed information, please visit http://www.apress.com/source-code.

Printed on acid-free paper

This book is dedicated to my husband who has always supported me in my endeavors.

Table of Contents

About the Author

 **Jessica Jolly** is a Microsoft Certified Trainer (MCT) who helps businesses, nonprofits, and individuals improve their business intelligence skills, bit by byte. She runs her own business, ALT-Enter, LLC. Before her reinvention as an entrepreneur (after 50!), she worked for Unilever, a global consumer products company, for 27 years, in a variety of managerial roles. Her business practice focuses on data visualization tools, specifically Microsoft's Power BI platform. She is living proof that you could cry through every math class you ever had and still fashion a career that focuses on data, charts, visuals, and code. When she is not training other adults, she is knitting and quilting (a refuge from all of the technology!), reading about the Civil War, swimming, gardening, biking, hiking, and canoeing.

About the Technical Reviewer

Ginger Grant is a Data Platform MVP who provides consulting services in advanced analytic solutions, including machine learning, data warehousing, and Power BI. She is an author of articles and books and at DesertIsleSQL.com and uses her MCT to provide data platform training in topics such as Azure Synapse Analytics, Python, and Azure Machine Learning.

Acknowledgments

I would like to thank Ginger Grant, my technical editor, for her kindness when correcting my errors. It takes tact and empathy to tell someone they are wrong, and she has both in spades.

Introduction

I cannot honestly say that I have always wanted to write a book. What I can say is that I have relied on books written by others throughout my learning journey with Power BI. Call me "old-school," but having the physical document available to write notes on, refer to, and reread helps me master a concept, technique, or idea. When Apress approached me with the idea of writing a book about the PL-300, I was excited and nervous. Excited because it would give me a chance to "pay it forward"—to help others who want to pass the PL-300 and, more importantly, become skilled Power BI practitioners. Nervous because I worried that I wouldn't be able to write cogently and succinctly about all the topics covered by the PL-300.

In the process of writing, I had to research some topics further, because I realized that I didn't fully understand them. I had to think deeply about each topic to come up with simple, clear language to explain complex elements. In other words, I had to really ensure that I understood each topic before I could write about it. This process has made me a better teacher and a better practitioner. Because teaching is my priority, I really hope that this book will reach folks who may feel intimidated by Power BI. I hope it will empower you, dear reader, to tackle the PL-300 exam. Even more importantly, I hope the book will encourage you to pick up other books written by other Power BI professionals. Apress publishes many of these titles, and they are all excellent.

Finally, let me share with you my personal mantra: #showup. Do not be afraid to take the exam; so what if you fail? Failure is integral to learning. Do not be afraid to speak at a conference; there are always folks who know less than you do and folks who know more than you do. Do not be afraid to become active in the Power BI community. We are a very welcoming, inclusive group of people who want everyone to succeed, and that includes you!

PART I

Prepare to Study

CHAPTER 1

Exam Overview

Welcome, reader. I hope that this book will be informative and helpful as you prepare for the PL-300 exam. I am a big believer in certification and want to encourage as many people as possible to get certified.

Why Certify?

The very premise of this book begs a question: Why certify? Lots of very talented professionals in the Power BI community are not, and don't feel the need to be, certified. You certainly can go this route if your "street cred" is high, that is, other professionals recognize your expertise. Building up your reputation over time is one way to accomplish professional recognition. But what if you are in a hurry? Or you don't have an extensive network to leverage? This is where a certification is valuable.

Any Microsoft certification test you take is rigorous and comprehensive—it is supposed to be! If you pass, that is a very good indicator to others (hiring managers, colleagues, your wider network) that you possess the minimum amount of expertise deemed necessary to be a competent Power BI practitioner. The PL-300 exam is what I call a "broad-spectrum" exam; it will test you on a wide range of concepts and techniques. To prepare for the exam, you need to make sure you are conversant with the full Power BI ecosystem. That's what makes the PL-300 (and the DA-100 before it) such a good indicator of your competencies and why certification is a great way to advertise them.

When Should You Take the Exam?

I take exams as part of my job; I am a Microsoft Certified Trainer (MCT) and am required to maintain active certifications to renew my MCT yearly. I was never terribly test-phobic and am certainly not now—I can't afford to be! But I recognize that lots of people are

© Jessica Jolly 2023
J. Jolly, *Microsoft Power BI Data Analyst Certification Companion*, Certification Study Companion Series,
https://doi.org/10.1007/978-1-4842-9013-2_1

terrified of taking a test. In my observation, there are two types of exam takers: (1) those who want to be completely prepared and won't sit for an exam unless they are close to 100% confident in their knowledge and (2) those who take the exam as soon as they feel even slightly ready. (Full disclosure: I am firmly in the second camp.) If you are in the "completely prepared" camp, you are your own best judge of when to take the exam. But I can say don't wait for the perfect moment. No such moment exists. I can't honestly say that this book (or any study material) will *completely* prepare you for every question on the exam. There will be questions even a seasoned professional may not have encountered. Nor do I expect that you will want to take exams the way I do: on a wing and a prayer. I use exams as a gauge of how far I am from competency. Occasionally, my approach works, and I unexpectedly pass an exam. But more frequently, I fail. I have a high tolerance for failure, which is *not the same* as saying it doesn't bother me. It does. But I work at taking it in stride. I respond to passing the same way I react to failing; it's a milestone along the way. In this way, I normalize *the taking of exams*, without overvaluing either outcome. In this book though, I am trying to prepare you for a middle way: taking the exam once you are *reasonably confident* in your knowledge.

What Is Reasonably Confident?

Determining if you are reasonably confident is subjective, but there are objective measures you can use. The first, and most important, method is to follow the list provided by Microsoft that outlines each of the subject areas (also called domains). This book is organized using those domains. Don't skip any chapters because you can be sure that some material from each domain will appear on the exam. Practice the techniques described as much as possible. Read or listen to other supplementary material, particularly on topics that you don't understand. (I will provide well-reputed sources for additional content in Chapter 15.) Attend as many user group meetings as you can. Post-COVID, most of them have a virtual option, so attending is much easier than it used to be.

To assess my understanding of a topic, I describe the concept using layman's terms— no technical terms at all. If I can't "translate" the idea into "plain English," I know I am not quite there. I also perform "teach-back" to someone else. Almost anyone in the Power BI community is a likely audience for a "teach-back." If the audience is more proficient than you are, they can give you feedback on aspects where you were unclear or, worse yet, incorrect. If your audience is not as knowledgeable as you are, they can tell you which parts you explained clearly and areas where your explanation was "muddied."

Taking the Exam

Before you take the exam, there are some steps you need to take.

Signing Up

The first step to taking the exam is signing up. You do this on the Microsoft website:

https://docs.microsoft.com/en-us/learn/certifications/exams/pl-300

The retail price for the exam is 165 USD. (You might have discounts based on your workplace or other memberships.)

Once you choose "Schedule exam," you will need to create a certification profile if you haven't taken an exam before. If you have taken an exam before, you will be taken to your profile page.

You will need to provide a copy of valid identification when taking the exam. Here are the acceptable forms of ID, taken from the Pearson VUE website:

- Passport
- Driver's license
- Non–US military ID (including spouse and dependents)
- Identification card (national or local)
- Registration card (green card, permanent residence, visa)

Unacceptable forms of identification include renewal forms with expired IDs and government-issued name change documents with government IDs. If your identification is not considered valid, you will not be permitted to complete your exam, and you are unlikely to receive a refund.

Tip 1   If you are creating a profile for the first time, make sure that the name that you provide matches the name on your identification you will use to validate your identity. If it doesn't, you may be challenged during your sign-in process.

Tip 2   Use an email address you will continue to have access to even if you change employers. Use a Microsoft email address for best results: Hotmail, Outlook, or your own domain.

After creating or verifying your profile, you will then be taken to the "Exam Discounts" page. If you have received a discount code, this is where you will be able to enter it.

Now proceed to the scheduling page.

Online or at a Testing Center?

You will need to decide if you want to go into a testing center or take the test online. Here are some factors to consider:

1.   Are there testing centers near you? A lot of them closed during the COVID pandemic and may not have reopened.

2.   Do you have a quiet, uncluttered space in which to take the exam? If you are taking the exam at home, you cannot have people coming into the room where you are taking the exam. You also need to clear out the space around your computer so there are no books or other potential sources of information near you. The exam proctor will ask you to take a picture of all four walls of your room to make sure there is nothing that could provide any extra information. This means removing any pictures from the walls, covering all screens but the one you are working on, and closing the door to the room.

3.   Do you do your best work later in the day or at night? If so, a virtual test may be the right option for you.

4.   Do you have lots of distractions you cannot control at home? If so, a testing center may be a better option.

5.   Does your computer have a microphone and camera attached? Both are required for an online exam.

6. Can your computer run the required software? Pearson VUE provides a test that you should run before your first online exam, to ensure you won't have any issues. If you are taking the test from a work-provided computer, make sure that you are not on the virtual private network or behind your company's firewall.

I have switched to online testing. Here are some things I have experienced or done that have worked well for me (or not!):

1. When my local library was open, I booked a conference room for two hours and took the test there. It was great because I didn't have to clear anything out. I put a handwritten sign "Do Not Disturb—Testing" on the door and then locked the door so no one could accidentally come in.

2. I took a test in my bathroom because it was the least cluttered of my rooms. I don't recommend this—it was very uncomfortable. The proctor didn't like it either as my device camera was at a strange angle because I had my laptop on my lap.

3. I have taken a test in a bedroom, with a door that I *thought* I had closed. My dogs came in and jumped up on the bed. I thought it would invalidate my test, but fortunately it didn't. (These dogs are poodles, so they are smart, but their data analysis skills are *not* renowned.)

4. I had a Dell laptop in which the camera was on the bottom of the screen. This created an awkward angle, which the proctor was not used to. She constantly asked me to adjust my camera, something that was not easy based on its position. I would recommend using a free-standing camera if you can, as it will be easy to adjust on request.

5. Proctors do not like it if you cover your mouth with your hand. Be aware of your habitual gestures because the proctor may object.

6. Proctors do not like it if you read the question to yourself, even silently. If that is a habit you have while reading, be aware of it.

7. Do not expect to have drinks or food. I have had proctors challenge my soda bottle.

These are just tidbits from my experience. **Please read the Pearson VUE website carefully, particularly if this is your first exam.**

Choosing Your Time Block

If you are scheduling an online exam, you will see a calendar with dates on which an appointment is available. (Grayed-out dates do not have available time slots.) You can choose the clock type you want to use (12-hour or 24-hour). Be sure to set the time zone where you will be when you are taking the exam.

The time you choose is the starting time for the exam. You can begin your check-in process *no earlier* than 30 minutes prior to the starting time. I recommend checking in as soon as you can—you can always start the exam a little early, but if you run into problems when checking in, you may need that entire 30 minutes.

Marking Your Calendar

Once you have successfully scheduled your exam, you will receive a confirmation email at the email address listed on your profile. (This may not be the email address you check regularly.) I forward the confirmation to my business email, where I keep my calendar. I then set up an appointment for the exam at the starting time of the exam and make a note that I can sign in up to 30 minutes early. I attach the confirmation to the appointment item. That way, I have all the relevant information I need right in the appointment entry.

You should block out two hours for the exam. The time allotted for the exam varies by exam, but two hours should be plenty for the PL-300.

Canceling or Rescheduling Your Exam

Up to 24 hours in advance, you can reschedule or cancel your exam. I have rescheduled exams several times. Each time the process worked seamlessly, until I forgot to reschedule an exam and therefore "lost" the exam. If you can't reschedule more than 24 hours in advance, you will need to contact Pearson VUE to discuss your individual situation.

I haven't taken an onsite exam since the beginning of COVID, so I can't speak to the rescheduling or cancellation policies of an onsite testing center. **If you choose to take the test at an onsite center, be sure to read the guidance documents carefully.**

The Exam Format

Now you are prepared to take the exam. You have scheduled, you have studied, and you are ready! What can you expect? I am not allowed to give you information about the content of the exam, but I can describe the format and structure of the exam.

Case Studies: You will have at least one case study, which will describe a scenario, with the current setup, the solution requirements, and the problems/issues/constraints fully described. You will then be given a series of specific questions, and you will need to determine if the proposed solution will meet the requirements. Case study sections are self-contained. You can mark a question for review, but you will only be able to review it while you are still in the case study.

My advice for Case Studies: Take your time and read *all* the descriptive material meticulously. Then read each question carefully and go back to the descriptive material and look for wording or specific points that could affect your answer. If you are uncertain about your answer, mark it for review and come back to it after answering the other questions in the case study. Sometimes answering other questions will jog your memory, and you will be able to confidently answer the question you weren't sure about.

Drag and Stack: These questions will require you to build an answer using various options that you can drag over from a list. For example, you will need to provide three steps, in sequence, and you are provided four options from which to choose.

My advice for Drag and Stack: Eliminate the clearly incorrect answer. There will usually, but not always, be one. Then, of the remaining options, identify the one that is clearly either first or last in the sequence. You have thus minimized the options you have to choose from and thereby reduced your risk of being incorrect. Read the options carefully (have I already said this?!). There are times when *the way* an option is written will make it clear whether it is correct or not.

Fill in the Blank: These questions provide you with options to use to fill in the blank (or multiple blanks) in an answer. Unlike Drag and Stack, you can use an option more than once or not at all.

My advice for Fill in the Blank: Look for the parts of the answer about which you are confident and fill in that blank. Then look at the other options and eliminate anything that is clearly wrong. After that, it is something of a guess. I do mark these questions for review because after finishing all the questions, I feel more confident in some of my answers.

Problem/Solution: These questions pose a particular problem and then provide a proposed solution. You are then asked if the proposed solution will solve the stated problem.

My advice for Problem/Solution: Read the problem statement carefully. (I know I am repeating myself, but I cannot overemphasize this enough. Sometimes there is a clue in the wording of the problem.) As you review the proposed solution, remember that there *can* be multiple solutions to a problem. Just because you marked a previous answer as a solution does not mean the next question is *not* a solution. Don't try to outwit the exam algorithm—there is not a predetermined set of solutions that always obtains. Read each proposed solution at face value.

General Tips for Exam Taking

I am someone who has never had exam phobia, so maybe I am exactly the wrong person to give you any tips. For what they are worth, here they are:

1. Don't be afraid to fail. Failing a test *does not mean you are a failure*. Rather, it is a gauge that tells you that more study is needed. As I said earlier, I have failed plenty of exams!

2. Get a good night's sleep. You are taking an exam, not facing a judge and jury.

3. Do not eat or drink anything unusual the night before your exam. You can step away for an unscheduled break, but this is a recent development, so I can't give you any specifics.

4. Breathe. Again, it seems obvious, but what I really mean is pay attention to your breath. Don't hold your breath or take shallow breaths. These breath patterns can increase your anxiety.

5. Wear comfortable clothing and make sure the room temperature is comfortable for sitting in one place for over an hour. Again, you won't be able to get up and put on a sweater or take off a garment.

6. Plan to keep your face in the camera's view and your hands resting on the table/desk or lap when you aren't using your mouse/touchpad. Proctors do not like it when you cover your mouth in any way.

7. Manage your exam clock. Don't spend too much time on one question. If I can't answer the question completely or confidently within two minutes, I answer to my best ability and then mark it for review. I rarely leave an answer completely blank. You would be surprised how much your nerves have settled toward the end of the exam. You can look at questions you weren't sure of and answer them confidently when you are reviewing them.

8. Read carefully. Yes, I am saying it again. I have passed exams for which I really didn't know the material very well. But because I read each question and answer carefully *and* I guessed very judiciously, I passed the exam. I don't recommend this as a surefire way to pass an exam, but it certainly helps.

9. Handle failure and passing with the same amount of reaction—don't overly celebrate a pass or overly accentuate a failure. Neither is anything other than a gauge of your knowledge. *There's always more to learn.*

You've Passed. Now What?

You will find out immediately whether you passed. Each Microsoft certification has a "badge" with an icon. I search for the badge icon, capture it (or get it in a .png format), and put it into a folder I keep for certification icons. I then add it to my email signature, my LinkedIn profile, and my website.

If an employer needs proof that you have passed the exam, you can share your transcript with them. You will have an MCID (once you've filled out your profile), and you will have a transcript code. You can provide your MCID and transcript code to any employer interested in your certifications.

You've Failed. Now What?

Plan to take the exam again. Do not be discouraged. At the end of each exam, you will get a profile of your answers by domain. Take note of these areas and tackle the ones that were scored the lowest.

Failed exams do not reflect on your transcript. No one needs to know if you failed. And even if they do, so what? There's a reason I am so public about failing exams—failure is just a necessary part of success!

CHAPTER 2

PL-300 Coverage

As I mentioned in Chapter 1, I consider the PL-300 exam a "broad-spectrum" exam. That means that the domains covered are comprehensive: from the Power Query Editor (PQE) to the Power BI Desktop and then the Power BI Service. Before we dive into each of these domains in turn (in subsequent chapters), I would like to provide an overview of the Power BI ecosystem. I start all my training classes with this overview, and invariably there are elements that surprise students.

A Note on Terminology   Power BI has a deep heritage in database technology. It should therefore come as no surprise that there is a lot of database terminology. Throughout this book, I will take pains to identify and explain terms that you will encounter while studying for this exam.

The Tools

There are three separate tool sets that are used in Power BI: the Power Query Editor, the Power BI Desktop, and the Power BI Service. You will need to be familiar with each of these tools and what their individual roles are in the product.

Power BI Desktop

The Power BI Desktop (hereafter called "Desktop") is the client where you will develop your data model and create reports. It is a free tool, which can be downloaded from the Microsoft Store. (See below for more information on downloading the Desktop.) You can use the Power BI Desktop without logging into the Power BI Service, but if you want to publish a report, you need to sign in.

13

Tip If you have Office 365 through your employer, your Power BI license will probably be connected to those credentials. If you are learning Power BI proactively and do not have employer-provided credentials (yet), you can sign up for a free Power BI license. However, to do so you must use a "business" domain. For example, you cannot sign up for a Power BI license using a Gmail email account.

The Power BI Desktop is a resource glutton; Microsoft recommends having a machine with at least 8 GB of RAM. If you can, get a "beefier" machine, with at least 16 GB of RAM, preferably 32 GB. With less than 16 GB of RAM, you may struggle with the responsiveness of the Desktop. *Additionally, the Power BI Desktop does not have a Mac version.* If you are planning to use an Apple computer, you will need to install a Windows virtual desktop, such as Parallels.

The Desktop is a development environment. Many of us come to Power BI through Excel, and we don't consider ourselves "developers." But you need to adopt a developer mindset when using the Desktop to develop your data model and your reports. There will be some features and functionality that won't be activated until the report is published. You also do not want to share your reports (in a PBIX file) directly with another user. Yes, they *can* open your report in the Desktop, but there will be things that won't work properly or as designed until you publish the report into the Power BI Service.

Desktop Updates

The Power BI team at Microsoft delivers updates to the Power BI Desktop ten times a year. The easiest way to ensure that you have the latest Power BI Desktop is to download the application from the Microsoft Store. (Scroll down to the bottom of the web page to find the download button.) If your organization does not allow you to download from the MS Store, you can download the Desktop application directly from here. If you cannot download from the MS Store, you will need to *manually update* the Power BI Desktop.

Reports and Dashboards

When I teach, I often hear students use the terms *report* and *dashboard* interchangeably. *Reports and dashboards are two different products*, and as I will be using these terms throughout this book, I want to define them here.

A **report** is a single-page or multi-page document with one or more visuals on each page. Reports are usually created in the Power BI Desktop but *can* be created in the Power BI Service. A report is *always* underpinned by a data model. A report typically covers a particular subject but doesn't have to.

A **dashboard** is a single-page document with one or more visuals taken from one or more reports. Dashboards can *only* be created in the Power BI Service. Visuals that are "pinned" to a dashboard do not interact with each other as they do on a report. (There is one exception to this rule, which we will cover in a later chapter.) Dashboards can have streaming content, such as IoT data, whereas reports cannot.

Report or dashboard? The favorite answer in the Power BI community is "It depends" because it often does. If the report consumers need to actively filter the visuals, a report is probably the best choice. On a dashboard, when a visual tile is selected, the reader is directed back to the original report. If you are creating something to provide information at a glance, a dashboard may be a better option than a report. I think of a dashboard as something that can be displayed on a big monitor hanging in the lobby, cafeteria, or factory floor. People look at the monitor to see updated information, but don't expect to interact with that information.

Power Query Editor

The Power Query Editor (PQE) tool is what you use to extract, transform, and load your data.

Extract, Transform, Load (ETL) describes the process in which you will connect to a data source, acquire the data you want (Extract), perform the changes you need to make (Transform), and then apply the changes you have specified to the selected data and import it into the Power BI Desktop (Load).

The Power Query Editor is a tool that is available through the Power BI Desktop. It is also available through Excel 2016 (or later) and from the Power BI Service. Any techniques and skills you use in the Power Query Editor within the Power BI Desktop you can also use in the Power Query Editor in Excel or in the Service. Just a quick note, new features are released to the Power Query Editor in this order: PQE Service, PQE Desktop, and, finally, PQE Excel. There may be features that you use in the PQE Service or in the PQE Desktop that you won't see in PQE Excel.

The Power BI Service

If you shouldn't send PBIX files to other users directly, what should you do? This is where the Power BI Service ("the Service") comes in. The Service is integrated into the Office 365 suite of products. You can access the Power BI Service in one of three ways:

1. Navigate to `www.app.powerbi.com`. To sign in, use your Office 365 credentials or the sign-in credentials you used when you registered for a free license and the trial.

2. From within Office 365, click the tile for Power BI. You may have to go to `All apps` to surface the tile if you have never used it.

3. From within the Desktop, after you have published your report, follow the hyperlink to the Service.

The Service has three main areas: `My workspace`, `Workspaces`, and `Apps`. For this exam, it is essential to have familiarity with `Workspaces`. If you are using a free Power BI account, you will not have access to `Workspaces`, only to `My workspace`. Practicing only with `My workspace` will not provide access to the full capabilities of the Service, which is why you should sign up for the 60-day trial Power BI Pro license as you study for the exam.

Workspaces, My workspace, and Apps

A **workspace** is a membership-based collaboration area within the Power BI Service. `Workspaces` are created by an Admin, who could be someone in the business or someone in IT. If you are added to a `Workspace`, it will appear on your list of `Workspaces`. `Workspaces` have four levels of membership:

- *Admin*: Has full control of the workspace

- *Member*: Can create, edit, and delete content. Can add other members. Can decide what is included in the workspace's app (if there is one)

- *Contributor*: Can create, edit, and delete content

- *Viewer*: Can view content

You will not see a specific workspace in the Service unless you have been added to it at one of the preceding levels of membership.

My workspace is a sandbox area where you can publish reports and experiment with the features of the Service. You should not publish content to My workspace that you wish to share with others.

An **app** is a vehicle for the distribution of reports and dashboards within the Power BI Service. It is *not* the same thing as the Power BI mobile app. I think of the app as a magazine that has curated content and is distributed at intervals (weekly, monthly, quarterly). An app is associated with a specific workspace on a one-to-one basis (one app, one Workspace). Someone with the right privileges in the workspace must create and update the app. Apps can contain reports, dashboards, and Excel content. I will cover Apps in more detail in a later chapter.

Licensing

You *can* use the suite of tools with a free license. However, you will be limited in your capabilities using a free license: primarily you will not have access to Workspaces. To use Power BI within a workplace infrastructure, you will need a Pro license, which can be a trial license. If you want to work with the full Power BI ecosystem and you don't already have a paid license, you will need to sign up for a Power BI Pro trial license, which is valid for 60 days.

Tip   You can't sign up for a trial license with a consumer email address such as Gmail or Yahoo or AOL. You will need a "work"-related email to sign up.

Languages

There are two languages that are used with the Power BI ecosystem: M and DAX (Data Analysis Expressions). You do not need to be an expert in either of these languages for the exam. But you will need to be familiar with basic DAX and M functions and syntax.

We will cover the basics of the M language in Chapter 4 and DAX in Chapters 6 and 7.

Practicing Before the PL-300

If you are working in Power BI already, you may not need a lot of practice prior to sitting for the exam. If, however, there are techniques or features that I refer to in this book with which you are unfamiliar, your best bet is to practice. The biggest challenge is acquiring a dataset that is easy to use. The good news is that Microsoft has several sample datasets available that you can use.

Northwind Excel and CSV Files

The easiest way to practice is to use Excel and/or CSV files. Almost every business user has familiarity with these two tools. Northwind is a set of data that Microsoft developed for use as sample data. This data is fake, which makes the data safe for you to use without worrying about confidentiality. If you are using the Excel (or CSV) version, you can review the data so that you are familiar with it prior to using it in Power BI. You can also calculate results using Excel formulas, which can help you check your DAX code. The disadvantage of this data is that it is a small set of data with a limited number of fields in each worksheet. But as a *starter* dataset, I think it is excellent. You can find it on GitHub:

`https://github.com/graphql-compose/graphql-compose-examples/tree/master/examples/northwind/data/csv`

AdventureWorks Database

If you want a more robust (and realistic) set of data with which to practice, Microsoft has developed several databases. AdventureWorks DW is the most commonly used, but there are others, such as Tailwind Toys.

AdventureWorks is available as a BAK file, which you can use to restore a database to your local device. This process was unfamiliar to me as I had no database background (and still don't); I assume it will be unfamiliar to many of you as well. I am going to outline the steps you will need to take to use the database so you understand the overall process. I will then provide a link to the Microsoft documentation where they give step-by-step instructions.

Step 1: Download the BAK file for AdventureWorks DW. Find the BAK file for AdventureWorks here.

Step 2: Install SQL Server Management Studio (SSMS). This is a free application (there are paid versions, but you don't need one) available here.

Step 3: Install Microsoft SQL Server on your local device. This is where the AdventureWorks database will be hosted.

Alternate Step 3: Set up an Azure AD account and use the Azure SQL Server option. Note that you will need an Internet connection to access a database hosted in Azure. *Read all the fine print if you choose this option so that you aren't surprised by any charges.*

Step 4: Use SSMS to restore the database from the BAK file. There are detailed instructions on how to do this at the following URL:

```
https://docs.microsoft.com/en-us/sql/samples/adventureworks-install-
configure?view=sql-server-ver15&tabs=ssms#restore-to-sql-server
```

Step 5: Use the credentials that you set up for the database to connect from the Power BI Desktop. Take care to note if you are going to use database credentials or Windows credentials to connect to your database.

What and Why?

When planning this book, I had to decide on both content and perspective. I could have made this a "how-to" book, but there are many excellent "how-to" books—many of them published by Apress! My approach is to explain a feature (*what is*) and *why* it is important to understand it. If I believe that knowing a feature or concept will make you a well-rounded Power BI practitioner, I have included it, even if it does not appear on the PL-300 exam. Don't misunderstand me: there are many features that I do not cover at all because they are more complex or advanced. In Chapter 15, I will provide a list of books, blogs, and YouTube channels that provide excellent "how-to" content. The feature set in Power BI is constantly changing, and it is better to use frequently updated sources to learn how to use a feature. In this book, I want to provide a road map for you so that you know *what* to study and *why*.

PART II

Prepare the Data

PART II

Prepare the Data

CHAPTER 3

Get Data from Different Sources

Power BI can connect to many different data sources. These connection options are called connectors. Take the time to review all the connectors available; you probably will not encounter a question on the PL-300 about an obscure connector, but you *should* know the commonly used connectors:

- SQL Server (all the flavors)
- Excel/CSV
- Folders (SharePoint and File Explorer)
- Power Platform
- Azure
- Power BI dataflows and datasets

Getting the Data

It is usual to initiate data extraction after launching the Power BI Desktop if you are starting a new report. The Home tab has multiple options for getting data, as shown in Figure 3-1.

© Jessica Jolly 2023
J. Jolly, *Microsoft Power BI Data Analyst Certification Companion*, Certification Study Companion Series,
https://doi.org/10.1007/978-1-4842-9013-2_3

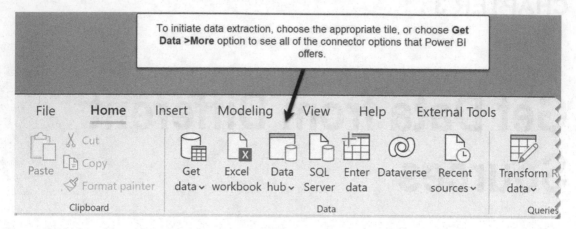

Figure 3-1. *The Home tab has several options for extracting data*

After initiating the extraction, you will be presented with the `Navigator` dialogue box, as shown in Figure 3-2. This dialogue box is where you can make further selections in your data source. For example, if you are connecting to an Excel workbook, you will see a list of worksheets and table objects in that workbook, as shown in Figure 3-2.

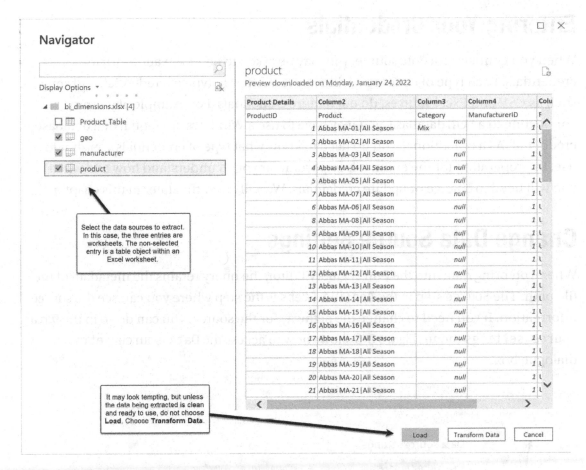

Figure 3-2. Selecting worksheets in the Navigator dialogue box

As shown in Figure 3-2, it is tempting to choose the Load button (because it looks like you should). But unless your data is clean and ready to work with, choose Transform Data instead because it will open the Power Query Editor window.

Tip   In the Navigator window, you will see three yellow dots that scroll across the top of the window. Do not be misled—they are *not* indicative that you must complete another step.

Entering Your Credentials

When you connect to a data source, you may be asked to enter the appropriate credentials. Each type of connector will require a different type of credential, and some, such as CSV and Excel sources, do not require credentials. For example, if you are connecting to a SQL database, you may have to use a Windows credential or a database credential. As a practitioner, you do need to know what type of credentials you should use. In preparation for the exam, it is important for you to understand how and when you will need to change or update credentials. We will cover that later in this chapter.

Change Data Source Settings

When you bring data into the Power Query Editor, the query retains the metadata of the file path. The `Source` step in the `Applied Steps` is the step where you can see the source information. If you need to change the pathway for the source, you can do so in the `Data source settings` menu. Figure 3-3 shows how to access the `Data source settings` dialogue box.

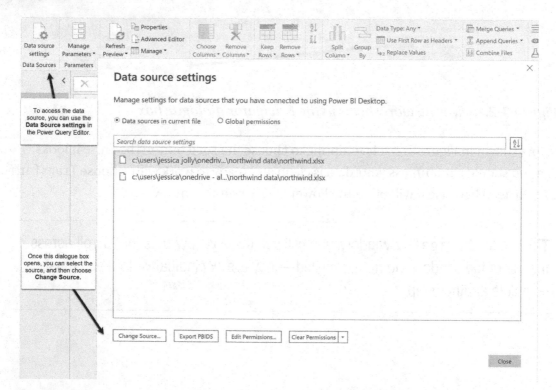

Figure 3-3. *Accessing the Data source settings in the Power Query Editor*

Changing Data Source Settings

It is quite common to need to change the file path for a particular file. For example, if a colleague shares a PBIX file with you, any files that were used in the PBIX file will have the pathway pointing to where your colleague stored the files. You will have an error until you change the pathway to point to the location on your device. The easiest way to do this is in the Data source settings dialogue box. But you can also correct the pathway directly from the error screen itself.

When a Data Source Moves

If you have moved a source file's location, the path that is stored will not resolve. In Figure 3-4, you can see an example of a broken file path.

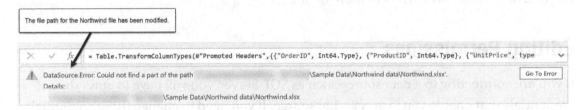

Figure 3-4. *A broken file path*

To change the pathway, you can use the Go To Error button, which selects the Source step and offers you an Edit Settings option, which you can see in Figure 3-5.

Figure 3-5. *Edit Settings within an error*

You will then be presented with a dialogue box, as shown in Figure 3-6.

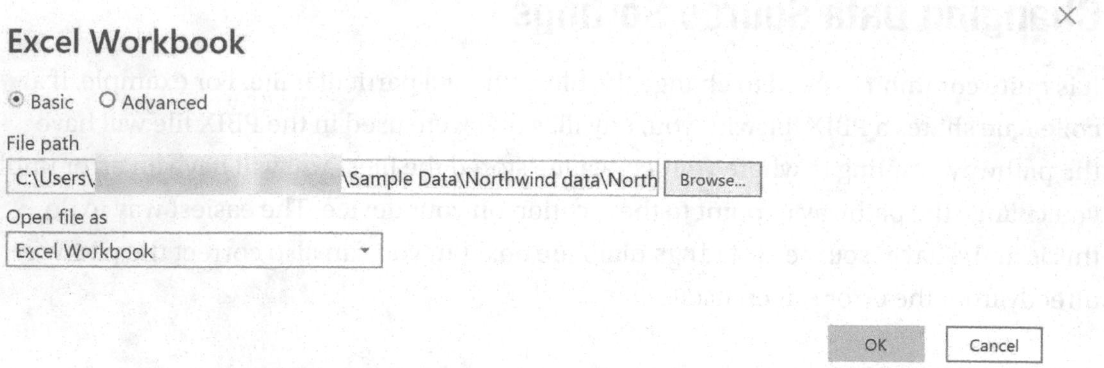

Excel Workbook

⊙ Basic   ○ Advanced

File path

| C:\Users\ _____ \Sample Data\Northwind data\North | Browse... |

Open file as

| Excel Workbook ▾ |

| OK | Cancel |

Figure 3-6. Browse to change the file path

This is one of the most common errors you can incur in the Power Query Editor. In Chapter 4, we will cover errors in more depth.

Editing Permissions

If you are connecting to a data source such as SQL Server, you will have to enter the credentials that enable you to access that source. If you need to change these credentials (e.g., your password changes), you can do so in the Data source settings ➤ Edit Permissions dialogue box, as shown in Figure 3-7.

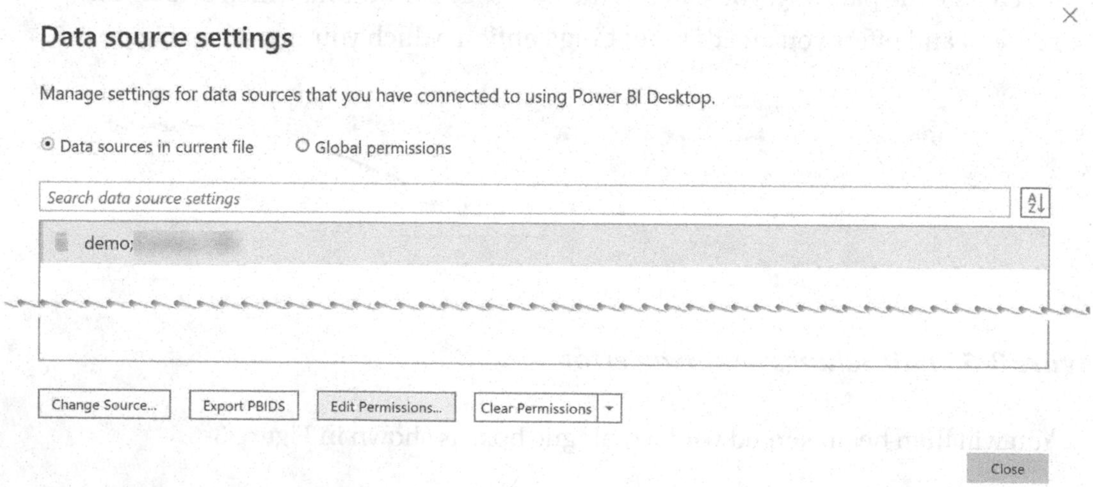

Data source settings

Manage settings for data sources that you have connected to using Power BI Desktop.

⊙ Data sources in current file   ○ Global permissions

| Search data source settings | A↓Z |

| demo; _____ |

| Change Source... | Export PBIDS | Edit Permissions... | Clear Permissions ▾ |

| Close |

Figure 3-7. Editing permissions on a file source

Once you have identified the source you want to change, choose `Edit Permissions`, as shown in Figure 3-8.

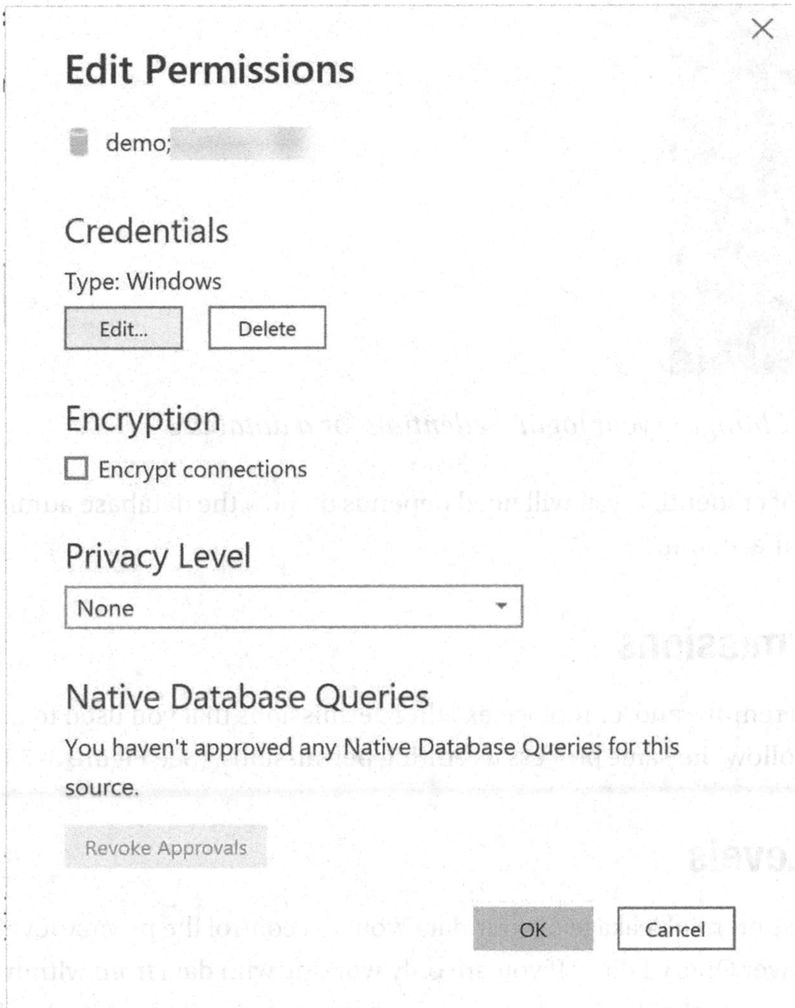

Edit Permissions

demo;

Credentials

Type: Windows

[Edit...]   [Delete]

Encryption

☐ Encrypt connections

Privacy Level

None ▾

Native Database Queries

You haven't approved any Native Database Queries for this source.

Revoke Approvals

[OK]   [Cancel]

Figure 3-8. *The Edit Permissions dialogue box*

Finally, you arrive at the dialogue box shown in Figure 3-9, where you can choose between three types of credentials: Windows, database, and Microsoft.

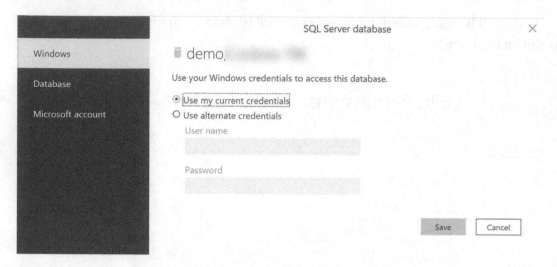

Figure 3-9. *Changing your login credentials for a database*

The type of credentials you will need depends on how the database administrator has set up your account.

Clear Permissions

If you need to remove and/or replace existing permissions that you used to connect to a data source, follow the same process as editing permissions. (See Figure 3-7.)

Privacy Levels

To control the potential leakage of your data, you can control the privacy levels of the data in the Power Query Editor. If you are only working with data from within your organization, you probably don't need to worry about setting the privacy levels for your data. However, it is important to understand what the options are both for the PL-300 and if you need to use them in your practice:

- *None*: There are no privacy restrictions on this data source. It can be combined with other data without any restrictions.

- *Public*: This data can be combined with other public or organizational data sources, and the data is visible to anyone. However, only files, Internet data sources, and workbooks can be marked as public.

- *Organizational*: If you mark a data source as organizational, that data source can be combined with other data sources classified as "organizational."

- *Private*: A data source classified as private will isolate that data completely. It cannot be combined with any other data source, even other data sources classified as private.

You can access the `Privacy Level` in the `Edit Permissions` dialogue box as shown in Figure 3-10.

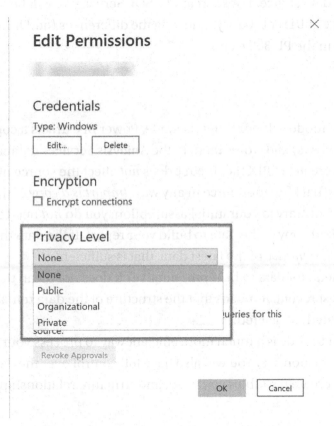

Figure 3-10. *The Privacy Level*

The challenge with setting privacy levels is that you can set them too rigorously. If you do so, you can incur a `Formula.Firewall` error in your query. Another concern with privacy levels is that they can slow down a refresh once your report is published in the Service. There is an option to disable the privacy levels in the File ➤ Options and settings ➤ Options ➤ Global ➤ Privacy menu. If you do choose to disable the privacy levels, you must be sure that you are only working with data within your organization's control.

Selecting a Storage Mode

In addition to entering credentials, you will also need to determine a storage mode (if applicable) for the data source. For sources like SQL Server, you will be presented with two options: Import or Direct Query. Knowing the differences (and limitations) of these modes is included in the PL-300 exam.

Import

The default storage mode is Import. In this mode, Power BI extracts a copy of the selected tables (or views) and stores them in the Analysis Services database that is spun up when you create a PBIX file. Import does *not* affect the source of the data—you are not "writing back" to the source in any way. *Import is a copy* of the data at the time of extraction. Contrary to your initial assumption, you do *not* need to work with a constantly refreshed copy of the data to build your report. If the data that you are working with is *representative* of the latest data, that is sufficient.

What does it mean for data to be representative? It does *not* mean that the values are the same or the most recent. It means that the structure of the data remains consistent as data is added, updated, or deleted.

Using the Import mode is a much more efficient way to process your queries: your report will be more responsive. You will also have full control over the data model—you can add measures, create the tables you need, and structure relationships optimally.

Direct Query

When I teach a class on Power BI and Direct Query comes up, invariably a student says, "You should always use Direct Query so you can have the latest data." Not to put too fine a point on it, this is not necessary. It *is* true that if you use Direct Query you will always be using the latest data. But you will pay a performance price for that timeliness. And you don't usually need to work with the most recent data. If the data you are working with is representative (see earlier) of all the data, working with older data is not an issue.

`Direct Query` creates a connection between the Power BI Desktop and the data source. Your report's responsiveness will be dependent on the latency of this connection, something that is probably not in your control but can negatively affect your report performance. You will not be able to perform any transformations or modeling of the data—you must use the data as is. If the data has been fully prepped for all your reporting requirements, this restriction may not be an issue. But you need to be sure that it meets your needs. Using `Direct Query` can also have a negative impact on the server that you are connecting to; be sure to talk to the database and/or server owner to make sure that your report doesn't create an inordinate burden.

Before you choose `Direct Query` as your storage mode, fully investigate whether the data really needs to be up-to-the-minute. Here are some questions you can ask yourself or your report consumers:

1. How often will the report consumers act on the data? If the data is only actioned once a day, or even twice a day, you don't need `Direct Query`.

2. Do you have a lot of historical data in your dataset? If you have data that is several years old, typically you do not need the data from five minutes ago, because you are making decisions across a wider time frame.

3. Does the data change significantly in real time? How often is the data refreshed at the source?

4. Are parts of the source data refreshed at different rates? If yes, you don't want to use `Direct Query` because parts of your report could conflict.

Don't choose `Direct Query` unless you have some overriding business justification for it; the disadvantages often outweigh any advantages.

For Future Reference: Writing Your Own SQL Code

In the same dialogue box where you see the `Import` and `Direct Query` options, you will also see an `Advanced` drop-down. This is where you *could* write your own SQL to extract exactly what you need from the source. Writing your own SQL statement immediately breaks "query folding" (explained in Chapter 4), which is a bad thing. If you choose to write a custom SQL query, do so only if you are confident that you can write a better query than Power Query can generate.

Live Connection

When you connect to an Analysis Services source, it is called a Live Connection. These three sources are SQL Server Analysis Services Tabular, SQL Server Analysis Services Multidimensional, and Power BI Service dataset.

Note on Hybrid Tables   In December 2021, Microsoft announced the ability to combine data that has been imported and data that is accessed via Direct Query. These are called hybrid tables and are accomplished by partitioning the data. The primary benefit of a hybrid table is you get the speedy performance of imported data and the latest data via Direct Query. Partitions are not covered in the PL-300 exam and are beyond the scope of this book, but I want you to know what is meant by hybrid tables.

Using Different Data Sources

The likelihood is that you will be connecting to data sources that are used heavily in your organization: your ERP system (finance, accounts payable/receivable, inventory) and your CRM system (customers, sales pipelines, marketing) are the most prevalent. You can browse the list of connectors under the Get data menu to find the right connector as shown in Figure 3-11.

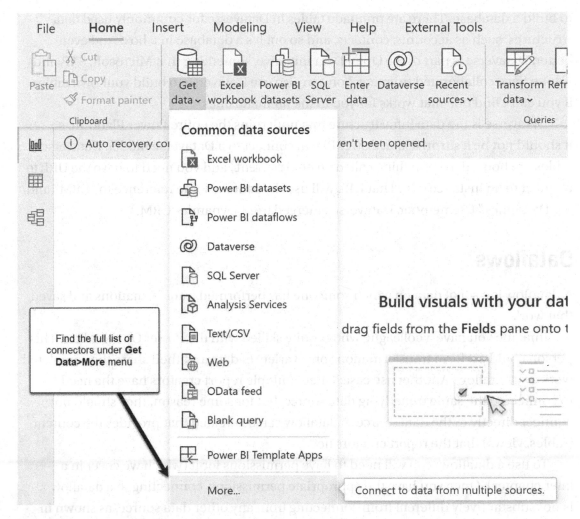

Figure 3-11. Reviewing all the connectors available

And of course, there are always good old Excel and CSV files. But there is a whole new world of data sources that you have (potentially) available to you. (Whether you have them available to you or not, you need to know *about* them for the exam.)

Dataverse

Dataverse is the new name for what used to be called the "Common Data Service." Approximately five years ago (don't quote me on the exact date), Microsoft realized that within their Dynamics CRM tool, they were sitting on a gold mine: a ready-made database infrastructure that could be used by non-database-literate folks (like me)

35

to build a database. There are premade tables in Dataverse for commonly used data structures, such as accounts, contacts, and so on. It's a database in a box. And even better, Dataverse is part of the Open Data Initiative, something that Microsoft, SAP, and Adobe have collaborated to create. You can also use Dataverse to build your own tables, if you can't find one that works for you in the premade ones.

Dataverse is the data infrastructure that underpins the entire Power Platform, so it should not be a surprise that Power BI can connect to a Dataverse model. Dataverse tables are housed in something called an `environment`, and you need to have the URL to connect to an instance of it. That URL will usually contain some reference to "CRM" and/ or "Dynamics." (Remember, Dataverse emerged from Dynamics CRM.)

Dataflows

A dataflow is a set of data on which someone has performed transformations and saved that work.

Imagine you have a colleague who is quite skilled with the Power Query Editor. This person could perform transformations on a variety of data and then share the completed work as a dataflow. Another use case: Often multiple report creators have the need to connect to the same underlying data source, but for some reason, they should not connect directly to the data source. A dataflow can be created that provides the content (tables, views) that the report creators need.

To use a dataflow, you will need to have permissions for it (which we cover in a later chapter). Once you have the appropriate permissions, connecting to a dataflow is not substantively different from connecting from any other data source, as shown in Figure 3-12.

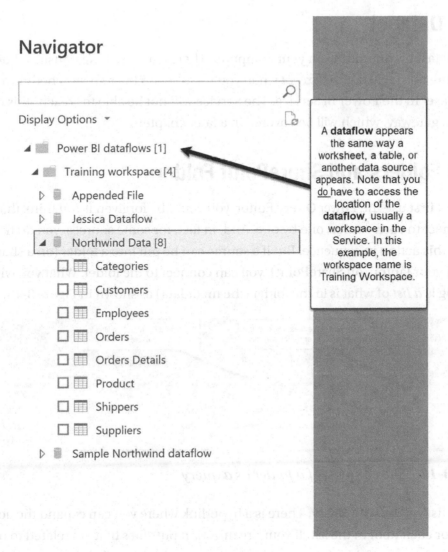

Navigator

Display Options ▾

◢ ▦ Power BI dataflows [1]

  ◢ ▦ Training workspace [4]

    ▷ ▤ Appended File

    ▷ ▤ Jessica Dataflow

    ◢ ▤ Northwind Data [8]

      ☐ ▦ Categories

      ☐ ▦ Customers

      ☐ ▦ Employees

      ☐ ▦ Orders

      ☐ ▦ Orders Details

      ☐ ▦ Product

      ☐ ▦ Shippers

      ☐ ▦ Suppliers

    ▷ ▤ Sample Northwind dataflow

> A **dataflow** appears the same way a worksheet, a table, or another data source appears. Note that you do have to access the location of the **dataflow**, usually a workspace in the Service. In this example, the workspace name is Training Workspace.

Figure 3-12. *Connecting to a dataflow in a workspace*

Shared Dataset

If someone in your organization has already put a lot of work into creating a dataset, anyone who has permissions to that dataset can use it to create a new report. We will talk further in a later chapter about datasets, but the benefit of using a shared dataset is the time savings. Someone else can do all the work of transforming and modeling the data, and you can use it all in a report. Just a side note: Using a shared dataset creates a Live Connection (see earlier).

37

Local Dataset

A local dataset is one sitting on your computer. There isn't anything unusual about connecting to a local dataset *except* when you try to set up the refresh schedule for the local dataset in the Power BI Service. The Service will not be able to "reach" this dataset without a gateway, which will be covered in a later chapter.

Using Folders and SharePoint Folders

When you first use the Power Query Editor, you could be forgiven if you think that you connect to each source, one by one. And, in fact, for some sources, you do have to perform this action in sequence. But if a source can be put into a folder (on a shared drive, on your laptop, on SharePoint), you can connect to the folder. What you will be extracting is *a list* of what is in the folder (the metadata) as shown in Figure 3-13.

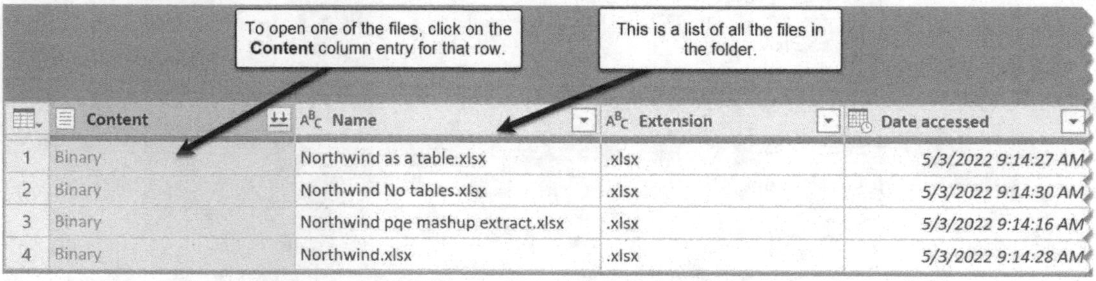

	Content		ABC Name		ABC Extension		Date accessed	
1	Binary		Northwind as a table.xlsx		.xlsx		5/3/2022 9:14:27 AM	
2	Binary		Northwind No tables.xlsx		.xlsx		5/3/2022 9:14:30 AM	
3	Binary		Northwind pqe mashup extract.xlsx		.xlsx		5/3/2022 9:14:16 AM	
4	Binary		Northwind.xlsx		.xlsx		5/3/2022 9:14:28 AM	

To open one of the files, click on the **Content** column entry for that row.

This is a list of all the files in the folder.

Figure 3-13. *The contents of a folder as a query*

That list will be your query. There is a hyperlink where you can expand the actual dataset for each item in the list. If your organization puts files that are related to one another in the same folder (e.g., monthly budget Excel workbooks), connecting to the folder is far more efficient than connecting to each workbook singly. You can also combine the individual files together as a single query, as shown in Figure 3-14.

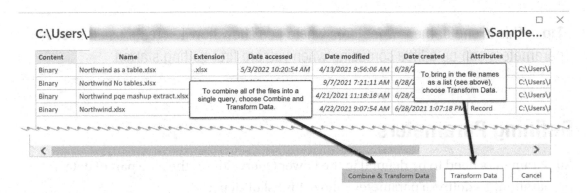

Figure 3-14. *Options for combining files*

Tip   You usually combine files that have the same structure: number of columns, names of columns. If you combine queries with different structures, there may be a lot of "messy" transformations to perform.

SharePoint folders work the same way, but there is one trick: you need the *top-level* URL to the SharePoint. Nothing else will work.

Parameters

A parameter is one of the terms that stumped me when I began to learn Power BI. I understood a parameter as a boundary or a limit. But within Power BI, it follows another definition: an arbitrary constant or an independent variable. (All three definitions courtesy of Merriam-Webster Dictionary.) A parameter does one of three things within Power BI:

- Provides a value to a function within the Power Query Editor

- Allows a user to enter a value in the Power BI Desktop

- Allows a user to enter a value in the Power BI Service

For the PL-300 exam, you will be expected to know how to change the value of a parameter, but I want you to understand what a parameter is, where you create them, and *some* of the ways you can use them.

> **Tip**   This is one of the few features where I do show how to create/use it because parameters can be a little confusing when you are first getting started.

Defining Parameters

All parameters need to be defined in the Power Query Editor; they are part of data preparation. To define a parameter, follow this list of steps:

Step 1: Select `Manage Parameters`.

Step 2: Select `New Parameter`.

Step 3: Populate the `New Parameter` dialogue box as shown in Figure 3-15.

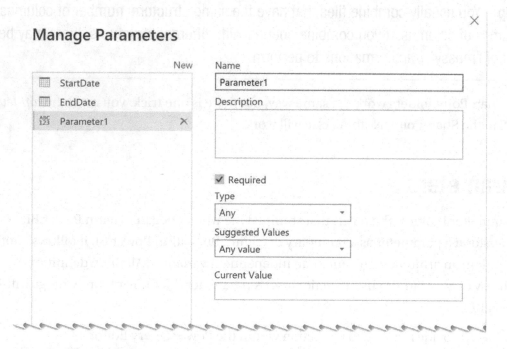

Figure 3-15.   *The New Parameter dialogue box*

Step 4: Provide a name and a description for your parameter. Use a name that is unique.

Step 5: Specify the data type for the value that will be supplied to the parameter (e.g., if you are going to enter dates, specify the `Date` data type).

Step 6: If there is only going to be a restricted list of possible values, you can provide these values in a list you create or use an existing query that has all the values already in it. If you want to use an existing column in an existing query, select that column, right-click, and choose `Add as a new query`. This will create a new query that is a list (a single column) that you can then provide as an input to the parameter as shown in Figure 3-16.

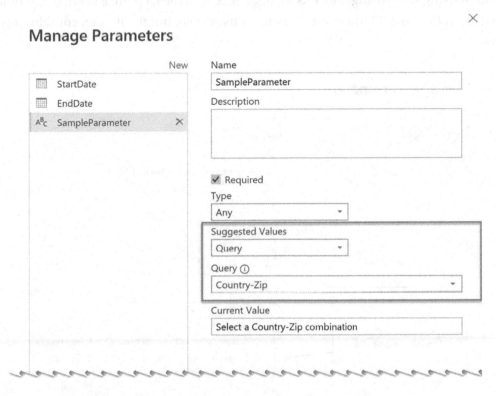

Figure 3-16. *Populating the Manage Parameters dialogue box*

Step 7: Provide a default value for the parameter. This will be the value that displays when a user first opens the parameter. You can enter a helpful message such as "Enter a date here" or choose a default value.

Tip   If you have ever used the `Data Validation` feature in Excel, this process will be very familiar. The only feature this dialogue box doesn't offer is the ability to add a message.

Within the Power Query Editor

One use case that is very common is to enable users to change file paths easily. Creating this parameter is straightforward.

Follow Steps 1–5 as outlined earlier in the section "Defining Parameters." For Step 6, instead of using an existing query as for Suggested Values, create a list that will hold the file paths. In Figure 3-17, there are two file paths shown, but the list can contain only one file path.

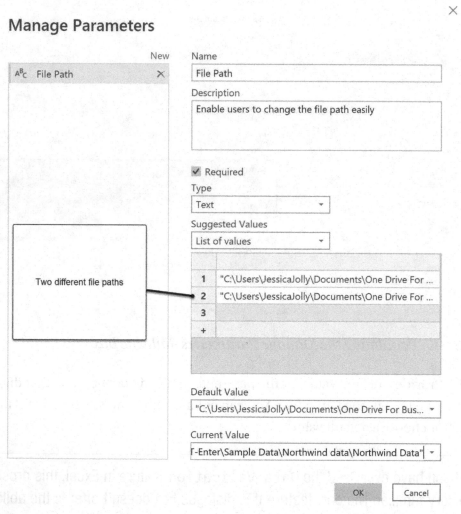

Figure 3-17. *Setting up a list of file paths as a parameter*

Once you set up the list of values, you can then change the parameter value as shown in Figure 3-18.

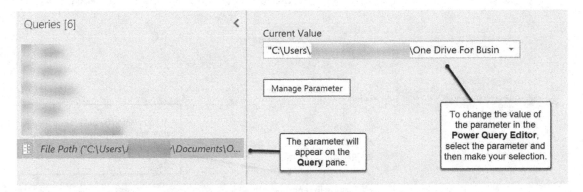

Figure 3-18. *Changing the parameter value in the Power Query Editor*

In the Power BI Desktop

Once you have created a parameter, you can then use it in the Power BI Desktop. In our file path parameter example, you can make the parameter available as a data source. The first step is loading the parameter to the data model, something that does *not* happen by default. You must Enable load for the parameter, as shown in Figure 3-19.

The other common use for a parameter is to set up a parameter with a server and database name pre-populated. This method is useful because it is not uncommon to need to connect to the same source for different tables or views.

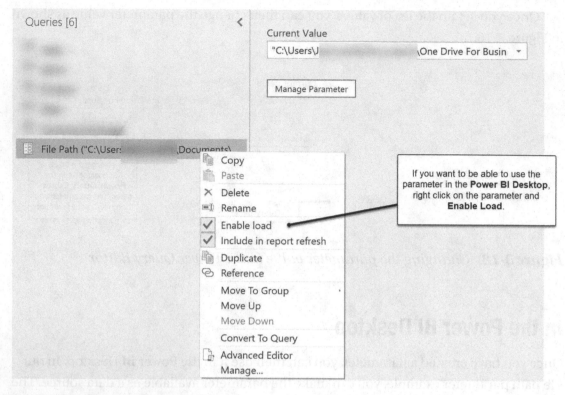

Figure 3-19. *Enabling the load for the parameter*

When you have enabled the load, the next time you choose Apply (or Close and Apply), the parameter will appear in your data model in the Power BI Desktop. To access the parameter, navigate to Transform data ➤ Edit parameters, and select the appropriate parameter as shown in Figures 3-20 and 3-21.

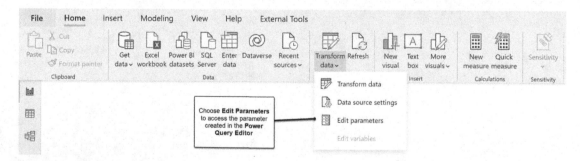

Figure 3-20. *Accessing the parameters created in the Power Query Editor*

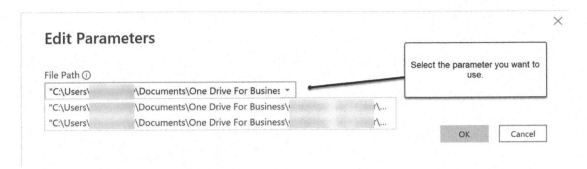

Figure 3-21. *Choosing the parameter*

Incremental Refresh   One of the most common uses of parameters is incremental refresh. The first time you publish your report in the Service (covered in a later chapter), you will set up a refresh schedule. Often, you want to bring in all the data when you first publish and, in subsequent refreshes, only bring in the new or changed data. Incremental refreshes allow you to specify the start date and end date of the data you want to target during the subsequent refreshes. Setting up a RangeStart and RangeEnd parameter is a prerequisite for setting up an incremental refresh.

Clean, Transform, and Load the Data

This chapter covers exam topics around cleaning data, transforming data, and loading that data into Power BI where it can be analyzed. We cover the Power Query Editor, the M language that underlies transformations, and various topics relating to data quality.

Accessing the Power Query Editor

After initiating the Get data procedure within the Desktop, the Power Query Editor (PQE) will open in a new, separate window. This is intentional—the two tools are *intended* to work side by side. While you are active in the PQE window, you can minimize the Desktop window.

What Is the Power Query Editor?

Let's set the scene. You have a project that requires you to gather data from a variety of sources. You didn't (necessarily) originate this data, and therefore it probably needs some shaping before you can use it. It may have columns you don't need, or it might be missing columns you do need. It may not have necessary calculations, or the data might not be in the right format for you to perform calculations on it. It might have misspellings, inconsistent abbreviations, blank rows, and null values. Any or all these things are invariably true for most data sources. Can you go back to the sources and fix them? Maybe, but most likely not. If the data comes from a database, it has been created for and is used by a lot of different people. The database owner is probably not going to change the data to meet your specific requirements. *The Power Query Editor to the rescue!*

47

© Jessica Jolly 2023
J. Jolly, *Microsoft Power BI Data Analyst Certification Companion*, Certification Study Companion Series,
https://doi.org/10.1007/978-1-4842-9013-2_4

I think the Power Query Editor is the best tool Microsoft has ever created! And you can use it through the Power BI Desktop, through Excel, or through the Power BI Service. The Power Query Editor is *not* a standalone application; it must be accessed through the Power BI Desktop or Service or through Excel. You can open it in one of two ways:

1) `Get data` on the Home tab

2) `Transform data` on the Home tab (as shown in Figure 4-1)

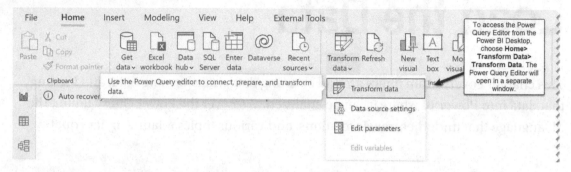

Figure 4-1. *Accessing the Power Query Editor using Transform data*

The PQE allows you to take the raw data (in the form of queries) and work with it to perform all the changes you need to make it work for you. What kinds of changes?

1. Deleting, merging, combining, and splitting columns

2. Deleting top, bottom, and alternate rows

3. Changing the data type of a column

4. Combining queries together (merging, appending)

5. Duplicating or referencing a query

6. Renaming and documenting columns, queries, and steps

7. Replacing values, blanks, and errors

8. Adding new columns

9. Adding new calculations

This is not a comprehensive list of all the types of changes (called transformations) you can perform, but to pass the PL-300 exam, you should be conversant with all the preceding transformations.

You use the ribbon tools to specify the transformations you want to perform for each query. Your mouse clicks are captured and recorded in individual steps, called Applied Steps. (If you are familiar with macros in Excel, this process will sound familiar.) Each step is "translated" into M and is visible using the Formula Bar (see Figure 4-6 for an example).

To become a very proficient "transformer" (sorry—couldn't help myself!), you need to be very familiar with the extensive available commands. You do *not* need to know how to write M from scratch, but some basic M skills are helpful on the exam (and in real life!).

Tip   Turn on the Formula Bar under the View tab. Leave it on because it is the fastest way to absorb M while going about your transformations. Each action you perform using the ribbon is recorded in M and is visible in the Formula Bar, as you can see in Figure 4-2.

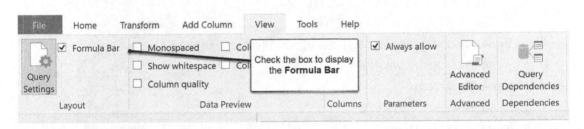

Figure 4-2. *The Formula Bar visible*

Let's examine an M statement, using a simple example shown in Figures 4-3 , 4-4, and 4-5. I am going to split a column into two columns.

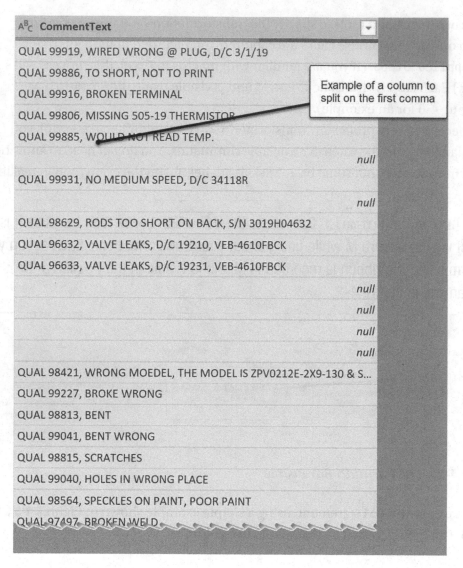

Figure 4-3. *Column to be split*

A^B_C CommentText		seCode ▼	A^B_C To Bin Numbe
QUAL 99919, WIRED WRONG @ PLUG, D/C 3/	📋 Copy		NC1
QUAL 99886, TO SHORT, NOT TO PRINT	✄ Remove		NC1
QUAL 99916, BROKEN TERMINAL	Remove Other Columns		NC1
QUAL 99806, MISSING 505-19 THERMISTOR	Duplicate Column		NC1
QUAL 99885, WOULD NOT READ TEMP.	Add Column From Examples...		NC1
	Remove Duplicates	null	
QUAL 99931, NO MEDIUM SPEED, D/C 34118F	Remove Errors		NC1
	Change Type	null	
QUAL 98629, RODS TOO SHORT ON BACK, S/N	Transform		NC1
	Replace Values...		
QUAL 96632, VALVE LEAKS, D/C 19210, VEB-4	Replace Errors...	By Delimiter...	
QUAL 96633, VALVE LEAKS, D/C 19231, VEB-4	Split Column	By Number of Characters...	
	Group By...	By Positions...	
	Fill	By Lowercase to Uppercase	
	Unpivot Columns	By Uppercase to Lowercase	
	Unpivot Other Columns	By Digit to Non-Digit	
	Unpivot Only Selected Columns	By Non-Digit to Digit	
QUAL 98421, WRONG MOEDEL, THE MODEL I!	Rename...		
QUAL 99227, BROKE WRONG	Move		NC1
QUAL 98813, BENT	Drill Down		NC1
	Add as New Query		

Figure 4-4. *Splitting the column by delimiter*

And here are the resulting two columns:

^{ABC} CommentText.1 ▼	^{ABC} CommentText.2 ▼
QUAL 99919	WIRED WRONG @ PLUG, D/C 3/1/19
QUAL 99886	TO SHORT, NOT TO PRINT
QUAL 99916	BROKEN TERMINAL
QUAL 99806	MISSING 505-19 THERMISTOR
QUAL 99885	WOULD NOT READ TEMP.
null	*null*
QUAL 99931	NO MEDIUM SPEED, D/C 34118R
null	*null*
QUAL 98629	RODS TOO SHORT ON BACK, S/N 3019H04632
QUAL 96632	VALVE LEAKS, D/C 19210, VEB-4610FBCK
QUAL 96633	VALVE LEAKS, D/C 19231, VEB-4610FBCK
null	*null*
null	*null*
null	*null*
	null

The resulting two columns, after splitting the column on the first comma

Figure 4-5. *One column split into two*

Now that we have the example set up, let's look at the M that was generated by this transformation, shown in Figure 4-6.

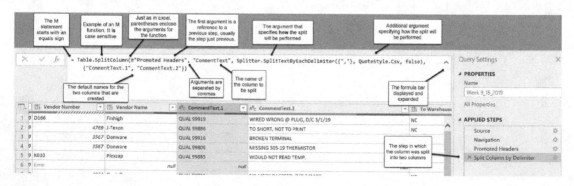

Figure 4-6. *The anatomy of a sample M statement*

The M Language

You don't have to be able to write M from scratch, but knowing some basic facts about M is helpful:

1. M is a separate language from DAX. It is used in the PQE, not in the Desktop.

2. *M is case sensitive.* Pay attention to upper- and lowercase!

3. M is a functional language. You use a function to perform an action.

4. An M function has arguments (just like in Excel) that are separated by commas.

5. In M, when you see curly braces "{}", that indicates a list.

6. To see the entire script you have written in the query you are working on, open the Advanced Editor on the Home tab.

Undoing and Redoing a Step

One of the first things I look for in any application is the Undo feature. It just makes me feel more secure. But in the Power Query Editor, you can look all day long, and you will not find an Undo feature in the ribbon. The way you fix mistakes is by working with the relevant Applied Step. Each step will have a red X if you mouse over it, as you can see in Figure 4-7. But don't be hasty—the Power Query Editor is very flexible. You can Redo a step that has a gear icon next to it. You can also rearrange steps by dragging them up or down the list.

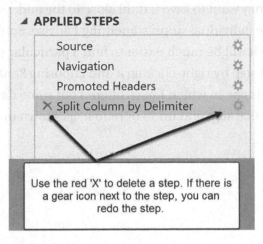

Figure 4-7. Undoing or redoing a step

53

Naming and Documenting

In addition to data not meeting your requirements, it often does not have user-friendly names. If your source is a database, you will often see column names prefixed with the term "DIM" or "FACT"—more on these prefixes in Chapter 5. You should rename columns and queries with names that make sense to your report readers. Two columns in the same query cannot have the same name, but you can have columns of the same name in different queries. In fact, you should make sure that your key columns have the same names in different queries. That will make it easier for you to relate them in the data model and easier for your report reader to know that they represent the same value.

You may have seen names where there are two words joined by an underscore (Name_Name2). Should you have spaces in the names of your columns and queries? Spaces are more familiar to your users, but if you have a space in your table name, you will always have to enclose it with single quotes (e.g., 'Name Name2').

Tip   Get in the habit of always putting your table name in single quotes—then, when a table name requires single quotes, you won't be wondering what is wrong.

If there is a naming convention in your organization, follow it. If there isn't a naming convention, establish one. Column and query names will be consistent.

Rename all your columns in the query as one `Applied Step`. That way, when you look for the step where you renamed a column(s), it will be in one step. It doesn't matter if you do it at the beginning or end of your process, but because you may be creating and deleting columns, you may want to save it until close to the end.

You can also rename individual steps, something I advise. Sometimes the `Applied Steps` list is quite long—it will be much easier to find a particular step if it is descriptively named. You can name a step by right-clicking it and choosing `Rename`. The one type of step I always rename is one in which I have filtered out some data. That way, when I panic, I can easily find that step and undo or redo it, as shown in Figures 4-8, 4-9, and 4-10.

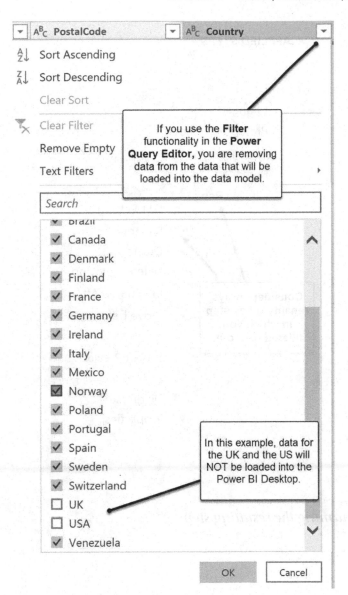

Figure 4-8. *Filtering out data*

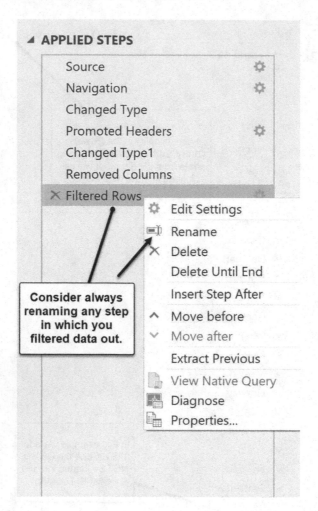

Figure 4-9. *Renaming the resulting step*

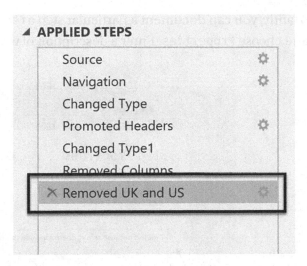

Figure 4-10. *Much easier to find when in a panic*

While you are naming things, it is a good time to document your query and your steps. On the Applied Steps panel (on the right of the Power Query Editor window), there is a hyperlink label All Properties. Click the hyperlink and enter a description of the query as shown in Figure 4-11. *Bonus:* When you bring the query over into the Desktop, the description will appear in the tooltip for the table!

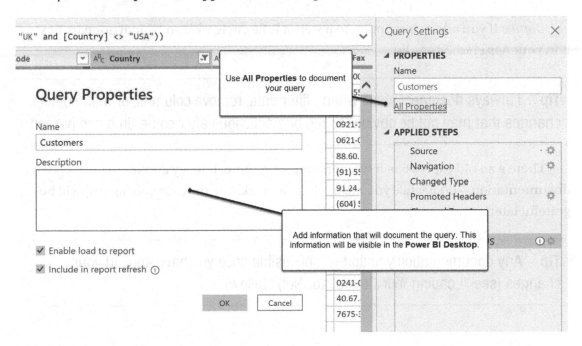

Figure 4-11. *Documenting a query*

Even more importantly, you can document a particular step as shown in Figure 4-12. Right-click the step and choose `Properties`. Enter a description of what you did and why.

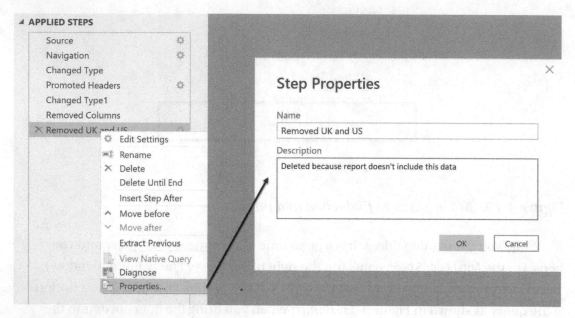

Figure 4-12. *Documenting a step*

Bonus: If you add a description to a step, a little circle with an "i" in it appears next to it in your `Applied Steps` list.

Tip   I always document steps when I filter data, remove columns, or make other changes that may not be obvious to me or a colleague after some time has passed.

There's an old expression a stitch in time saves nine. It really applies to documentation—do it while you are during the work. You (or your colleagues) will be grateful later!

Tip   Any documentation you add will be visible once you have applied your changes (see "Loading Your Queries (or Not)" below).

Data Quality and Distribution

If you are connecting to a data source you are not familiar with, you don't necessarily know what to expect. Will the data have lots of errors? Will there be a lot of blanks or null values? Inconsistencies? We all hope that the data will be perfect "out of the box," but this is usually not the case, which is why one of your first steps should be to enable the Data Preview tools on the View tab as shown in Figure 4-13. Specifically you should enable:

Column quality
Column distribution
Column profile

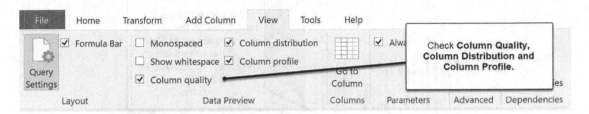

Figure 4-13. *Turning on column profiling*

Each of these features will introduce new elements to your screen real estate, so you may not want these features on all the time. Looking at them when you first bring in the data is a good practice; then you can turn them off after you have assessed your data.

Here are some suggestions for things to look for in these boxes:

1. Are there empty or blank values in a column? Decide what your
   strategy will be for filling these blanks. Do you want to put in a "0"
   or an "N/A" or a "blank"? Using Replace Values is a simple way to
   make these changes, but make sure you know if the empty value is
   truly blank or is a null. Blanks and nulls are treated differently in
   the Power Query Editor.

CHAPTER 4   CLEAN, TRANSFORM, AND LOAD THE DATA

2. What is the ratio of **distinct** to **unique** values? **Distinct** indicates
    the number of different values present in the column. (If you have
    a list {1, 2, 3, 4}, there are four distinct values.) **Unique** indicates
    the number of values that are not repeated. (In a list {1, 1, 2, 2, 2,
    3, 4, 4}, there is only one unique value.) A ratio of one to one (or
    close to 1/1) means that this column has very high cardinality
    (shown in Figure 4-14)—a term I will explain below. A ratio of 1
    to 0 or 1/0 is good (shown in Figure 4-15). This means that every
    value is repeated *at least* once.

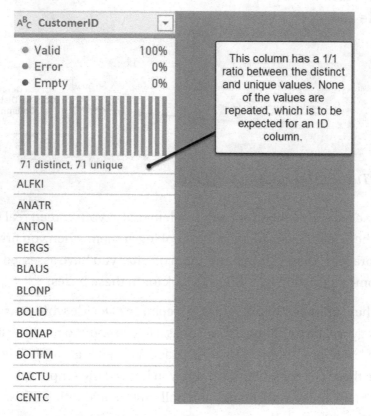

Figure 4-14. *Example of a high-cardinality column*

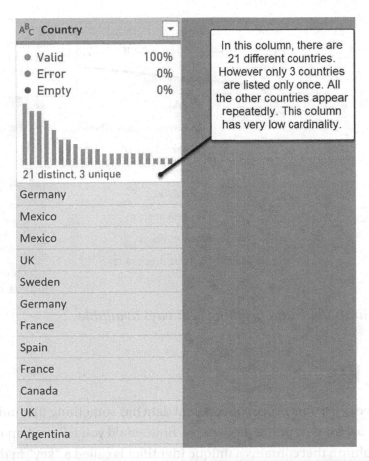

Figure 4-15. Example of a low-cardinality column

3. What is the distribution of values? Do you see different types of
data in the same column (i.e., text and numeric)? Part of your
work will be to make the values in a column a consistent type
(either a text or number).

Once you have scanned your data and noted any "problem" areas, you can return
to the View tab and turn off the Data Preview tools. You will always have the Profile
shortcut bar visible, right under the column headers as shown in Figure 4-16.

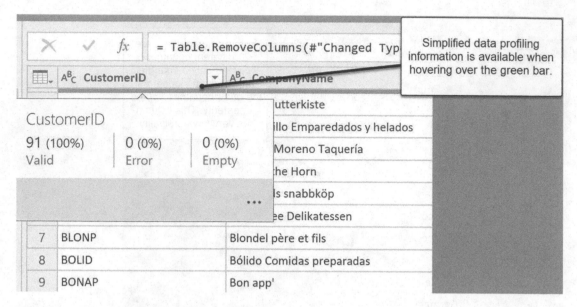

Figure 4-16. Simplified data profiling is always available

Keys and IDs

It makes intuitive sense that every collection of data has something that uniquely identifies each row (or data point). Otherwise, how would you tell rows apart? Or identify duplicates? A column that contains a unique identifier is called a "key" in database terminology. A key can be native to the data (e.g., an employee ID number in a table with employee information). It can also be something that the database designer has added. Regardless of where the key comes from, it is a unique identifier for the data, and there must be one present for the data model to be constructed.

If you are extracting your data from a data warehouse or a database, a column that is the unique identifier is usually going to have the word "key" in its title. But if you don't see a column with "key" in its name, open the Data Preview tools and look for a column with a 1/1 ratio for distinct/unique: it is likely to be a "key" field, as shown in Figure 4-17.

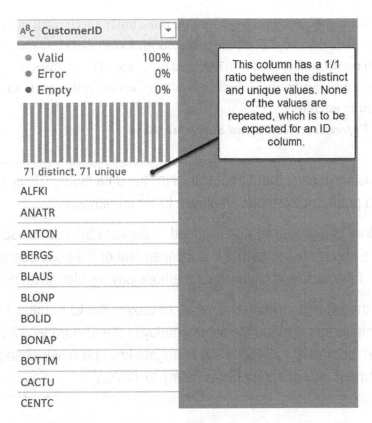

Figure 4-17. *A good example of a key column*

If you have two columns with a 1/1 ratio, scrutinize each of them to see which you should keep. A key column has (by definition) high cardinality, which means it will be very "expensive" to "store." I hate to keep putting you off, but we **will** get to cardinality. (It gets its own section!)

When a key column is present in another table, it is called a "foreign key." When it is in its own "home" table, it is called a "primary key." You may not see these terms directly on the exam, but the concepts they represent are critical. You can connect two tables together by matching the primary and foreign key columns. If we were working in a database, we would call this process "joining." In Power BI, the term "join" is not used; rather, we create "relationships." You need to have relationships between tables for the data model to work. (See Chapter 5.)

As part of your transformation process, you must ensure that each query has a column that serves as the "key." Simplify this column as much as you can. For example, if the ID has two components (1234-56789) and only one of the components can serve as an ID, split the column and reduce the key down to the minimum number of characters to uniquely identify each row.

For Future Reference: Native and Surrogate Keys

A **native key** is something that the business (or the data owner) uses to uniquely identify a data point, for example, employee ID for employees.

A **surrogate key** is a unique ID that is added to the data by a database owner. The advantage of a surrogate key is that it is independent of the business, so does not change, even if the business changes its methodology for identification.

For example, the HR department assigns an employee the ID number XYZ123. The database administrator assigns the same employee the ID number 123456. Both IDs are unique, but the ID 123456 is the surrogate key and never changes even if the HR department changes their ID taxonomy to 123XYZ.

Data Types Matter!

When I taught Excel to beginners, one of the points I emphasized was to *not* leave a column's data type as General. This is equally (if not more) true in Power BI. The wrong data type is *not* a net-neutral decision. There are some rules that you need to follow when assigning a data type to a column:

1. Currency should be stored as a Fixed Decimal type. This data type stores a number at four digits of precision *after* the decimal point.

2. A Fixed Decimal type is *not* the equivalent of a Decimal type.

3. A Decimal type stores up to 15 digits, including numbers before *and* after the decimal place. For example, if I have a number that is 13 digits *before* the decimal place, the Decimal data type will only store two digits *after* the decimal place, resulting in a loss of precision.

4. Dates should be stored as a Date data type. If you need to store a value for Time, store it in a separate column. (Don't worry about formatting a date column—that happens in the Power BI Desktop.)

5. If you know your PBIX file will be consumed by someone in a different region of the world, you should assign Date, Fixed Decimal, and Decimal using the Locale option, shown in Figure 4-18. This feature will properly convert a date from US format (Month/Day/Year) to rest-of-the-world format (Day/Month/Year) automatically. It will do the same for Fixed Decimal and Decimal—it switches the decimal place to a comma and vice versa—all without any manual intervention.

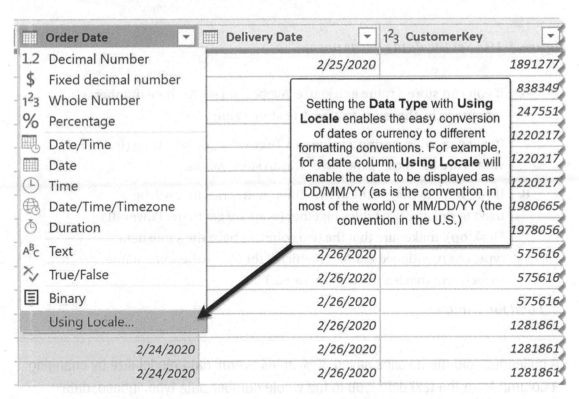

Figure 4-18. *Accessing Using Locale in the Data Type menu*

Once you have accessed Using Locale, set the data type as normal, as shown in Figure 4-19.

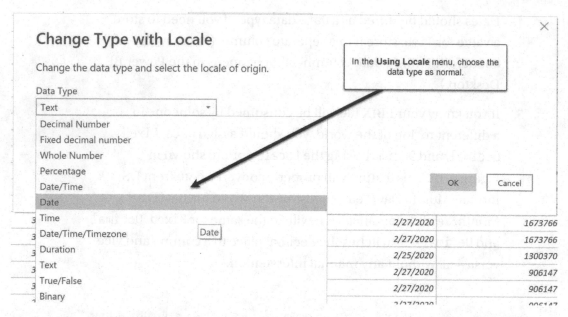

Figure 4-19. *Set the data type as normal*

6. If you can store a value as a Whole Number, do so. A whole number is going to be the "cheapest" way to store values.

7. If you can avoid storing a value as a Text value, do so. String (text) values are the most "expensive" way to store values.

8. If you have two columns in two different queries that will be used to link the two tables together (once we get to the Power BI Desktop), make sure that the two columns have the same data type. (As mentioned earlier, it is nice if they have the same name as well, but that isn't strictly required.)

Food for Thought

A colleague told me he once saved 30% in his overall data model size by changing a column from the text data type to the whole number data type. Indeed, data types matter!

Be deliberate and intentional in your data type choices. Checking the data types should be the last thing you do before you finish your query transformations. Watch out for extra Changed Type steps. You are usually safe removing these as they appear in your list of steps. Most of the time they are unnecessary. (There are always exceptions. If the Changed Type is necessary to perform a step below it, do not delete it. You will break the subsequent steps.)

For Future Reference: Query Folding

This is the feature you don't know you need until you break it. When you connect to a data source that is powered by something (meaning a server), you can "fold" the work of doing the transformations back to that engine. For example, if you connect to a data source on SQL Server, there's an excellent chance that the server supports folding. If so, the PQE is going to fold back the transformations to the server to perform them and thus get them done faster. (Servers *typically* have more power than our laptops.) *But there are some transformations that will break query folding, and changing a data type is one of them (usually).* That's why I said that you should delete any gratuitous Changed Type steps that the PQE creates. That is also why I said that changing data types should be the *last* step you perform on your query. All the previous steps will be folded back, speeding up the process.

There are sources that have no underlying "engines": Excel, CSV, and PDF come to mind. When a query originates from one of these types of sources, there is no query folding. One school of thought is "don't worry about breaking query folding in these queries." But I disagree.

Tip   Practice the same good habits regardless of whether the query type supports folding. Then you won't accidentally break folding when it *is* available because of sloppy practices.

How do you know if query folding is happening (or not)? On your Applied Steps panel, select a step and right-click. If the View Native Query is grayed out, then query folding is *not* happening. In Figure 4-20, query folding is happening.

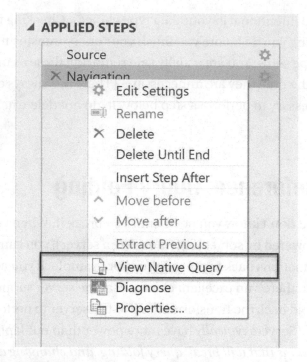

Figure 4-20. *Query folding is occurring in this step*

If you think it should be, go back up your list of steps until you find the step where it was broken. (Remember, it will *never* work with Excel, CSV, or PDF.) If View Native Query is an active option, click it. A window will then open in which you can see the M translated into the "native" language of the source server as shown in Figure 4-21.

□ ✕

Native Query

```
select [$Table].[ProductKey] as [ProductKey],
    [$Table].[Product Code] as [Product Code],
    [$Table].[Product Name] as [Product Name],
    [$Table].[Manufacturer] as [Manufacturer],
    [$Table].[Brand] as [Brand],
    [$Table].[Color] as [Color],
    [$Table].[Weight Unit Measure] as [Weight Unit Measure],
    [$Table].[Weight] as [Weight],
    [$Table].[Unit Cost] as [Unit Cost],
    [$Table].[Unit Price] as [Unit Price],
    [$Table].[Subcategory Code] as [Subcategory Code],
    [$Table].[Subcategory] as [Subcategory],
    [$Table].[Category Code] as [Category Code],
    [$Table].[Category] as [Category]
from [dbo].[Product] as [$Table]
```

Figure 4-21. *Example of a native query*

One final note: Query folding is probably *not* going to show up on the PL-300, but while I want to help you pass the exam, I *also* want you to become a skilled Power BI practitioner. Knowing how to use query folding to speed up your transformations is one skill that you should have.

Your Chance to Practice

Look up Alex Powers' 30 days of query folding on YouTube. It is a great opportunity to understand what steps do (and don't) break folding.

Replacing Data
Blanks and Nulls

The Power Query Editor treats Null and Blank values differently. For both values, you use the same technique to replace them: Replace Values as shown in Figures 4-22 and 4-23.

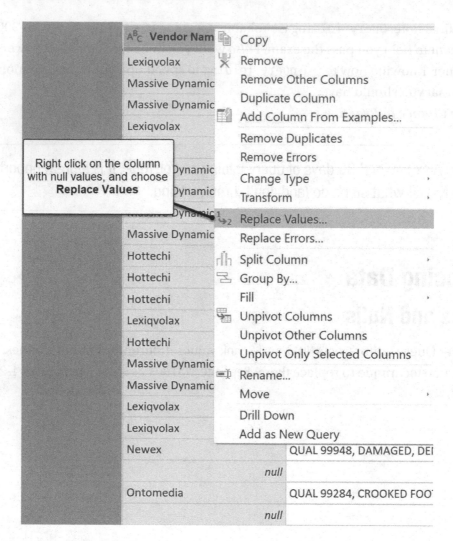

Figure 4-22. *Replacing values in a column*

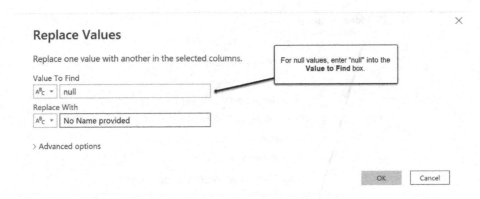

Replace Values

Replace one value with another in the selected columns.

For null values, enter "null" into the **Value to Find** box.

Value To Find

A^B_C ▾ | null

Replace With

A^B_C ▾ | No Name provided

> Advanced options

OK   Cancel

Figure 4-23. *For null values, be sure to enter "null"*

For blank values, leave the Value To Find box empty.

Errors

Errors are a little trickier. If you are lucky enough to have all the errors show up in the first 1000 rows, you can review them and determine the issue. You can see the error source by clicking the cell with the error, as shown in Figure 4-24.

	Part Number	Description	Quantity	Trans Date	Vendor Number	
	● Valid 100% ● Error 0% ● Empty 0%	● Valid 100% ● Error 0% ● Empty 0%	● Valid 100% ● Error 0% ● Empty 0%	● Valid 100% ● Error 0% ● Empty 0%	● Valid - % ● Error 32% ● Empty - %	
1	11P709-01	HARNESS COMPRESSOR K5 3PH 41in YEL BLK RED w/PL...	1	9/16/2019	D166	
2	11P826-07	WIRE HRNS-AURORA-P3 CONDENSATE 180 IN		9/19/2019	4769	
3	11P853-01	Harness-Compressor to VS Drive Power		9/19/2019	3567	
4	11P879-03	Wire Harness Perform 55 w/o DSH 022-042 (See Memo)		9/16/2019	3567	
5	12P531-06	Well Type 2.5 in Temp Probe 10k ohms NXW		9/19/2019	K010	
6	14P512B01	MOTOR PSC 1/2 HP HE3K132 230/1 (SEE NOTES)	1	9/20/2019	Error	
7	14P512B02	MOTOR PSC 1/2 HP 460/1	18	9/19/2019	4974	
8	14S551-02	PROGRAMD MOTOR 1/2HP 277/60/1 FERRITE	1	9/16/2019	Error	
19	40P816-01RG	ACCS PNL SD COMP NV5 036-72 RIVER GRAY	1	9/16/2019	1633	
20	40P824-01RG	ACCS PNL LWR FRNT NV5 022-30 RIVER GRAY	2	9/16/2019	3585	
21						

Click into a cell with an **Error**. The type of error will be displayed below.

⚠ DataFormat.Error: Invalid cell value '#N/A'.

Figure 4-24. *Displaying the reason for the error*

You can also click the hyperlink for the error. This will result in a new step being added, which may not be necessary for diagnosis. If you right-click the Data Quality peek bar, there is a contextual menu specifically for handling errors, as shown in Figure 4-25.

71

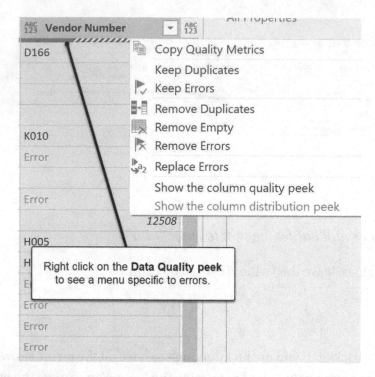

Figure 4-25. *Several options for handling errors*

You can remove or replace the errors from this menu. But what if you suspect that you have errors in rows that are not included in the first 1000 rows? You can set the Power Query Editor to profile all the rows of your data. There is a drop-down box on the bottom left-hand side of the screen you can toggle, as shown in Figure 4-26.

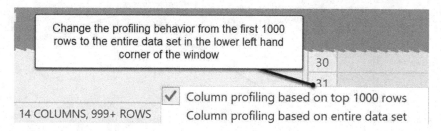

Figure 4-26. *Changing the profiling behavior*

Once the profiling behavior is changed, the Data Quality peek will reflect all the rows. If there are errors, they will be highlighted under the Error category, shown in Figure 4-27.

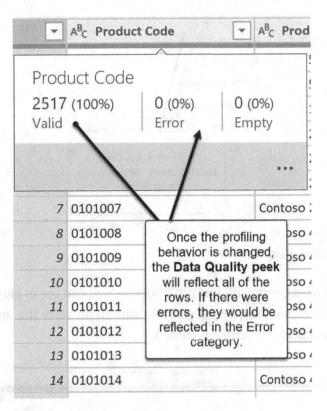

Figure 4-27. *After changing the profiling behavior*

This example does not have errors, but if it did, they would be reflected in the Error category in the Data Quality peek.

If the errors are not present in the first 1000 rows, how can you determine how to fix them? Use the Keep Errors option in the Data Quality peek context menu, as shown in Figure 4-28.

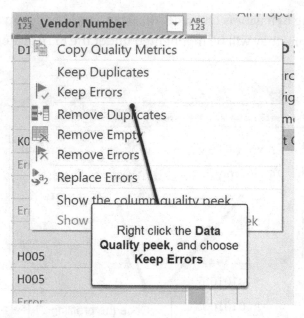

Figure 4-28. *Choose Keep Errors*

You will now have a query with just the errors, as you can see in Figure 4-29. (It might be a good idea to duplicate the query first if you want to preserve the query in its original state. Duplicating a query is discussed below.)

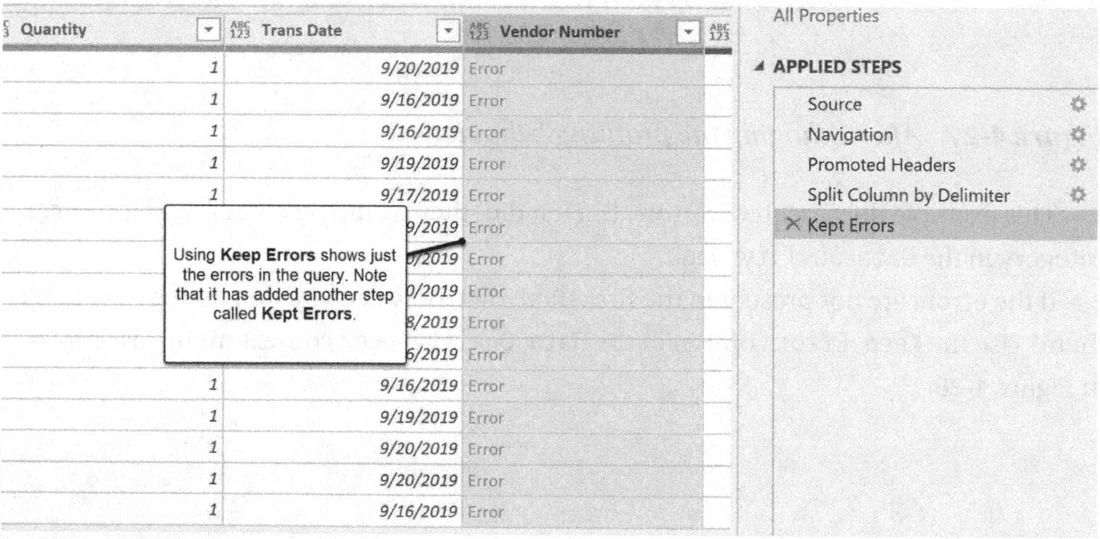

Figure 4-29. *Now only the errors are displayed*

Now you can diagnose the errors and take the appropriate measures to fix them.

Adding New Data

If only the data sources to which we connect had all the data we needed! But all too frequently the source(s) you are using lacks something important. There are two types of new data you can create in the Power Query Editor: a new column or a new table.

Adding a New Column

There are several ways to create new columns:

- Column from Examples
- Custom Column
- Conditional Column
- Index Column
- Duplicate Column

The correct option is the one that most efficiently performs the necessary task. For example, if you want to add a new column with the country "United States," you could use either `Column from Examples` or `Custom Column`. Figures 4-30 and 4-31 show both methods.

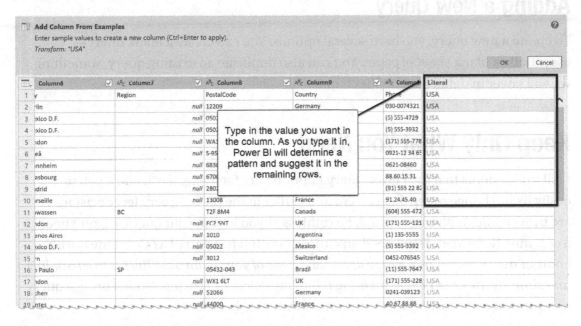

Figure 4-30. *Adding a column from examples*

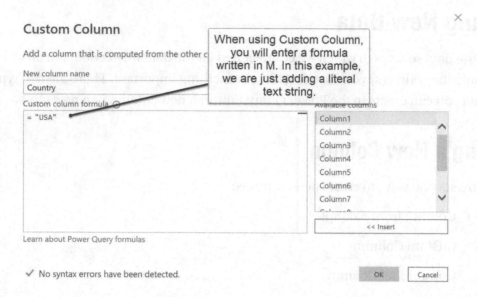

Figure 4-31. *Adding a custom column*

I have provided these two examples to illustrate that there will often be several ways to perform the same task. Which method you choose will vary based on your understanding of each technique and the requirements of your task.

Adding a New Query

To create a new query, you have several options. You can create a blank query—essentially a blank sheet of paper. You can also duplicate an existing query, something we will cover in detail later in this chapter.

Keep Only What You Need

I tell my students that the Power Query Editor is very forgiving. It will allow you to easily fix or change a step that you created earlier in the process; very few decisions are irreversible. With that in mind, be ruthless as you look at your queries. Don't need a column? Remove it. Don't need an entire query but just part of it? Combine it with another query, either as a merge or append. *One of your main objectives is to streamline and simplify the data before you bring it into the Power BI Desktop*. Do *not* bring a query or a column over "just in case." You can always come back for it.

Combining Queries

Append

Imagine a scenario in which you have 12 different Excel worksheets, each for a different month in the year. You bring each of them into the PQE, and now you have 12 different queries. You have a perfect opportunity to streamline the queries. You can choose to append all of them into one new query (e.g., Append Queries as New) or append them into an existing query (e.g., append February into the January query and so on). In Figures 4-32, 4-33, and 4-34, there are four queries that will be combined into one separate query. (In these examples I am using Append, but these remarks apply equally to Merge.)

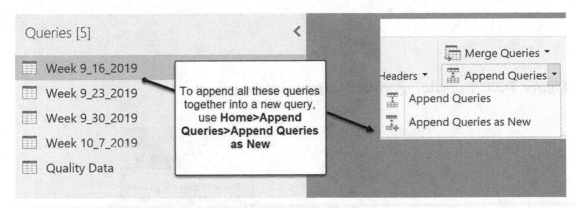

Figure 4-32. *Appending queries as a new query*

The following dialogue box will open:

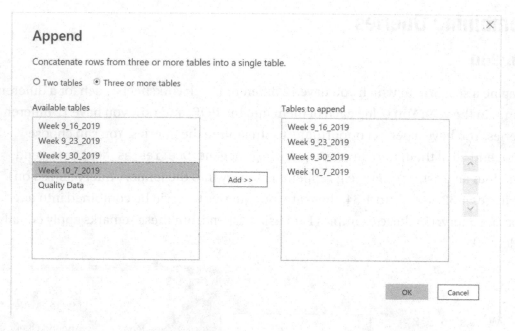

Figure 4-33. *Appending multiple queries into a new one*

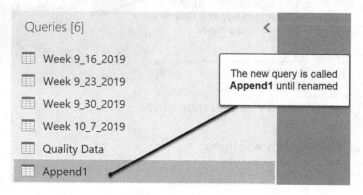

Figure 4-34. *The new query*

Merging

The mechanics of merging two queries are like those you use when appending, with one key difference. When appending, it is a good idea to ensure that the structures of both queries (number, name, data types of columns) are the same. With a merge, it is important to understand exactly how you want to merge the two queries. There are seven different join patterns, which I will explain in the following.

The default join is a left outer join (Figure 4-35). In a left outer join, records in one query are compared with records in a second query. Because a picture can replace 1000 words, I am illustrating each type of join with a simple diagram.

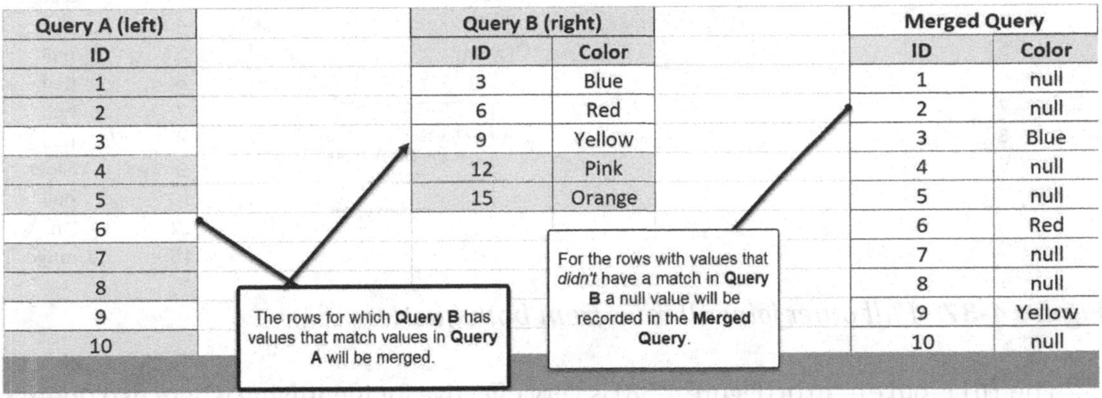

Query A (left)	Query B (right)		Merged Query	
ID	ID	Color	ID	Color
1	3	Blue	1	null
2	6	Red	2	null
3	9	Yellow	3	Blue
4	12	Pink	4	null
5	15	Orange	5	null
6			6	Red
7			7	null
8			8	null
9			9	Yellow
10			10	null

The rows for which **Query B** has values that match values in **Query A** will be merged.

For the rows with values that *didn't* have a match in **Query B** a null value will be recorded in the **Merged Query**.

Figure 4-35. *Left outer join: all rows from the left, matching from the right*

The next most common type of join is a right outer join. This is the inverse of a `left outer join` (Figure 4-36).

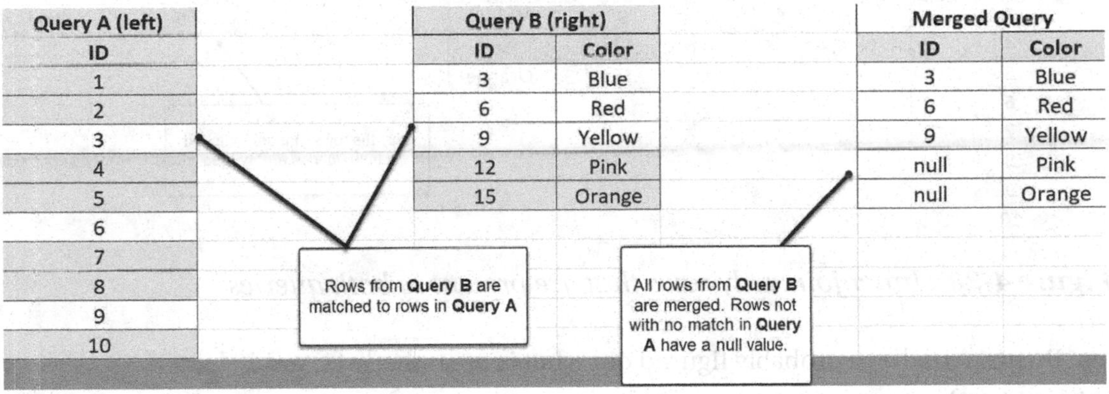

Query A (left)	Query B (right)		Merged Query	
ID	ID	Color	ID	Color
1	3	Blue	3	Blue
2	6	Red	6	Red
3	9	Yellow	9	Yellow
4	12	Pink	null	Pink
5	15	Orange	null	Orange
6				
7				
8				
9				
10				

Rows from **Query B** are matched to rows in **Query A**

All rows from **Query B** are merged. Rows not with no match in **Query A** have a null value.

Figure 4-36. *Right outer join: All rows from the right, matching from the left*

Next up is a `full outer join` (Figure 4-37). This type of join merges the two queries regardless of matches.

Query A (left)	Query B (right)		Merged Query	
ID	ID	Color	ID	Color
1	3	Blue	1	null
2	6	Red	2	null
3	9	Yellow	3	Blue
4	12	Pink	4	null
5	15	Orange	5	null
6			6	Red
7			7	null
8			8	null
9			9	Yellow
10			10	null
			12	Pink
			15	Orange

All the rows from **Query A** and **Query B** are merged.

Figure 4-37. *Full outer join: all rows from both queries*

The full outer join (Figure 4-38) is very effective for identifying where two queries do not match up. The direct opposite of the full outer join is the inner join.

Query A (left)	Query B (right)		Merged Query	
ID	ID	Color	ID	Color
1	3	Blue	3	Blue
2	6	Red	6	Red
3	9	Yellow	9	Yellow
4	12	Pink		
5	15	Orange		
6				
7				
8				
9				
10				

Only the rows that are matched in both queries are merged.

Figure 4-38. *Inner join: only rows that are present in both queries*

By now you have probably figured out what is next: the left anti join (Figure 4-39).

Query A (left)

ID
1
2
3
4
5
6
7
8
9
10

Query B (right)

ID	Color
3	Blue
6	Red
9	Yellow
12	Pink
15	Orange

Merged Query

ID	Color
1	null
2	null
4	null
5	null
7	null
8	null
10	null

> Only rows from **Query A** that are *not* matched in **Query B** are merged

Figure 4-39. *Left anti join: only rows in Query A that are not matched*

Next up, the `right anti join` (Figure 4-40).

Query A (left)

ID
1
2
3
4
5
6
7
8
9
10

Query B (right)

ID	Color
3	Blue
6	Red
9	Yellow
12	Pink
15	Orange

Merged Query

ID	Color
12	Pink
15	Orange

> Only rows in **Query B** that are *not* matched in **Query A** are merged.

Figure 4-40. *Right anti join: only rows in Query B that are not matched*

Finally, the `full anti join` (Figure 4-41).

Query A (left)

ID
1
2
3
4
5
6
7
8
9
10

Query B (right)

ID	Color
3	Blue
6	Red
9	Yellow
12	Pink
15	Orange

Merged Query

ID	Color
1	null
2	null
4	null
5	null
7	null
8	null
10	null
null	Pink
null	Orange

> Rows from both **Query A** and **Query B** that are *not* matched are merged.

Figure 4-41. *Full anti join: only rows in both queries that are not matched*

Duplicating a query

In the preceding example, one option you have is to duplicate one of the queries and then append all the other queries into the duplicate. When you duplicate a query, you are making an exact copy, shown in Figure 4-42. There are other times when duplicating a query is helpful, for example, when you need to preserve the original query as it is.

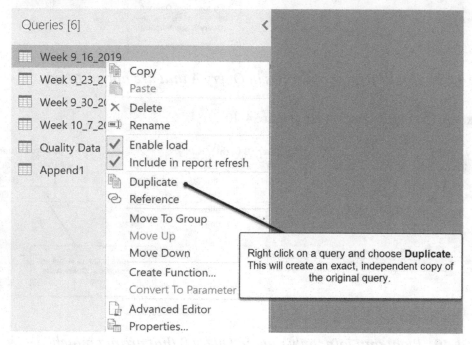

Figure 4-42. Duplicating a query

A Matter of Style

Lots of choices you make in the Power Query Editor are questions of style. When appending files, I prefer to append (or merge) them all into one new query, leaving the originals as is. But this isn't a "must-do." Experiment with different methods so that you can choose the right one in each circumstance.

Referencing a Query

Now let's think about it another way. What if the original query has many `Applied Steps` (transformations) and you are still working on it, but you need to copy the query and have it reflect all the work you are *continuing* to do on the original query? Reference the original query as shown in Figure 4-43. It will create a second version of the query, but any changes you make in the original query will cascade to the second version.

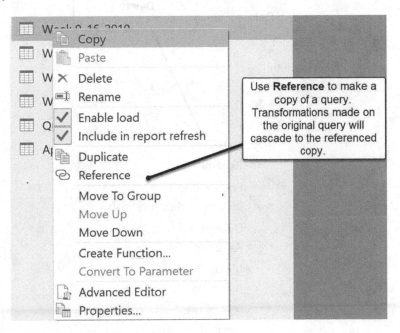

Figure 4-43. *Referencing a query*

Deleting a Query

You can delete a query if you don't need it as shown in Figure 4-44.

Figure 4-44. *Deleting a query*

You *can't* delete a query that is being used in another query (e.g., if you have appended or merged it into another query).

Working with Some Data

If your data has millions of rows, you do not need (or want) to work with all the rows to decide on your transformations. Or you may not want certain rows to appear in the final report. Either way, you can filter your data in the PQE to limit what you are working with. Filtering *excludes* rows that do not meet the filter conditions. *These rows will not appear in the finished report.* If you want to work with only a subset of the data during the report development process, remember to remove the steps in which you limited the rows *before* publishing the report.

Only 1000 Rows?

In the lower-left corner, the Power Query Editor displays the number of columns the query has and how many rows it has scanned (previewed)—*up to 1000 rows.* At first glance this seems problematic, but it isn't because you are not *actually* transforming the data right now. You are writing a script of transformations that will be performed on the data when you load the data into the Desktop. (Don't worry. You haven't missed that part—we haven't gotten there yet.) All you need is a *representative* sample of the data. The presumption is that 1000 rows are sufficient for you to understand the structure and layout of the data and make appropriate decisions. If you need to see more values, you can use Filters ➤ Load more to see up to 1000 unique values in each column, as shown in Figure 4-45.

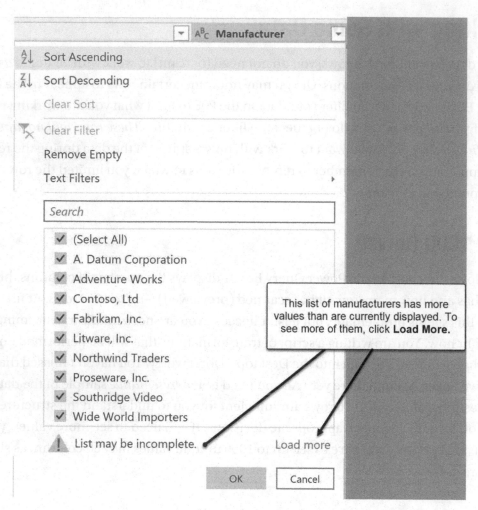

Figure 4-45. *Using the Filters panel to see all the unique values in a column*

But there's a hitch: the Filters panel cannot display more than 1000 unique values, as you can see in Figure 4-46.

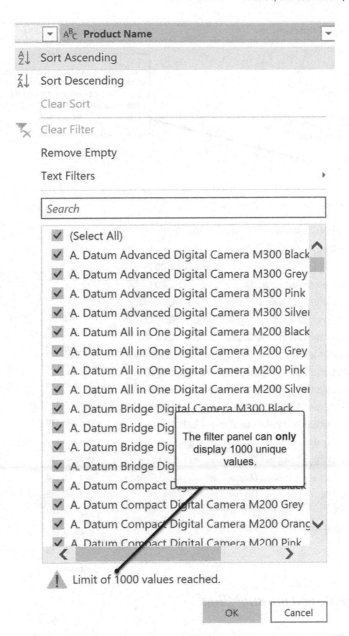

Figure 4-46. *Only 1000 unique values can be displayed*

If you have more than 1000 unique values and you need to filter some out, you must use the manual filters to create the filter you need as shown in Figure 4-47.

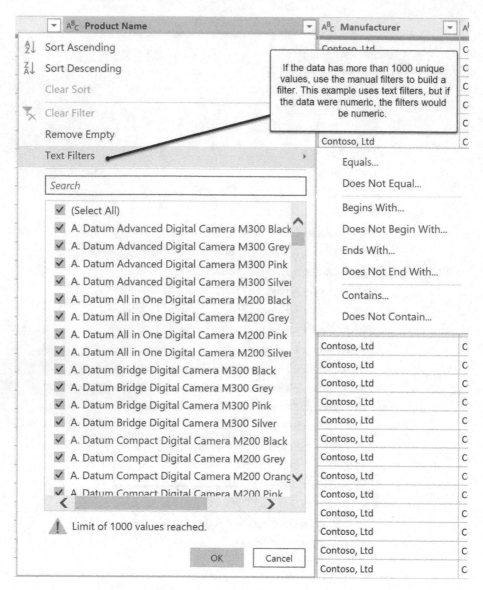

Figure 4-47. *Creating a manual filter*

If you cannot filter without seeing all of the data, you *can* scroll through your data, shown in Figure 4-48.

Figure 4-48. *Scrolling through data in the Preview window*

Scrolling through thousands of rows of data is tedious at best and impracticable at worst, which is why working with representative data is so important. If the data you have is very inconsistent, you may need to go back to the source to clean it prior to being able to use the Power Query Editor.

Once you create a step to filter out rows, I would *strongly recommend renaming and documenting* that step (see earlier).

For Future Reference: Future-Proofing Your Work

If only data would stay the same. If only users would never remove or add columns to an Excel worksheet. We often don't have much control on the data we work with; therefore, we should never assume that there won't be any changes. Here are just a *few* of the types of changes that can occur:

1. Columns are renamed, added, or deleted.

2. Files are moved, added, or deleted.

When you are working with a database, the data is probably much more stable. But if your data source is Excel, you have a higher likelihood of having columns changed. You need to build your transformation script such that if a change happens, your script can handle it without breaking. This is called future-proofing. The first step is to make sure your Formula Bar is visible and *read the M for every step you create.*

Excluding and Including Columns

When removing multiple columns, depending on how you make your selection (as a Remove Columns, Remove Other Columns, Select Columns), the M will be constructed differently. In Figure 4-49 a column will be removed. In Figure 4-50 only explicitly named columns will be kept.

```
= Table.RemoveColumns(#"Split Column by Delimiter",{"Vendor Number"})
```

Figure 4-49. *This step will remove a column called "Vendor Number"*

```
= Table.SelectColumns(#"Removed Columns",{"Vendor Name", "CommentText.1", "CommentText.2"})
```

Figure 4-50. *This step will only keep the explicitly named columns*

In Figure 4-49, one column has been *excluded* explicitly by using Remove Columns. What happens if the next time the data is refreshed another column is added? Will the new column appear in the report? In this example, the answer is yes because it has not been specifically excluded.

In Figure 4-50, three columns have been specifically *included* using Select Columns. What happens if the next time the data is refreshed another column has been added to the data source? Will the new column appear in the report? The answer is, no, it will *not* because it has not been specifically included.

There are many techniques to write M so that it is flexible and can handle changes to the source data, almost all of which are beyond the scope of this book. But there are several good books that have been published in which you learn how to future-proof your queries, which I will list at the end of the chapter. For the PL-300, learn to recognize an M expression that will break your query or perform unexpectedly. For real life, invest some time in learning how to future-proof your queries—your future self, and colleagues, will thank you.

Resolving Errors in Your Query

When you see the dreaded yellow error symbol in a query, it can be a little alarming (Figure 4-51)!

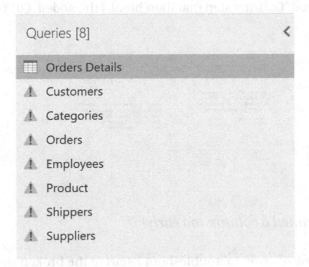

Figure 4-51. A lot of alarming errors!

Hopefully you won't often see this many errors, but the resolution process is always the same. Start with the step that has the error and then select each step preceding the one with the error, until you find a step that *isn't* broken. Then identify what happened between the last working step and the first broken step.

The good news is that most errors are one of two types: a broken file path or a prior step in the wrong sequence. I covered broken file paths in the previous chapter, so here I will talk about a few common *types* of steps that break other steps. (I can't cover every possible error type.)

Incorrect Data Type

Usually, you set your data types as your last step in the query because the Changed Type step will break query folding (see earlier). However, there are times when you need to perform an operation on a column or columns. If the existing data types are not compatible with that operation (e.g., you try to multiply two text columns), you may produce an error. The solution in this case is to insert a Changed Type step *before* the operational step.

Missing or Renamed Column

If you rename or delete a column that a subsequent step depends on, the Power Query Editor will generate an error. In Figure 4-52, I have engineered an error by renaming a column in the `Renamed Columns` step that then breaks the `Added Custom` step (and all following steps).

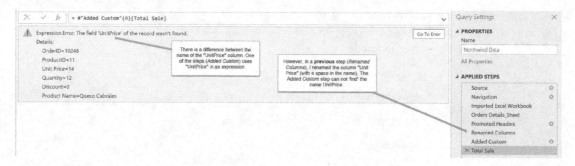

Figure 4-52. *I renamed a column too early!*

No matter the type of error, to troubleshoot I start at the broken step and then look at each step above it in turn. In this case, I would find that the `Renamed Columns` step caused the problem, and I can fix the error by deleting that step. Sometimes you must do more radical surgery and rearrange or redo your steps.

For Future Reference: Reusing Your Work

A well-written M script can be a work of art. That may seem an extravagant statement, until you spend a considerable amount of time building one! A lot of thought goes into choosing the correct steps, in the right order, preferably without breaking `query folding` (see earlier), and planning for future changes to the data. It is nice to know you can reuse your work.

The Advanced Editor

The `Formula Bar` reflects the M that has been generated for the step currently selected. If you want to see *all* the M that has been generated for a particular query, you need to open the `Advanced Editor` on the Home tab, shown in Figure 4-53.

Figure 4-53. *The M for a query, in the Advanced Editor*

While using the Advanced Editor is beyond the scope of the exam, I want you to know what it can do for you. If you need to modify several steps and you feel confident in your M coding skills, you can edit the M directly in the Advanced Editor. Additionally, M steps that you see in the Advanced Editor can be copied as plain text and pasted into another query.

When you first start editing M in the Advanced Editor, there are some common pitfalls:

- Make sure that you have a comma after each step *except* the last one (the one just above the in statement).

- Make sure that your M script starts with a let statement and ends with an in statement (unless you are using functions).

- The in statement usually references the last step name.

- The Source step (the first one) *must* point to the right location for *your* data source.

- When copying and reusing M in another query, check anything that is "hard-coded" (in double quotes) to ensure that an item with that name is present in the destination query.

- When copying and reusing M in another query, check all the step references to ensure that they are present in the new query.

Copying a Query

An even easier way to reuse the M script is to copy the query on the Queries panel. Select the query on the Queries panel (on the left side of the PQE) and then Ctrl+C. Open the PQE window for another PBIX file and Ctrl+V. The entire query is now available to the second PBIX file.

Copying Parts of an M Script

In the Formula Bar, you can see the M for each step. In the Advanced Editor, you can see the entire script. You can edit the M here (and in the Formula Bar), but it might be easier to copy the script and drop it into a text editor. (I use plain-old Notepad.) You can copy elements of the script (shown in Figure 4-54) and then paste those elements into the Advanced Editor for a different query in which you want to reuse the M.

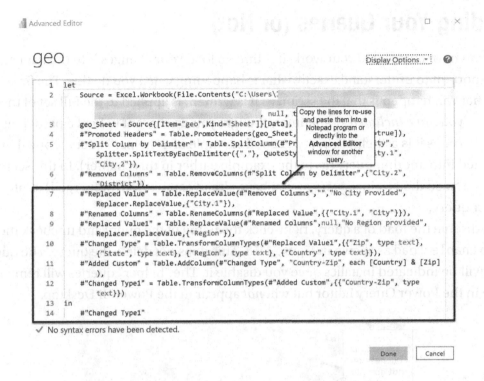

Figure 4-54. *Sample of an M script to be copied into another query*

Like all surgery, be careful when you do this. Here are some common "gotchas":

1. Step names are not the same in the two queries.

2. Column names are not the same in the two queries.

3. The source reference is different (this is usually in the top step).

4. Omitting the comma at the end of a step.

5. Including the comma in the last step.

Take your time and pay attention to the details. *Don't try to edit in a hurry; that is the fastest way to break your M script.*

Loading Your Queries (or Not)

Once you have completed your work, it is time to load your changes into the data model. It is important to understand exactly what is happening when you do this. The first thing that will happen is that the script, as it is written, is applied to the full set of the data that *you have included*. Sometimes, though, you don't want to load a particular query. Perhaps it is a "helper" query. A good example of a "helper" query is one that you appended into another query (as in the example earlier in this chapter). In this scenario, you don't need the original query as you have already appended (or merged) it into another query.

To disable the load of a query, right-click the name of the query and uncheck the box next to Enable Load as shown in Figure 4-55. This does *not* delete the query. The query name will be indicated in italics once you disable it. The "helper" queries will remain visible in the Power Query Editor but will *not* appear in the Power BI Desktop.

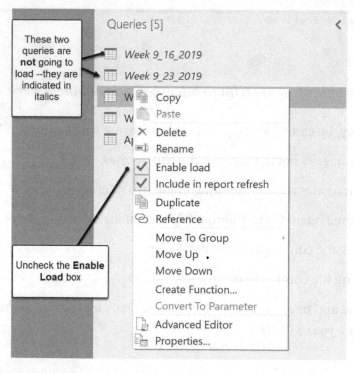

Figure 4-55. *Disable loading to the Desktop*

A Few Tips and Tricks

Here are a few tips and tricks that I hope you take from this chapter. Not all of these are covered on the PL-300 exam, but they will all serve you well:

1. Document your queries and steps.

2. Keep like steps together.

3. Name your steps.

4. Data types matter—be intentional in selecting them.

5. Keep the Formula Bar open and read the M for each step.

6. Future-proof your queries to the best of your current ability.

7. Reuse your M script as/when appropriate.

8. Change data types as close to the last step as you can.

Additional Resources

It is impossible to cover everything about the Power Query Editor in a single chapter. With that in mind, I want to recommend a few books that can further your knowledge.

- *Collect, Combine, and Transform Data Using Power Query in Excel and Power BI* by Gil Raviv

- *Master Your Data with Excel and Power BI* by Ken Puls and Miguel Escobar

In Chapter 15, I will provide additional resources, including YouTube and other Internet resources.

PART III

Model the Data

CHAPTER 5

Design a Data Model

What is a data model and why is it necessary? This is (perhaps) the most difficult concept to understand for a business user because Excel works in a flat world. Any summarization you want to perform requires that all the data is on the same worksheet. So, at most, you must use some LOOKUP functions to "retrieve" the data you need to include. While having everything on one worksheet is easy to comprehend, it is unwieldy and inefficient. Enter the data model.

A data model allows the logical combination of different groups of data (arranged in tables) *without physically combining them*. The model is the structure within which you will define these connections (relationships) between the tables.

Of all the skills we cover together in this book, data modeling may be the most critical to your success as a Power BI practitioner. Certainly, there are questions on the exam that test your knowledge of data modeling, and that *is* our main purpose here. However, when you use Power BI, by far most of your challenges will arise because of your data model structure. A good data model is vital for a performant Power BI report; a bad data model will hinder the speed and responsiveness of the report despite your best efforts. In this chapter I explain the basic principles of data modeling that you should know, both for the exam and in real life.

Define the Tables

As we saw in Chapter 4, a query is the form your extracted data takes in the Power Query Editor. Once you finish all your transformations and apply your changes, those queries become tables inside the Power BI Desktop. (For example, if you extract data from an Excel worksheet, it first becomes a query in the Power Query Editor and then a table once it is loaded into the data model. The same is true for any extracted data.) Once all your data has been loaded, you will have at least one table and usually many more. Now we need to define the connections between all these disparate tables. (Remember, they

101

© Jessica Jolly 2023
J. Jolly, *Microsoft Power BI Data Analyst Certification Companion*, Certification Study Companion Series,
https://doi.org/10.1007/978-1-4842-9013-2_5

may come from a wide variety of different sources and may never have been combined before. That's part of the magic of Power BI!) Before we explore relationships, I need to define some important terminology.

Dims and Facts

There are two primary types of tables in a data model: a fact table and (usually) several dimension (dim) tables.

Fact Tables	Dimension Tables
A fact table contains the data you are reporting on. In retail, it could be sales transactions. In medicine, it could be appointments and/or outcomes. In manufacturing, it could be data from each production line. Fact tables record things that have happened (usually), and so you will almost always see a date (and maybe time) stamp as part of a fact table record. A fact table *ideally* only contains values that are in numeric format (quantity; date; time; price; unique IDs for customers, patients, and products; etc.).	Dimension (dim) tables describe the elements of your fact table in greater detail. A dim table usually has a lot of columns (very wide), many of which are "strings" or alphanumeric.
For example, if the fact table contains sales transactions, each record will have an ID for the customer and for the product. Ideally, this ID will be an integer (whole number). This ID is a foreign key that allows the fact table to be related to the dim table for the customer (or product).	In the dim table, the ID number for the product (or customer or patient) is a primary key. (See Chapter 4, "Keys and IDs," for more information.) In the dim table, the record for that ID number is very detailed: the customer's name, address, birth date, demographic info, etc.
The fact table is usually the longest (the greatest number of rows) of the tables in the model. There *can* be two fact tables in a model, but that is a more advanced modeling problem, so I assume only one fact table in this book.	Dimension tables have *just one row* for each element being described (customer, product, store, etc.).
Fact tables can have *many* rows for each element such as product or customer or store.	Models usually have multiple dimension tables. Ideally, dim tables connect directly to the fact table, but they can be related to other dimension tables.

A quick note about other types of tables: There can be other types of tables in a data model such as a factless fact table or a bridge table. This book does not tackle those concepts, nor will the PL-300.

Using Fields in Visuals

We will be tackling visuals in a later chapter, but I want to introduce the concept of which *types of fields* you will use in a visual:

- Dimension table fields are descriptive; they should be used as labels on charts (e.g., rows, columns, and axes).

- Fact table fields are the values that are analyzed in a visual (e.g., summarized, averaged, counted).

Relationships: A Model's Connective Tissue

There are multiple types of relationships that Power BI supports. Let's walk through each of them. But first a word for those of you with a database background: relationships in Power BI are similar to but *not the same as a* join. *The purpose of a relationship in the Power BI context is to transmit filters.* (Much more on filters later.)

One-to-Many Relationship (1-Many)

Dimension tables have *one* row for each record (customer, product, store, etc.). (See the preceding definition.) Fact tables usually have *many* rows for each element described in a particular dim table (see the preceding definition). Therefore, the relationship used to connect a dim table to a fact table is a one-to-many relationship as shown in Figure 5-1.

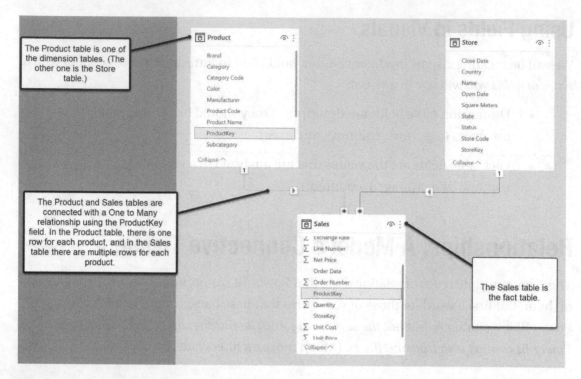

Figure 5-1. *A one-to-many relationship between a dimension and fact table*

In Figure 5-1, both the Product and the fact table have a field called ProductKey. Because there is only *one* row for each product in the Product (dim) table and there are *multiple* rows for each product in the Sales (fact) table, the relationship is one-to-many. The one side of the relationship is indicated by a tiny 1. The many side of the relationship is indicated by an asterisk, as shown in Figure 5-2.

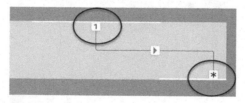

Figure 5-2. *The one-to-many icons*

Tip   If you can't figure out which table is your fact table, look for the table that has lots of rows with repeating customer IDs or product IDs or store IDs (the ID will depend on what data you are reporting on). Each fact will usually have a date (and maybe a time) associated with it.

Using the preceding example, if you choose a particular ProductKey in the Product table, the relationship will convey that selection to the Sales table as outlined in Figure 5-3. The Sales table is then filtered to only show facts related to the selected product (or selected products).

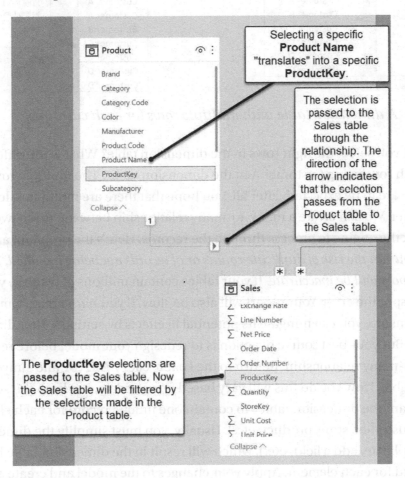

Figure 5-3.   Filter transmission from the Product to the Sales table

Many-to-Many Relationships (Many-Many)

The opposite of a 1-many relationship is a many-to-many relationship. If your model has two tables with multiple rows for the same customer (or store or product), the only way to connect these two tables is with a many-to-many relationship (meaning there are multiple rows for each customer in both the fact and the dimension table). I ask my students to visualize two sheets of paper, each with a list that has multiple lines for the customer they are interested in. I have illustrated the challenge in Figure 5-4.

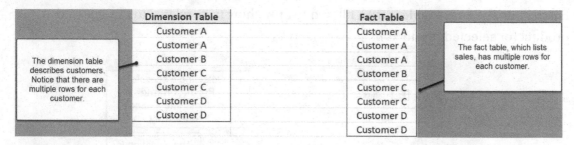

Figure 5-4. *A dimension table with multiple rows for each customer*

How can you select the right rows in the dimension table? What is the difference between each row listing Customer A in the dimension table? The multiple rows in the fact table are to be expected; after all, you hope that there are multiple sales for each customer. We can create a many-to-many relationship between these two tables and then ask the engine to process through the records. Here's the problem, and it is a big one: *You run the risk of duplicate counts or of records not being included. Either way, your report will be inaccurate.* If your tables contain millions of records, you are not likely to spot the error. Your report will also be slow. If you *must* create a many-to-many relationship, you can mitigate its potential ill effects by setting a filter direction (see below). But your best course of action is to redesign your model before resorting to a many-to-many relationship. Return to the Power Query Editor and simplify the dimension table. How you do this will vary based on your data, but keep the goal in mind: you want the dimension tables to contain one unique record for each element described (customer, store, product, etc.). Usually, you must simplify the dimension table (de-duplicate, add a field, etc.), which will result in the dimension table having a unique record for each element. Apply your changes to the model and create a one-to-many relationship.

One-to-One (1-1)

The third type of relationship is a one-to-one relationship. A one-to-one relationship is created between two tables when there is a unique row in *both* tables for a particular customer (store, product, etc.). (Don't confuse this with a fact table that *currently* only has one row for a particular customer. In that case, the fact table *can* have multiple rows for a customer. It just does not right now.) If Power BI suggests a one-to-one relationship, this is an opportunity to simplify your data model, as shown in Figure 5-5.

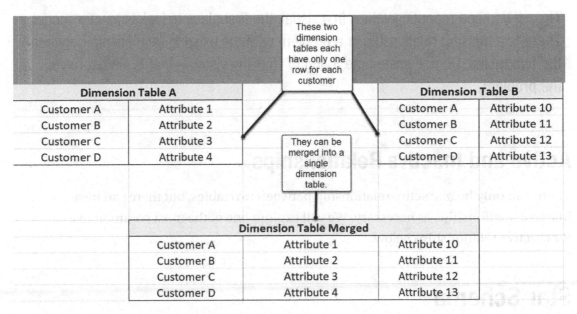

Figure 5-5. *Two dimension tables merged*

Return to the Power Query Editor and combine the two tables (it will probably be a merge operation). Apply your changes; you will only have one table and can proceed to create the standard one-to-many relationship.

Unlike the many-to-many relationship, the one-to-one relationship doesn't come with any significant disadvantages. Notwithstanding, if Power BI suggests a one-to-one relationship, you should try to merge the two tables to streamline your data model.

For Future Reference: Disconnected Tables

What happens if a table does not have a relationship with any other tables in the model? If you try to use a field from the disconnected table in a visual with a field from another table in the model, you will usually see repeating values. There *are* situations in which a disconnected table can be useful, but they are not in the scope of this book and are not included in the exam.

Tip   If you see repeating values in a visual, the first place to look is in your model. There is a missing relationship or a problem with the existing relationship between the two tables. Do not waste time trying to "fix" the visual—that is almost never the problem.

Active and Inactive Relationships

There can only be *one* active relationship between two tables, but there can be as many inactive relationships as necessary. We will explore one of the most common use cases for inactive relationships below.

Star Schema

As soon as you get started with Power BI, you will start reading and hearing about star schemas. This term refers to the "shape" of your data model, but it is much more metaphorical than physical. In a star schema, the fact table (usually just one) sits at the "virtual" center of your tables. The dimension tables are arranged in a circle around the fact table. Each dimension table is connected to the fact table through a relationship.

The star schema is not required. Rather, you should consider it the ideal that you are striving toward as you create your model. There is a common variant called the "snowflake" schema.

For Future Reference: Normalized Tables

A normalized schema is one in which tables have been deconstructed into their constituent parts. For example, if you have a Product table that has Subcategory and Category information in it, in a normalized schema, this table is broken down into three separate tables (or maybe even further). You will see this type of schema referred to as Third Normal Form, and it is quite common in data modeling generally.

Power BI aims for a happy medium. You don't want to break down your tables to their furthest extreme, but you also don't want all your data in one table (as in Excel).

Snowflake schemas are not the worst design for a data model, and sometimes they are necessary. Remember, the star schema is your *ideal* data model structure.

Relationships and Directions

Now that we have covered relationships, we must address the direction of the relationship. Yes, relationships have a direction. In Power BI a relationship is *not* a join; rather, it is a method to convey a filter from one table to another.

Single-Direction Relationships

By default, when Power BI creates a 1-many relationship, the direction will be single, flowing from the one side (usually the dim table) to the many side (usually the fact table). Recall the example from earlier (Figure 5-6).

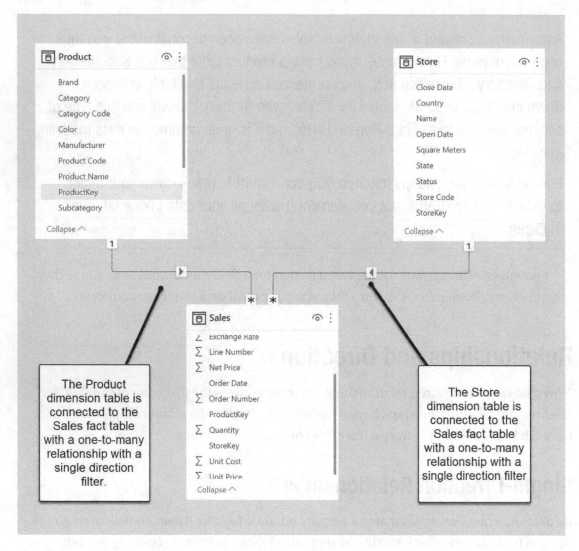

Figure 5-6. *Two dimension tables connected by single-direction one-to-many relationships*

This behavior enables you to make a selection in the dim table where there is only one row for each customer (or product or store), thereby avoiding ambiguity in your selection. This selection is then transmitted from the dim table to the fact table via the direction of the relationship. As long as the direction is one way, you don't have to worry about incorrect results arising from a bidirectional relationship.

Bidirectional Relationships

A bidirectional relationship is one in which a filter can be transmitted from *either* table in the relationship. This may sound very convenient, and there will be times you will be tempted to use a bidirectional relationship to solve a data modeling problem, as shown in Figure 5-7. *Avoid this if you can.* Bidirectional relationships can introduce ambiguity (or, worse, errors) in your reports. They can also slow your report down significantly. With that warning out of the way, there are ways to mitigate the potential damage a bidirectional relationship can do.

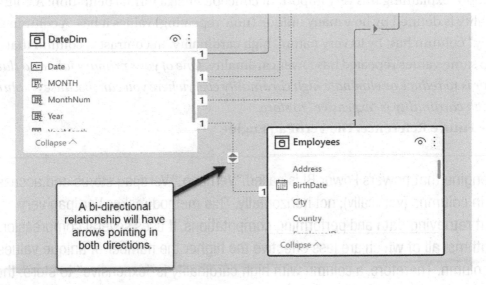

Figure 5-7. Bidirectional relationship

You will be presented with a bidirectional filter in two scenarios:

1. *In a 1-1 relationship*: These relationships are automatically created as bidirectional, and largely in this instance, the bidirectional filter won't do much damage to your report. The risk of ambiguity is not present, because both tables have unique rows for each element.

2. *In a many-many relationship*: This is the scenario in which you do not want a bidirectional relationship, but *a many-to-many relationship is always created as bidirectional.* Usually, you are going to use one of the tables to filter the other table, so in this situation, mimic a single-direction relationship by setting the

filter direction artificially. This selection will mitigate the potential for ambiguity because the selection is made in one table and is filtered to the other one.

With all that said, avoid bidirectional relationships as much as possible!

Finally, Cardinality!

In the previous chapter, I mentioned cardinality, and I promised that I would go into great depth explaining this very important concept. First, a formal definition: A column's cardinality is defined by how many unique (non-repeating) values it has. A column that is a "key" column has, by its very nature, high cardinality. In contrast, a column that has the same values repeated has lower cardinality. *One of your primary jobs as a data modeler is to reduce or eliminate high cardinality everywhere you can, because a column with high cardinality is "expensive" to store.*

For Future Reference: The VertiPaq Engine

The engine that powers Power BI is called "Vertipaq." Vertipaq stores and accesses data in columns (vertically), not horizontally. This method makes Vertipaq very fast at retrieving data and performing computations. It uses several compression algorithms, all of which are less effective the higher the number of unique values in a column. Therefore, a column with high cardinality is "expensive" to store: the engine cannot perform as much compression.

The best place to reduce cardinality is in the Power Query Editor. Can you eliminate the column entirely (is it necessary for your reporting)? Can you split the column into smaller units with more repeating values? For example, here's a single column with values separated by a pipe (|) symbol:

Contoso | Mountain Bike| MB-200

This column could be split into potentially four columns:

Contoso || Mountain Bike || MB || 200

Each of the columns, except the last one (with the "200"), would have much lower cardinality than the original column. Another common opportunity to lower cardinality is a date/time column:

4/15/2022 09:43 am

If you are using the time component, you can split the column into two (date and time), each of which will have much lower cardinality than the original column:

4/15/2022 || 9:43 am

If you are not using the time component, change the contents to date only.

When you do have a column with high cardinality that you cannot simplify (e.g., a key column), try to store that column as an integer, preferably a whole number. Integers are easier to compress, so even if the column is "expensive," you can mitigate the impact by selecting the most efficient data type.

Selecting the data type for the column is best done in the Power Query Editor, but you *can* change the data type in the Power BI Desktop if needed. There are a few other things you can set for the column in the Desktop:

1. *The format of the data*: You are not changing the data type (which is how the data is stored); rather, you are changing how it is displayed in your report. The only place you can change the format of the data type is in the Desktop; you *cannot* change the data format in the Power Query Editor.

2. *The categorization of the data*: There are certain types of data that benefit from being correctly categorized. The most frequently categorized data is geographic data, shown in Figure 5-8. For example, if you have a column with a city name and a column with country names, both columns are text data types. By categorizing columns—these respectively as "City" and "Country"—you can ensure that they won't be inaccurately mapped. (Cities and countries can have the same name: Columbia, South Carolina, and Columbia the country.)

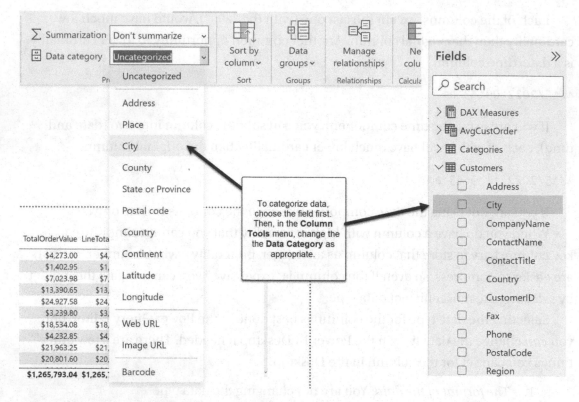

Figure 5-8. *Categorizing data using the Column tools menu in the Report view*

Another use case for categorization is if you have a column with a URL that points to a storage location for an image. When you categorize that column as Image URL, and then use that column in a visual, it will display the image, not the text string for the URL.

Once you have successfully categorized a geographical field, a globe symbol will appear next to the field.

Tip   This is a Microsoft tool, which means that there are almost always *at least* two ways to perform a task. You can categorize data in the Model view as well, as shown in Figure 5-9.

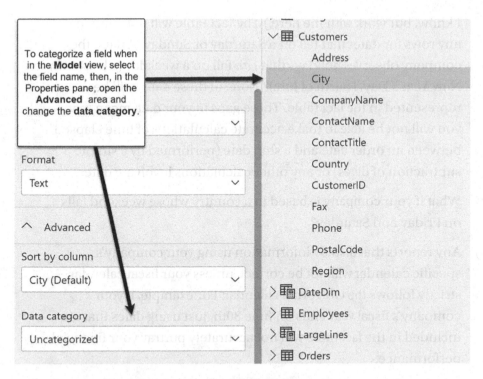

Figure 5-9. Data categorization in the Model view

3. *The name of the column*: Ideally, this is something you did in the Power Query Editor, but if you forgot or need to change the name of a column, you can do so in the Desktop. The change will propagate back to the Power Query Editor, if the data was loaded from the Power Query Editor.

Adding a Date Table

Almost every data model will have fields with dates in them; quite frequently, there will be several fields that store dates. In a data model that contains information about orders (for example), the fact table may have three fields related to dates: order date, ship date, delivery date. You *could* use these date fields in your reports, but this will present some problems:

1) The fact table may not have *all* the dates between the earliest and latest dates represented. What if the company in question does not accept orders, ship, or deliver on the weekends? (Improbable,

115

I know, but work with me here.) The fact table will not contain any rows for dates that fall on a Saturday or Sunday. What if the company observes holidays that *can* fall on a weekday (Christmas, New Year's Day, Fourth of July)? None of these dates will be represented in the fact table. These gaps in your data mean that you will not be able to make accurate calculations of time elapsed between an order date and a ship date (performed by a simple subtraction of dates) or any other calculations involving dates.

2) What if your company is based in a country whose weekend falls on Friday and Saturday?

3) Any reports that display information using your company's specific calendar will not be correct, unless your fiscal calendar strictly follows the Gregorian calendar. For example, if your company's fiscal year ends on June 30th, just using dates that are included in the fact table will not accurately portray your financial performance.

4) The built-in time intelligence functions in DAX will not work as designed. These functions will be covered in the next chapter, but here's a sneak preview: you will *want* to use the time intelligence functions!

By now you are wondering what to do to avoid all these dire circumstances, and well you might! The answer is simple: *add a dimension table specifically for dates*. And the good news is that it is (relatively) easy to do so. A date dimension table (often shortened to "date dim") can be constructed in one of three ways, all of which are equally effective. Which one you should choose depends on your company's particular data environment:

1. Use one that has been created by someone else and stored in a data warehouse. If you are lucky enough to have one of these, rejoice! All you do is to import that table the same way you would any other table from a data source. The good news is that it will be accurate, standardized, and complete.

Tip   If your company does not already have a corporate date table, make it your mission to get one created and stored in an area where anyone using Power BI can access it.

2. Create one in the Power Query Editor. This method has the advantage of taking up less "space" in your model (more on that in the next chapter). You can readily find the M code for date tables that have been created by experts in M such as Ken Puls and others. Or you can watch one of the several excellent YouTube videos on the subject and create one yourself.

3. You can use DAX to create a date table in the Power BI Desktop. As with the M code date tables, there are excellent examples readily available on the Internet. Most would agree that the best examples are those provided by SQLBI (I have no affiliation with them, just a big fan). In the next chapter, wherein we explore DAX more fully, I will return to using DAX for your date dimension table.

Whichever method you choose (or have available), *you need a date table in your model*. Once the date dimension table has been created, there are several steps you must take for it to be useful:

1. Establish a numerical sort column for the months of the year. Otherwise, when you use the month column in a report, it will be sorted alphabetically (e.g., April, August, February, etc.).

Best Practice   In your sort column, include the year number *and* the month number (e.g., 202101, 202102, 210203). That way, the months and years will be sorted appropriately in your report.

2. Mark your date table. You will need to have one column that *has a row for every date* between the earliest and the latest date present in your model. *This column must be formatted as a date.* Once you have successfully marked the date table, you see a little icon next to your date column that looks something like an ID card as shown in Figures 5-10 and 5-11.

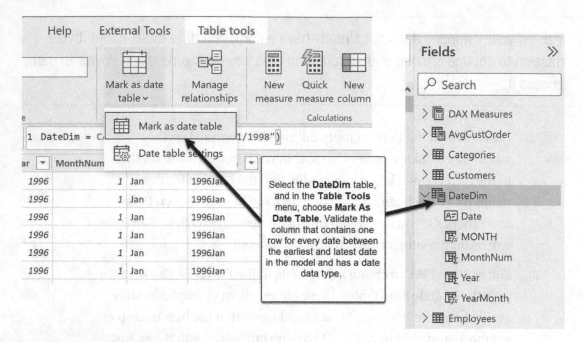

Figure 5-10. Marking a date table

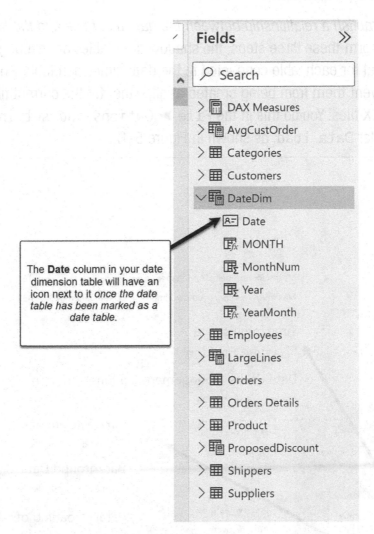

The **Date** column in your date dimension table will have an icon next to it *once the date table has been marked as a date table.*

Figure 5-11. *The date column indicates that the date table has been marked*

For Future Reference: Shadow Date Tables

Without a date table, Power BI creates mini date tables "behind" every date field in your model; these tables are called "shadow" date tables, and they are problematic for several reasons: 1) You have no control over them. You can't add to or modify them. 2) They bloat the data model unnecessarily. 3) They don't work *reliably* with DAX time intelligence functions. There are several ways to get rid of them. The first is to create a date table (using one of the methods listed earlier), *mark it as a date*

119

table, and establish a relationship between the date dim table and the fact table. Once you perform these three steps, the shadow date tables are expunged from the data model for each table connected to the date dimension table. The second way is to prevent them from being created at all, either for the current file or for all of your PBIX files. You do this in the File ➤ Options and settings ➤ Options under Data Load, as shown in Figure 5-12.

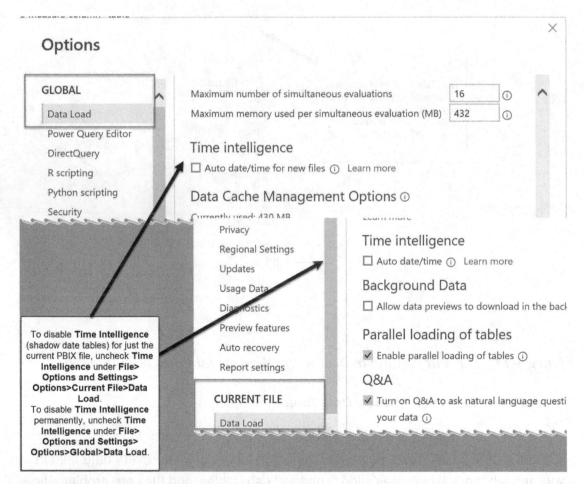

Figure 5-12. Disabling "shadow" date tables forever

3. Connect the date dimension table to the fact table via a 1-many relationship. (Remember, the date dim table is a dimension table just like any other in your model. There is one row for each date between the earliest and the latest date in your model.)

Now that I have covered the why and the how of creating a date dim table, we can return to the first statement of this section: almost every data model will have multiple fields that are dates. To use each date field in a report visual accurately, the field must be connected to the date dimension table. But remember: there can only be *one* active relationship between two tables, which leads us to inactive relationships.

Inactive Relationships

If you create a second relationship between two tables, the second one will automatically be inactive. You can't manually activate a relationship once the report is published, which is why there is a DAX function called UseRelationship. I will address DAX in Chapter 7, so don't worry if you are not sure what a DAX function is. For now, the important thing to know is that you can create as many inactive relationships as you need between two tables. Returning to our example, you would create one active relationship and two inactive relationships between the fact table and the date dim table (as shown in Figure 5-13):

'FactTable'[OrderDate] to 'DateDim'[Date] (active)

'FactTable'[ShipDate] to 'DateDim'[Date] (inactive)

'FactTable'[DeliveryDate] to 'DateDim'[Date] (inactive)

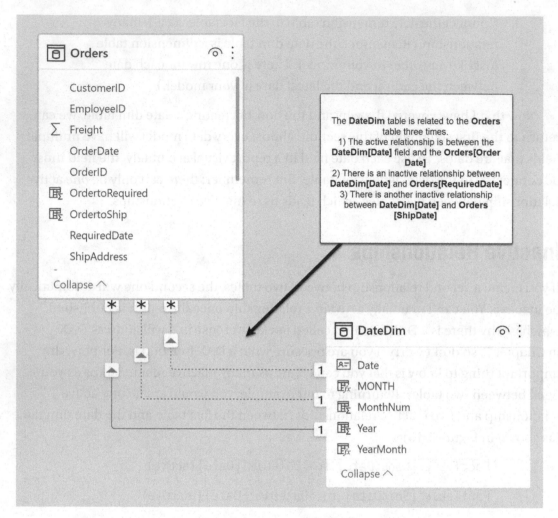

Figure 5-13. *Active and inactive (dotted lines) relationships*

Usually, the field that you use most in your reports is the one that has the active relationship. In this example, the `'Orders'[OrderDate]` field is the most used in reports, which is why it is the active relationship. If `'Orders'[ShipDate]` is more commonly used in reports, then the active relationship could be between `'Orders'[ShipDate]` and `'DateDim'[Date]`.

Role-Playing Dimensions

There are scenarios in which you don't want to use the imactive relationship technique. Perhaps you can't identify which date field will be used the most in reports. There is another way to model the data so that you can use the `OrderDate`, `ShipDate`, and `DeliveryDate` without having to activate a relationship: role-playing dimensions. In our example, you would duplicate the `DateDim` table twice (so you have three total), and each `DateDim` table would have an active relationship to the appropriate date field in the fact table:

> `FactTable[OrderDate]` to `OrderDateDim[Date]` (active)
>
> `FactTable[ShipDate]` to `ShipDateDim[Date]` (active)
>
> `FactTable[DeliveryDate]` to `DeliverDateDim[Date]` (active)

Every table that you add increases the size of your model, so think carefully before you choose role-playing instead of using active/inactive relationships. If your model is small overall, then the penalty for the extra tables may not be important for performance. But if your model is already complex, with lots of tables, opting for active/inactive relationships is probably a better choice.

Critical to Success

Creating the correct relationships is critical to the success of your report. Without the proper relationships, your visuals will be, at best, inaccurate. At worst, they will be wrong. Relationships play an important role in the performance of your report. A bidirectional relationship can slow your report significantly, among its other drawbacks.

There is a rule of thumb in the Power BI community that you will spend 80% of your time cleaning, transforming, and modeling your data. If you find yourself wondering when you can get to building a report, be patient! Once the model is complete, you will be amazed at how fast the report comes together. In the meantime, let's move to perhaps (?) the most challenging part of modeling: writing DAX.

CHAPTER 6

Develop a Data Model

In the previous chapter, we covered the basic principles of creating a data model. A star schema, dim and fact tables, and relationships are the building blocks of a data model. Once you have those in place, you can proceed to refine your model. The one assumption that we made was that all the data we needed was either in the source(s), or we created it using the Power Query Editor. But sometimes that isn't sufficient or possible; we need to explore how to add data using DAX in the Power BI Desktop.

Wait! What Is DAX?

Data Analysis Expressions (DAX) is the language that is used to perform four types of content in the Power BI Desktop:

- Calculated tables

- Calculated columns

- Measures

- Security roles

In this chapter we will cover calculated columns and tables and security roles in some depth. We are saving measures, and a deeper examination of DAX, for Chapter 7.

Adding Data to Your Model

It is best to add data that you need "as far upstream as possible," meaning at the source. But quite often you do not have access to the source data or permission to change it. The next best option is to add the data in the Power Query Editor. Let's assume that adding the data in the source or in the Power Query Editor is not possible. In that situation, you will need to use DAX to add the content in the Power BI Desktop.

125

© Jessica Jolly 2023
J. Jolly, *Microsoft Power BI Data Analyst Certification Companion*, Certification Study Companion Series,
https://doi.org/10.1007/978-1-4842-9013-2_6

> **Tip**   The Formula Bar isn't visible unless you are creating something (table, measure, column) using DAX or you select something that was created using DAX. If you want the Formula Bar not to display, check the X. Don't worry—you won't delete anything that has already been created.

Calculated Tables

The easiest way to add a table is to copy an existing one. The DAX syntax is simple. For example, if you want to make a copy of an existing table, you could use this DAX expression, as shown in Figure 6-1:

```
NewTableName='Existing Table Name'
```

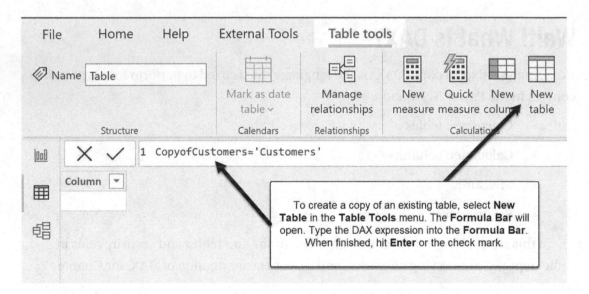

Figure 6-1. Adding a table by copying an existing one

You can also construct new tables using more complex DAX. It is beyond the scope of this book to provide detailed information about DAX functions. For the PL-300 exam, there are two concepts to understand:

1. Creating a calculated table *can* be a significant drag on the performance of your report because it is not compressed as effectively by the VertiPaq engine.

2. Calculated tables (and columns) are initiated when the report opens. Their values do not get recalculated unless the model is reinitiated.

In Figure 6-2, you can see examples of calculated tables.

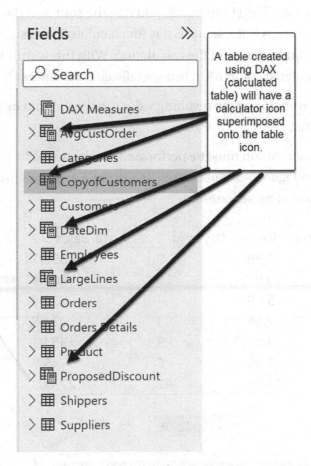

Figure 6-2. Calculated tables are marked with a different icon

Avoid creating calculated tables if you can. Your best option is to create the needed content (tables or columns) at the source. Because modifying the source is often impossible, the next best option is to have tables and columns in the Power Query Editor.

Calculated Columns

Calculated columns present a temptation for newer Power BI practitioners, especially those of us coming from Excel. Let's stipulate that you need to perform a calculation not present in your existing data; a common one is Total Sales. In Excel this is easily solved by adding a formula in a new column that multiplies Unit Price by Quantity. Once over in the Power BI Desktop, creating a column is our first instinct. There are times when creating a calculated column *is* the correct option, but if so, you should create it in the Power Query Editor if possible. (Even better, add it to the source of the data.) The reason to avoid calculated columns is the same as it is for calculated tables: the impact on performance and the static nature of the calculation. With this warning in mind, when should you use a calculated column? In two specific circumstances:

1. When you want to use the resulting values in the column in a slicer or filter.

2. When the calculation must be performed row by row to be accurate. In Figure 6-3, you can see an example, using an Excel table for ease of presentation.

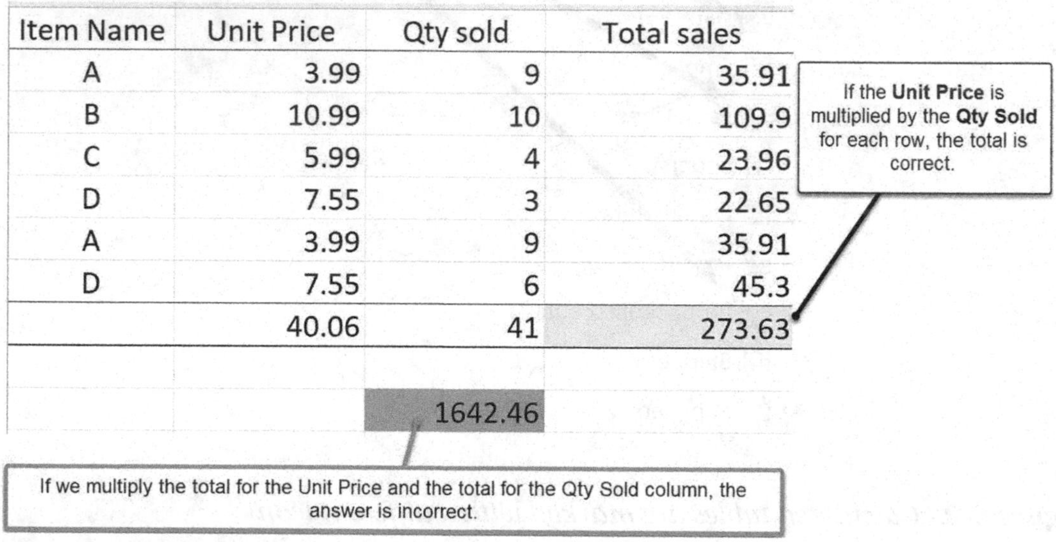

Item Name	Unit Price	Qty sold	Total sales
A	3.99	9	35.91
B	10.99	10	109.9
C	5.99	4	23.96
D	7.55	3	22.65
A	3.99	9	35.91
D	7.55	6	45.3
	40.06	41	273.63
		1642.46	

If the **Unit Price** is multiplied by the **Qty Sold** for each row, the total is correct.

If we multiply the total for the Unit Price and the total for the Qty Sold column, the answer is incorrect.

Figure 6-3. Example of a row-by-row calculation

If the calculation needs to be performed for each row for the total to be accurate, then you should use a calculated column. In Figure 6-4 is a screenshot of the base columns in the 'Orders Details' table.

OrderID	ProductID	UnitPrice	Quantity	Discount
10508	39	$18.00	10	0.0000
10521	35	$18.00	3	0.0000
10530	76	$18.00	50	0.0000
10546	35	$18.00	30	0.0000
10553	35	$18.00	6	0.0000
			10	0.0000
			30	0.0000
			10	0.0000

These are the original columns in the **'Orders Details'** table. Note that there isn't a column that calculates a subtotal, or a net total without the Discount applied.

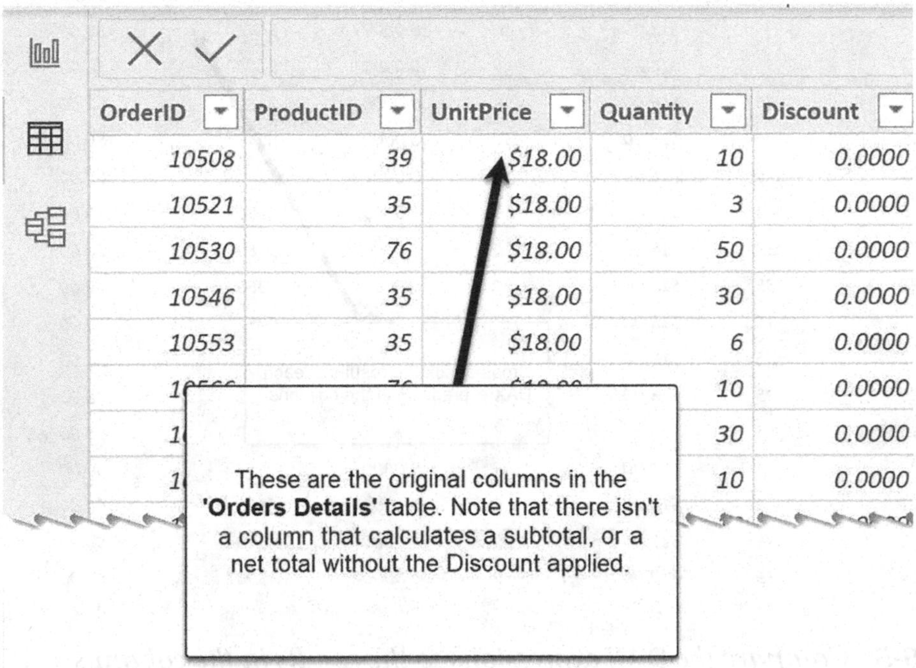

Figure 6-4. *The original columns in the query; none provide a total*

Here are the DAX calculations to create the necessary columns such as subtotal and total:

```
Subtotal=
'Orders Details'[UnitPrice]*'Orders Details'[Quantity]
Discountvalue =
'Orders Details'[Subtotal]*'Orders Details'[Discount]

LineTotal =
'Orders Details'[Subtotal]-'Orders Details'[Discountvalue]
```

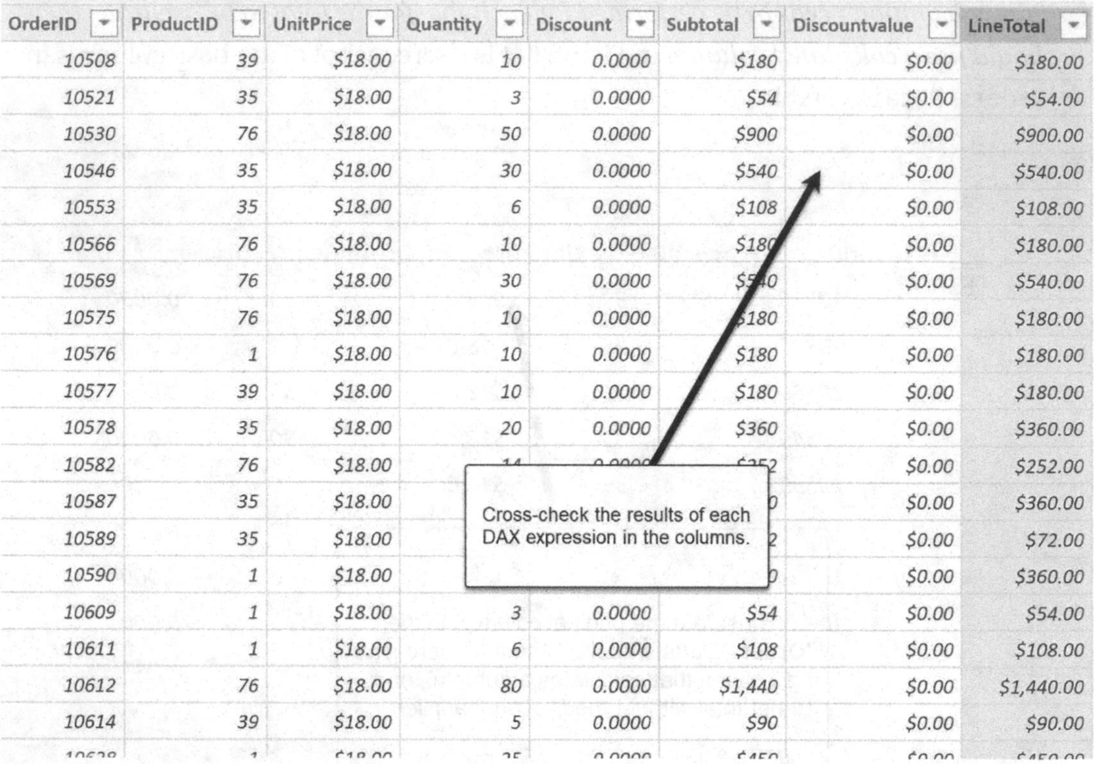

OrderID	ProductID	UnitPrice	Quantity	Discount	Subtotal	Discountvalue	LineTotal
10508	39	$18.00	10	0.0000	$180	$0.00	$180.00
10521	35	$18.00	3	0.0000	$54	$0.00	$54.00
10530	76	$18.00	50	0.0000	$900	$0.00	$900.00
10546	35	$18.00	30	0.0000	$540	$0.00	$540.00
10553	35	$18.00	6	0.0000	$108	$0.00	$108.00
10566	76	$18.00	10	0.0000	$180	$0.00	$180.00
10569	76	$18.00	30	0.0000	$540	$0.00	$540.00
10575	76	$18.00	10	0.0000	$180	$0.00	$180.00
10576	1	$18.00	10	0.0000	$180	$0.00	$180.00
10577	39	$18.00	10	0.0000	$180	$0.00	$180.00
10578	35	$18.00	20	0.0000	$360	$0.00	$360.00
10582	76	$18.00	14	0.0000	$252	$0.00	$252.00
10587	35	$18.00				$0.00	$360.00
10589	35	$18.00			2	$0.00	$72.00
10590	1	$18.00				$0.00	$360.00
10609	1	$18.00	3	0.0000	$54	$0.00	$54.00
10611	1	$18.00	6	0.0000	$108	$0.00	$108.00
10612	76	$18.00	80	0.0000	$1,440	$0.00	$1,440.00
10614	39	$18.00	5	0.0000	$90	$0.00	$90.00
10628	1	$18.00	25	0.0000	$450	$0.00	$450.00

Cross-check the results of each DAX expression in the columns.

Figure 6-5. *Compare the DAX expressions to the results in the columns*

Note several things about these expressions:

1) They are written the same way you would write them in Excel.

2) There are no functions (e.g., SUM, AVERAGE, COUNT) in the expressions.

3) Each column has a unique name.

4) Column names (in square brackets) are fully qualified by their table name.

5) Common mathematical operators are used (*, –, +).

6) Table names have single quotes around them.

When you create a calculated column, you are performing a specific calculation row by row. This behavior is called "iterating." A calculated column is an iterated calculation. We will be getting deeper into DAX in Chapter 7, but it's never too early to start introducing key DAX concepts—here's your first one:

DAX "thinks" primarily in columns. It can also "think" in rows, and when it does, it is iterating over a table or a column.

(Yes, I am speaking as if DAX is a living breathing organism, which of course it is not. But bear with my literary flights of fancy. Maybe once you have worked with DAX, you too will think it has a mind of its own!)

Refining Your Model

There are several ways to refine your model. They aren't all necessary, but they are useful touches that make your model easier for your report consumers to understand.

Hierarchies

Many types of data lend themselves readily to hierarchies. Here are just a few examples that come to mind:

- *Dates*: Year, Quarter, Month, Date
- *Products*: Category, SubCategory, Product
- *Organization*: President, Vice President, Director, Manager, Supervisor

You *can* use these individual fields without congregating them in a hierarchy, but if you organize them into a hierarchy, you accomplish several things:

1. You make it clear to the user that the fields relate to each other in a hierarchical structure.

2. You make it easy for the report creator (who might be you!) to drag all the related fields on to a visual at once.

3. You create a clear "path" for drilling down in a visual.

Hierarchies can be created either in the Report view or in the Model view. In the following examples, I am using the Model view.

In Figure 6-6, there are several fields in the "Product" table that could be combined into a hierarchy. (I say "could" because there is no requirement to create hierarchies. They are a nice touch though.)

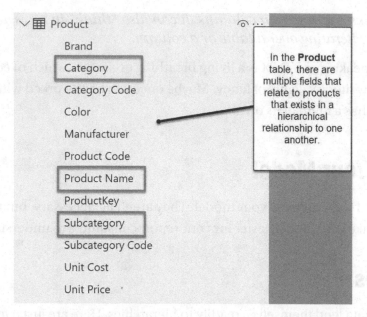

Figure 6-6. *Several fields that can be combined into a hierarchy*

To initiate a hierarchy, right-click the field that will be at the top of the hierarchy. In Figure 6-7, the top of the hierarchy is Category.

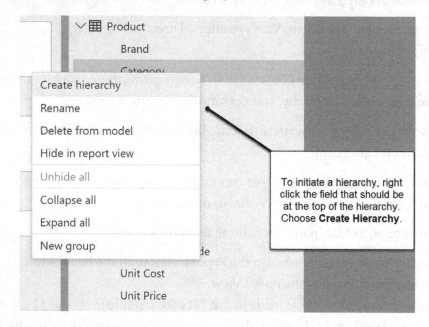

Figure 6-7. *Initiating a hierarchy*

Once you have the hierarchy created, you can add fields to it in several different ways. Shown in Figure 6-8 is how to initiate a hierarchy using the Properties panel of the Model view.

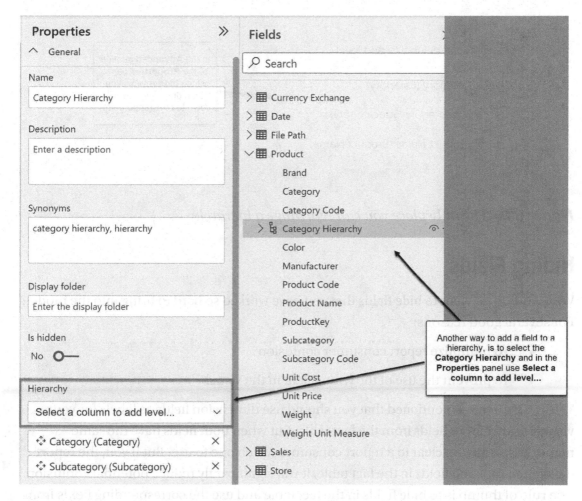

Figure 6-8. *Adding to a hierarchy on the Properties panel*

Tip   If you don't see the Hierarchy option on the Properties pane, make sure that you have selected the hierarchy.

A second way to add fields to your hierarchy is to right click. What happens if you don't start with the field at the top of the hierarchy? Or if you add the fields in the wrong order? You can rearrange the fields, but the *only* place you do so is in the Model view on the Properties panel. To rearrange the fields, drag them up or down, as shown in Figure 6-9.

Figure 6-9. *The only place you can rearrange a hierarchy*

Hiding Fields

Why would you want to hide fields that you have worked so hard to bring into the model? For several good reasons:

- To minimize report consumer confusion

- To prevent the use of the wrong field in the visual

In Chapter 5, I mentioned that you should use dimension fields as labels for your visuals and analyze fields from the fact table. But when both fields have the same name, it isn't always clear to a report consumer which one to use. But if you, the report developer, hide the fields in the fact table, it will significantly reduce potential confusion. The rule of thumb is to hide fields in the fact table and use the corresponding fields from the dimension table. In Figure 6-10, observe that the two tables (`Product` dimension and `Sales` fact) are connected by a relationship on `ProductKey`.

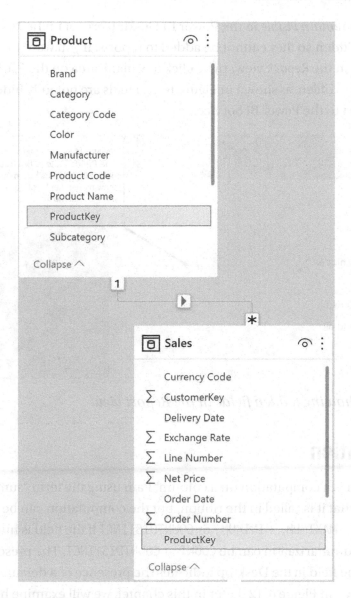

Figure 6-10. *The Product dim table and the Sales fact table*

In this example, it would be best practice to hide the `ProductKey` field in the `Sales` table. The report consumers would have to use a field from the `Product` dimension table as a label in a visual.

It is also best practice to hide "helper" fields—fields that are present to provide a needed function but are not useful in a visual. An index field or a field that provides a sort order is a good example of a "helper" field.

Hidden fields remain visible in the Power BI Desktop except in the Report view, where they are hidden so they cannot be added to reports. If you want to see fields that you have hidden in the Report view, right-click any blank area on the Fields pane, and choose View hidden, as shown in Figure 6-11. Fields are not fully hidden until you publish the report to the Power BI Service.

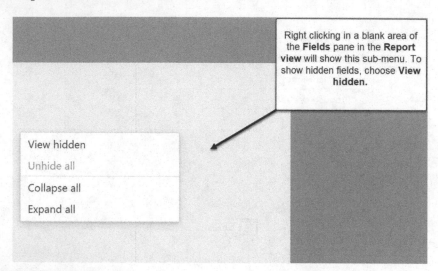

Figure 6-11. *Showing hidden fields in the Report view*

Summarization

A summarization is a computation on a column. I am using the term "summarization" because that is what it is called in the ribbon, but the computation can be a SUM, AVERAGE, COUNT, MAXIMUM, MINIMUM, or COUNTDISTINCT if the field is numeric. If the field is text, the summarization can be COUNT or COUNTDISTINCT. The presence of a sigma symbol next to the field in the Desktop indicates the presence of a default summarization behavior, as shown in Figure 6-12. Later in this chapter, we will examine how to either change this behavior or remove it.

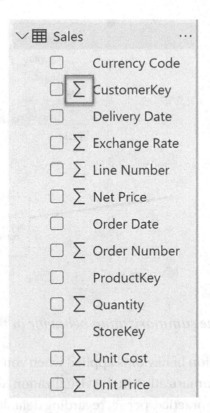

Figure 6-12. *The sigma symbol indicates a summarization behavior*

Default Summarization

The default summarization that Power BI applies is a SUM if the field's data type is a number. During the refinement of your model, you should examine each field that has a sigma symbol next to it and decide if that is an appropriate operation to apply. You can perform this operation in any of the three views within the Power BI Desktop.

From either the Report or Data view, *after selecting the field* as shown in Figure 6-13

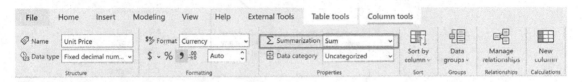

Figure 6-13. *Set the summarization behavior*

From the Model view, *after selecting the field,* as shown in Figure 6-14

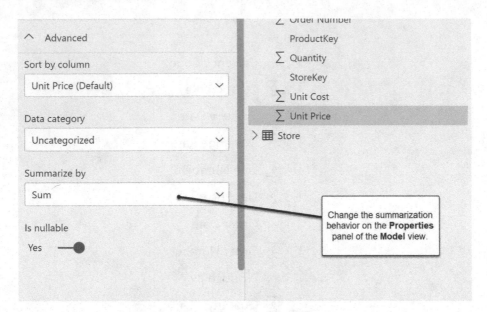

Figure 6-14. *Changing the summarization behavior in the Model view*

The default summarization behavior is applied when you use that field in a visual. You can also change the summarization in the visualization, which we will explore in Chapter 7. There isn't a best practice, per se, regarding default summarization. As a data modeler, you decide if you want to leave the summarization in place. You can remove it without a deleterious impact on your model as shown in Figure 6-15. On the other hand, you can also leave it in place without a negative impact.

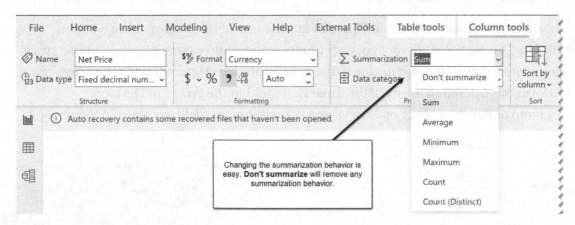

Figure 6-15. *Changing the default summarization behavior on a field*

Categorization

For certain types of data, categorization can enable additional uses for the field in question. Geographic data is most frequently categorized data. In Figure 6-16, you can see how to categorize a field (in this case `City`), after selecting it.

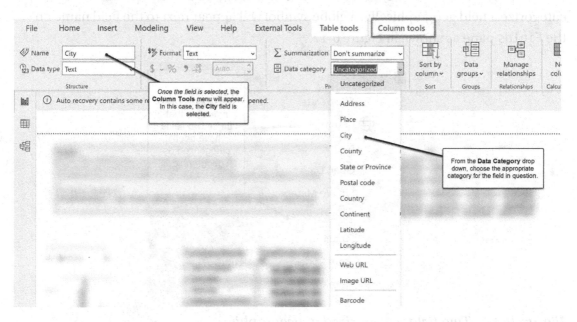

Figure 6-16. *Categorizing a field*

There are a couple of interesting points about categorization:

1. You can categorize a place (e.g., an airport or a stadium).

2. You *cannot* categorize a region (or any geographical unit not used in standard maps).

3. Make sure your zip/postal codes are in a text data type; if they are not, they cannot be categorized as a postal code.

Maps *will* work without categorization, but performing this step can remove ambiguity. For example, if you have a column with an abbreviation CA, is that California or Canada? Is AR Arkansas or Argentina? It is usually clear from the column heading (Country or State); nonetheless, categorization is a form of insurance. Finally, categorization will help the Q&A feature properly interpret a question about an address or place (see in the following for more discussion about Q&A).

Another interesting example of categorization is for URLs. If your data has a URL that points to an image or a web page, you want Power BI to display the image (or web page), not the text of the URL. Categorizing the data as either an Image URL or a Web URL will enable this capability.

The only indication that you have successfully categorized a field is when you categorize a field geographically, a globe symbol will appear next to the field name on the Fields pane as shown in Figure 6-17.

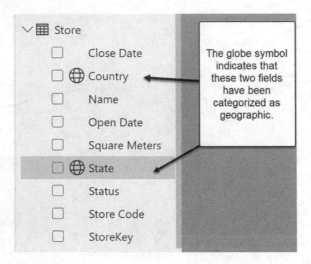

Figure 6-17. *Two fields categorized as geographic*

Setting Up Q&A Functionality

Imagine a day when we can simply speak a question and Power BI will recognize and answer that question. This is what the Q&A function supports: the ability to use natural language to ask a question about the data. While Power BI will deliver results without any special preparation, you can enhance the user experience by completing a few steps in advance.

Q&A is available for reports and dashboards. In both mediums, you "activate" Q&A by asking a question. In a report, you do this by choosing the Q&A visualization as shown in Figure 6-18.

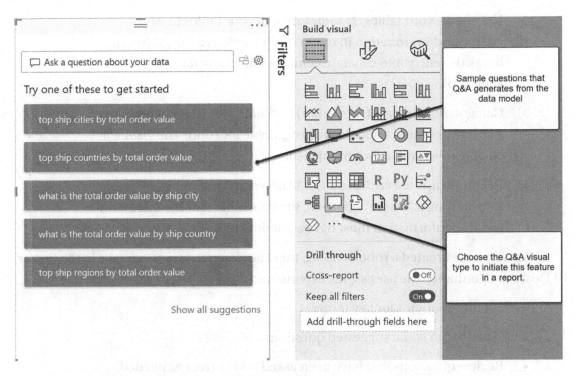

Figure 6-18. *Q&A visualization with sample questions*

The Q&A engine reviews the data model and generates questions based on the relationships between tables. (See Chapter 5 for more details on relationships.) The questions use the names of the columns in each table, so naming the columns with a user-friendly name (see Chapter 5 again) contributes to the success of Q&A.

Preparing for Q&A

There are two places to enable Q&A: in the Power BI Desktop and in the Service. This chapter addresses the steps you can take in the Desktop to set up (and optimize) Q&A. The good news? All these steps are ones you are already taking while building a good model:

1) Make sure to set the appropriate data types. For example, when working with date columns, set them as Date data type. The Q&A will be able to map the relevant date column to a "when" question.

2) Normalize your tables, *to some extent*. If your tables have compound information in one column (such as a full address), break the entry into separate columns (such as street address, city, state, zip).

3) Categorize your data (see earlier) so that Power BI recognizes that a specific column references a geographic location. The Q&A will be able to answer a "where" question.

4) Relationships are critical for Q&A success. For example, to answer a "when" and "where" question, the date table and the table with location information must have a relationship.

After you have created a robust model, there are four steps you can take in the Power BI Desktop to enhance the user's Q&A experience:

- Set up synonyms for key terms.

- "Seed" with some suggested questions.

- Review questions that have been asked and correct as needed.

- "Teach" the model by supplying some sample questions.

To access the Q&A setup within the Power BI Desktop, go to Modeling ➤ Q&A setup as shown in Figures 6-19 and 6-20.

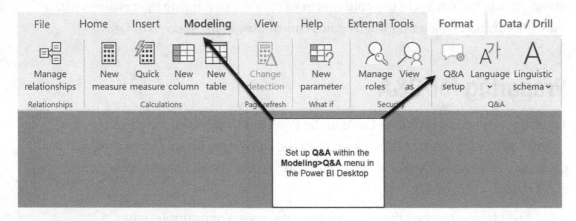

Figure 6-19. *Accessing the Q&A setup menu*

Figure 6-20. *The Q&A setup menu*

If the organization uses terminology that is significantly different from the field names used in the model, setting up synonyms as you build your model is very helpful. You can do this in either the Q&A setup menu or the Model view, as shown in Figure 6-21.

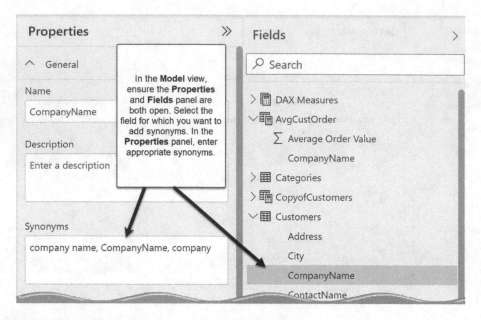

Figure 6-21. *Entering synonyms in the Model view*

Security

Like setting up Q&A, setting up security is a two-step process. The first step happens in the Desktop, and the second happens in the Service. This chapter covers the steps you complete in the Desktop. A subsequent chapter will address the steps that are completed in the Service.

Multilayer Security

There are multiple layers to the security options available in the Power BI Desktop.

Access Credentials

When connecting to a data source, you must enter your credentials. Those credentials determine what you can access (as in a database). These credentials control what *you* can access, not what the report viewer can see.

Row-Level Security

Once the data has been extracted, loaded into the data model, and combined, the model creator must set up the security controls that will determine what data the viewers can see in the report. This is called row-level security because the security controls the rows that a viewer can see.

The key step in this process is setting up roles. Each role is limited to specific data, based on DAX expressions. To set up these roles, click the `Manage roles` tile on the Home tab as shown in Figure 6-22.

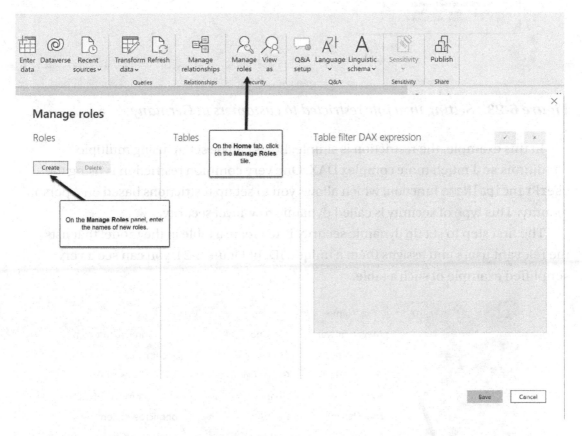

Figure 6-22. *The Manage roles dialogue box*

Set up the role with the appropriate DAX to restrict the data that the reader can view. In the following example, the role is restricted to viewing the data of customers who are based in Germany as shown in Figure 6-23.

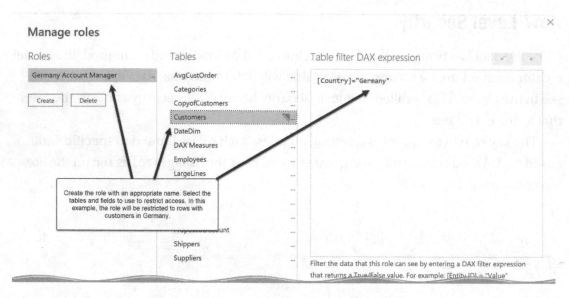

Figure 6-23. *Setting up a role restricted to customers in Germany*

In this example, the restriction is simple. Roles can be set up using multiple conditions and much more complex DAX. One very common restriction is using the UserPrincipalName function, which allows you to set up restrictions based on a person's identity. This type of security is called dynamic row-level security.

The first step to set up dynamic security is to create a table in the model that lists the relevant users and assigns them a unique ID. In Figure 6-24, you can see a very simplified example of such a table.

ID	Full Name	UPN
1	Megan Bowen	MeganB@ .onmicrosoft.com
2	Adele Vance	AdeleV@ .onmicrosoft.com
3	Gradie Archer	GradieA@ .onmicrosoft.com
4	Henrietta Mueller	HenriettaM .onmicrosoft.com
5	Joni Sherman	JoniS@ .onmicrosoft.com
6	Lee Stein	LeeS@ .onmicrosoft.com

Each user is assigned an ID number. This would probably be an actual ID for that user in an employee table.

Figure 6-24. *An example of a simplified user table*

146

The next step is to assign user access to specific data using the user's unique ID. In Figure 6-25, you can see that only Megan Bowen has access to the A. Datum and Litware brands.

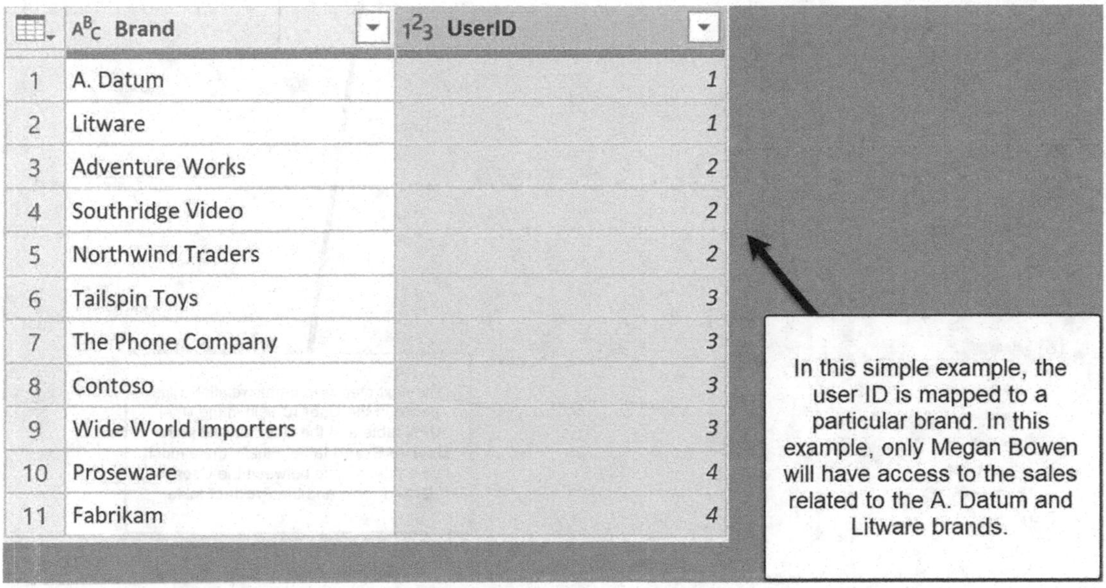

	A^B_C Brand	1^2_3 UserID
1	A. Datum	1
2	Litware	1
3	Adventure Works	2
4	Southridge Video	2
5	Northwind Traders	2
6	Tailspin Toys	3
7	The Phone Company	3
8	Contoso	3
9	Wide World Importers	3
10	Proseware	4
11	Fabrikam	4

In this simple example, the user ID is mapped to a particular brand. In this example, only Megan Bowen will have access to the sales related to the A. Datum and Litware brands.

Figure 6-25. The brands and the associated user IDs

Dynamic security uses the mechanism of filter transmission through a relationship, so it makes sense that the next step is to wire the two new tables into the model and create the appropriate relationships, as shown in Figure 6-26.

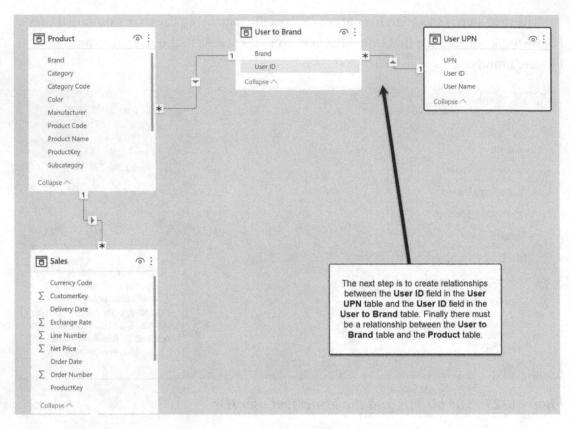

Figure 6-26. *The key to dynamic security is the relationships in the model*

Now that the relationships are in place, there is one more step: to create a new role that explicitly states that the data a user will have access to depends on their **User Principal Name (UPN)**. In Figure 6-27, you can see an example of such a role.

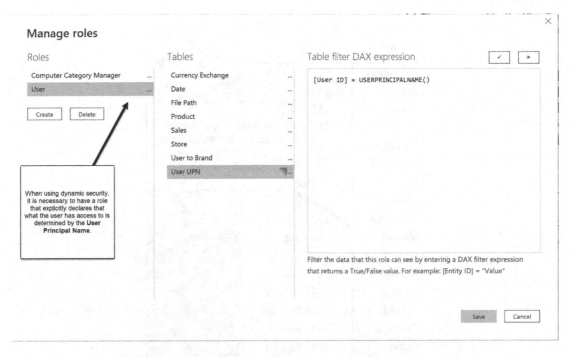

Figure 6-27. *Setting up a role that explicitly ties visibility to the UPN*

Once you have set up the necessary roles, the next step is to test the role, which you can do using the View as function. In the following are two figures—Figure 6-28 that has no row-level security in place and Figure 6-29 when viewed as the Germany Account Manager role.

Country	All_Sales
Argentina	$8,119.10
Austria	$128,003.84
Belgium	$33,82...
Brazil	$108,78...
Canada	$50,19...
Denmark	$32,66...
Finland	$19,25...
France	$8...,918.32
Germany	$226,916.58
Ireland	$49,979.91
Italy	$15,770.16
Mexico	$23,582.08
Norway	$5,735.15
Poland	$3,531.95
Portugal	$12,883.36
Spain	$17,983.20
Sweden	$54,495.14
Switzerland	$31,692.66
UK	$58,971.31
USA	$245,678.26
Venezuela	$56,810.63
Total	**$1,265,793.04**

Without any row level security, the sales for all customers in every country is visible.

Figure 6-28. *Without row-level security, all data is visible*

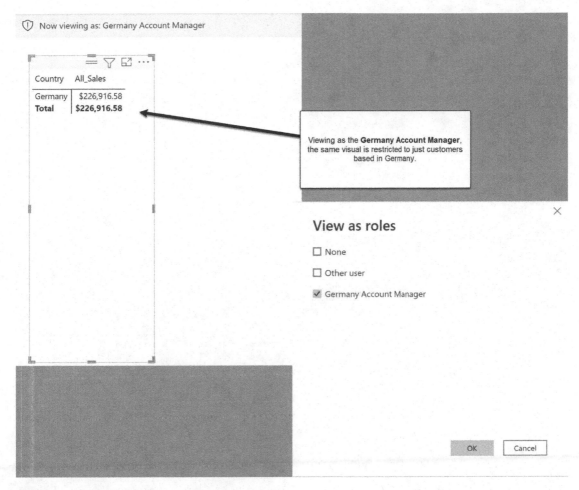

Figure 6-29. *Using the View as feature*

Once the roles are established and tested, the second step is to assign users to roles in the Service, which will be covered later.

For Future Reference: Object-Level Security

The PL-300 does not cover this topic, but as always, I want you to be fully prepared for the terminology and concepts you will read about when studying for the exam. Unlike row-level security, object-level security controls access to an entire object or entity. For example, you can restrict access to a table or a field such that it is not visible or useable by a report viewer. Object-level security must be implemented with an external tool, such as Tabular Editor.

CHAPTER 7

Create Model Calculations Using DAX

DAX (Data Analysis Expressions) is the language Power BI uses to create content: tables, columns, security roles, and measures. We covered the first three uses of DAX in the last chapter. In this chapter, we will focus on measures. Measures are calculations that your data doesn't already have. What kind of calculations? They can be anything from a simple addition to a way to conditionally format a visual or to create a dynamic title for a visual.

Measures

What do you use when a calculated column is not necessary? For example, in the earlier chapter, we created a column that calculates the total for each row ([LineTotal]), but we need to know the total for *all* sales, not just the total line by line. We need a measure, which is a calculation not currently present in the data. In Figure 7-1, you can see how to enter a measure in the Formula Bar:

```
All_Sales=SUM('Orders Details'[LineTotal])
```

© Jessica Jolly 2023
J. Jolly, *Microsoft Power BI Data Analyst Certification Companion*, Certification Study Companion Series,
https://doi.org/10.1007/978-1-4842-9013-2_7

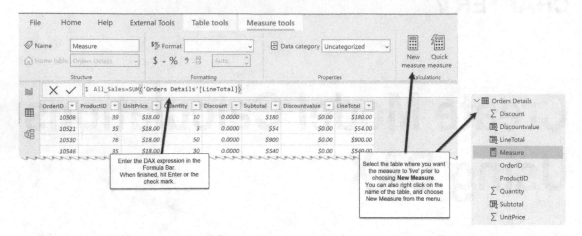

Figure 7-1. *Entering a measure*

This expression adds up the entire column called LineTotal in the table called 'Orders Details' and creates a measure called All_Sales. A measure is stored inside the data model (which is why the topic is introduced in this chapter). Because a measure is not materialized, *it does not require resources from the engine* until it is used in a visual.

Tip   You won't see a measure in the Data view because it is not materialized.

Let's revisit DAX's basic behavior. In my classes, I search for analogies that may resonate with my audience. I have started to call DAX the "Cookie Monster." (For folks who did not grow up with *Sesame Street*, "Cookie Monster" is known for gobbling down cookies.) DAX's innate behavior is to "gobble" up columns and produce the result, unless it is iterating (going row by row), as we covered in the previous chapter. With this in mind, let's analyze the simple measure used in Figure 7-1:

All_Sales=SUM('Orders Details'[LineTotal])

Right away, you should notice that *unlike calculated columns*, a measure *requires* a function, such as SUM, AVERAGE, MIN, or MAX. In our simple example, the measure is using SUM. The function tells DAX what operation you want to perform. The result of this measure is that the entire 'Orders Details'[LineTotal] column is added up.

All_Sales_Average=AVERAGE('Orders Details'[LineTotal])

In the preceding example, the `'Orders Details'[LineTotal]` column is added up and then divided by the number of rows in the column—in other words, it is averaged.

And just to remind you, let's reverse the question. When must you use a calculated column and not a measure? If you need to use the values that are calculated in a slicer or filter, you *must* use a calculated column. If the calculations must be performed row by row to be accurate, you *must* use a calculated column or an iterator function (covered later in the chapter).

DAX Syntax: A Quick Review

I covered the syntax rules for DAX in the previous chapter, but as you are probably new to DAX, I think they are worth repeating:

- DAX is *not* case sensitive (unlike M in the Power Query Editor).

- Every column name is enclosed in square brackets.

- Every column name is "fully qualified" with its table name.

- Table names do not require single quotes around them unless the name has a space in it. (Nonetheless, I make it a practice to always enclose my table names with single quotes because that way I won't forget to put them in when necessary.)

- Measures are enclosed in square brackets, *without* a table name.

- After a function, the arguments required by the function are enclosed in parentheses and separated by commas (exactly as formulas are entered in Excel).

- You can nest functions within other functions.

- You can reuse measures within other measures.

- Functions have mandatory arguments and optional arguments. In the `IntelliSense` menus, optional arguments are enclosed in square brackets.

When you are first learning to write DAX, it can be confusing. One helpful tool is IntelliSense built into the Power BI Desktop. As soon as you start typing in the `Formula Bar`, `IntelliSense` initiates.

As you start typing the name of a function, it will prompt you with the available functions that start with the letters you have typed in as shown in Figure 7-2. You can select the appropriate function from the list.

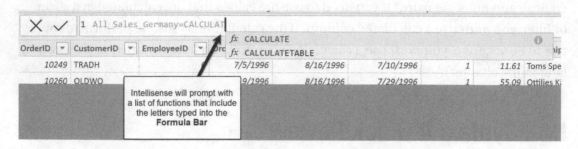

Figure 7-2. *IntelliSense suggestions for functions*

After selecting the function, IntelliSense will prompt with an explanation of the function and a list of the mandatory and optional arguments. Optional arguments are enclosed in square brackets, as you can see in Figure 7-3.

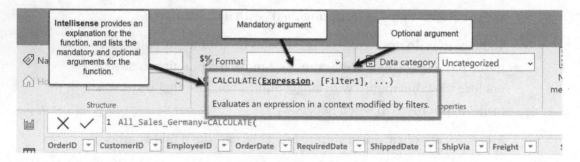

Figure 7-3. *IntelliSense explanation of the selected function*

To see a list of tables (and columns) available in the model, simply type in a single quote. You can select from the provided list of tables and fields, as shown in Figure 7-4.

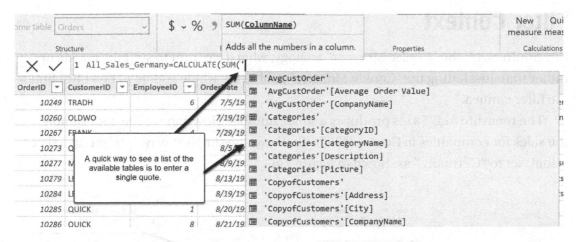

Figure 7-4. *Enter a single quote to see a list of tables (and columns)*

To see a list of measures available in the model, type in a left square bracket, as shown in Figure 7-5.

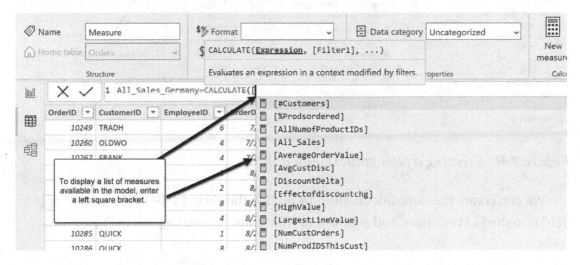

Figure 7-5. *Enter a left square bracket to display a list of measures in the model*

If you are new to DAX, using IntelliSense can guide you toward writing DAX that is syntactically correct. This does *not* mean that the DAX you write will work. You should test every measure in a simple visual to see the results of the DAX you have written.

Tip   Many people test their DAX by using simple data and performing the same calculation in Excel. This is a great way to understand what DAX is doing.

Filter Context

Continuing with the "Cookie Monster" analogy, what if we want to split the cookie up, rather than just letting the "Cookie Monster" gobble the whole cookie in one bite? Enter the filter context.

The measure All_Sales produces a single number. How can we see, for example, the sales for companies in Germany? The first way, the simplest way, is to set up a slicer visual, set to "Germany," as shown in Figure 7-6.

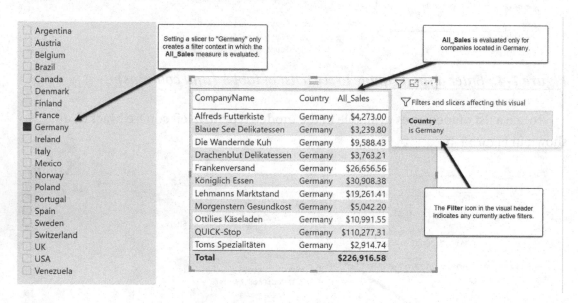

Figure 7-6. *Creating a filter context with a slicer*

We can create the same filter context by putting the 'Orders Details'[Country] field into the Filters pane and setting it to "Germany," as you can see in Figure 7-7.

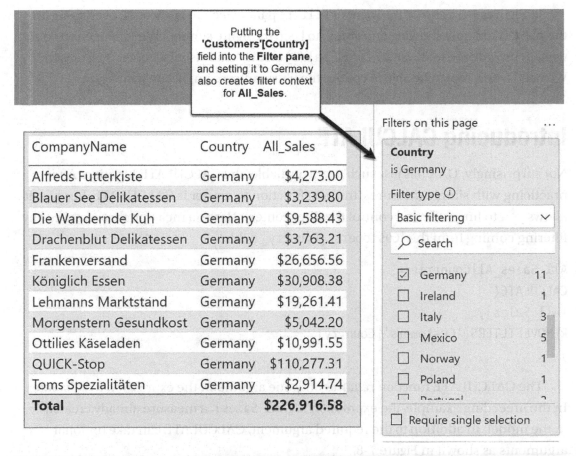

Figure 7-7. *Creating a filter context with the Filters pane*

There are numerous ways that a filter context can be introduced. In the preceding figures, you can see the obvious ways: using a slicer or the Filters pane. Some other ways include

- A drill-through from another page (or report)

- A selection on another visual on the same page

- A synced slicer

- Any combination of slicers, filters, drill-throughs, and/or hard-coded filters

You should always be aware of the current filter context because it can affect the results of any measure you are using in a visual.

In Figures 7-6 and 7-7, the slicer or `Filters` pane selection is affecting everything on the page. (I am only showing one visual, to keep the figure simple.) What happens if you want to include the total value of `[All_Sales]` on the same visual where it is also filtered? We need a new tool to be able to control the filter context's impact on a measure.

Introducing CALCULATE

Not surprisingly, DAX has just such a tool available: the CALCULATE function. After practicing with simple measures, the next function to master is CALCULATE, because it allows you to fine-tune and control the filter context. Here's a measure that removes any filtering coming from the `'Customers'[Country]` field:

```
All_Sales_AllCountries=
CALCULATE(
[All_Sales],
REMOVEFILTERS('Customers'[Country]
)
```

The CALCULATE function *requires* only one argument: the expression to calculate. In the preceding example, the expression is `[All_Sales]`, a measure already created in the model. In addition to the required argument, CALCULATE can take optional arguments as shown in Figure 7-8.

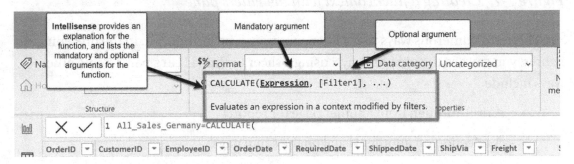

***Figure 7-8.** Optional filter context modifiers*

The optional arguments are of two types:

1) A filter context modifier that adds, modifies, or removes filters. Examples of filter modifiers include REMOVEFILTERS, ALL, and ALLEXCEPT (and there are many more).

2) A model modifier that alters the functionality of the model. Examples of model modifiers include USERELATIONSHIP and CROSSFILTER.

CALCULATE does *not* wipe out the existing filter context. It superimposes the filter conditions you have included in the CALCULATE measure *onto the existing filter context*.

In our measure All_Sales_AllCountries, the REMOVEFILTERS function scans the filter context for any filters coming from the 'Customers'[Country] field and removes them prior to calculating the measure, as you can see in Figure 7-9.

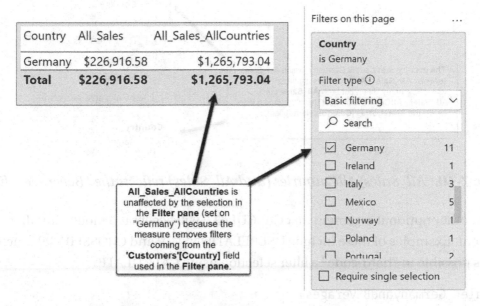

Figure 7-9. *Removing filters coming from the Filters pane*

It is *very important* to realize that this measure will *not* remove any filters coming from another field in the 'Customers' table or from a field in another table. If, for example, we add the 'Product'[Category] field to the Filters pane, the All_Sales_AllCountries *will* reflect that change in the filter context as shown in Figure 7-10.

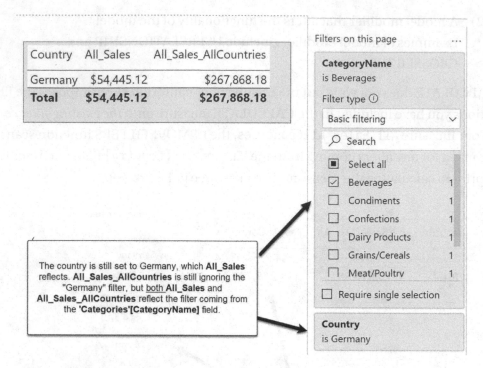

Figure 7-10. *All_Sales_AllCountries (and All_Sales) reflects the "Beverages" filter*

The other optional argument that CALCULATE will accept is a model modifier argument. Examples of these include USERELATIONSHIP and CROSSFILTER functions.

It is possible to "hard-code" a filter selection using CALCULATE:

```
All_Sales_GermanyandBeverages=
CALCULATE([All_Sales],
'Customers'[Country]= "Germany",
'Categories'[CategoryName]= "Beverages"
)
```

In this example, there are two filter modifier arguments:

> `'Customers'[Country]` = "Germany" hard-codes the country to Germany during the evaluation of the measure.

> `'Categories'[CategoryName]` = "Beverages" hard-codes the category to Beverages during the evaluation of the measure, as shown in Figure 7-11.

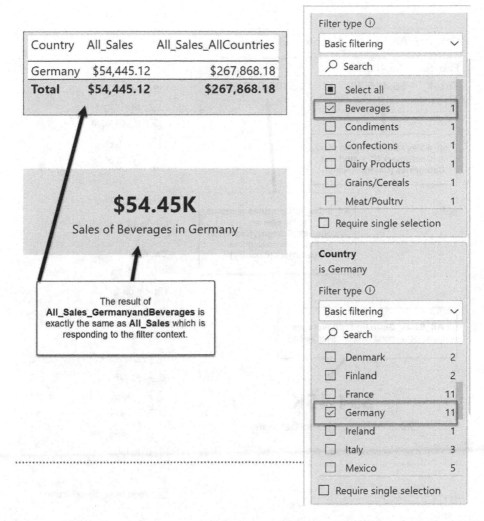

Figure 7-11. *All_Sales_GermanyandBeverages returns the same value as All_Sales filtered*

But what happens if we set the filters on the Filters pane to a different country and a different category? Spoiler alert: The hard-coded measure does not respond to the filter context, as shown in Figure 7-12.

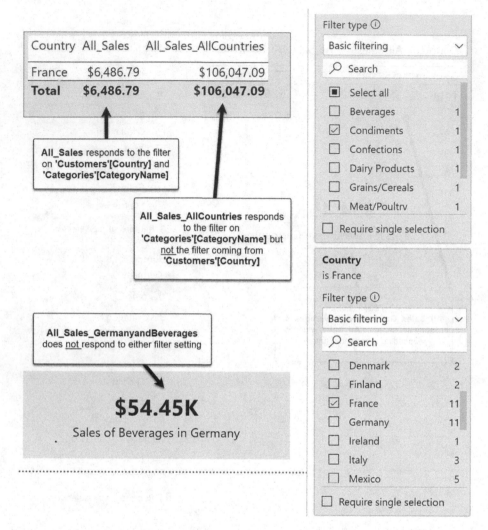

Figure 7-12. *All_Sales_GermanyandBeverages does not respond to filter selections*

In the following table, I have listed all three example measures and how they are (or are not) modifying the filter context.

The Measure	All_Sales(Measure 1)	All_Sales_AllCountries (Measure 2)	All_SalesGermanyand Beverages(Measure 3)
The DAX	=SUM('Orders Details' [LineTotal])	=CALCULATE([All_Sales], REMOVEFILTERS('Custo mers'[Country])	=CALCUATE([All_Sales], 'Customers'[Country]= "Germany", 'Categories' [CategoryName]= "Beverages")

(continued)

The Measure	All_Sales(Measure 1)	All_Sales_AllCountries (Measure 2)	All_SalesGermanyand Beverages(Measure 3)
The explanation	This measure does not use CALCULATE. Therefore, it is not performing any *additional* manipulation of the filter context. Its results depend on the external filter context. In this example the external filter context is Country=France and Category= Condiments.	This measure uses CALCULATE to remove any filters that are coming from the Country column in the 'Customers' table in the external filter context. The external context stipulates that Country = France, and *this is still true*. But the presence of the REMOVEFILTERS is imposed *in addition to* the external filter context. In this example, because the measure removes any filters coming from 'Customer' [Country], the Country=France is "overwritten" *for this measure.* By contrast, the external filter context also has a filter Category=Condiments. This external filter is included when calculating the measure, because nothing in the CALCULATE statement changes this external filter.	This measure uses CALCULATE to set the Country=Germany and the Categories=Beverages. Anything in the external filter context that conflicts with these two filter settings will be overwritten. The fact that the external filter context sets Country=France and Category=Condiment is "overwritten" *for this measure*. Any other filters present in the filter context *are unaffected.*

Modifying the Filter Context

In the preceding measure 3, we hard-coded two filter settings. In measure 2, we used the function REMOVEFILTERS. This is one of several functions you can use to modify the filter context. I have listed some of these functions in the following. You are *not* expected to be a DAX expert to pass the PL-300 exam, but to continue your DAX learning, you should familiarize yourself with some of these functions:

- KEEPFILTERS

- ALL

- ALLEXCEPT

- ALLSELECTED

Every filter modifier argument for CALCULATE does one of two things: removes existing filters or adds a filter. Two different modifier arguments can be combined as well.

Modifying the Model (Temporarily)

There are times when the optimal model structure is different from what you need for a specific reporting requirement. Imagine an orders table that has multiple fields related to dates: order date, ship date, delivery date. Let's assume that the primary reporting requirement is on order date, so the active relationship should be between the date field in the date table and the order date field in the orders table. But on occasion, there is a requirement to report on ship date or delivery date, but the active relationship is still between order date and the date table. (Remember, you can only have one active relationship between two tables.) The answer is to create inactive relationships between tables. But how can you "activate" the inactive relationship? You can use USERELATIONSHIP with CALCULATE in a measure to activate the needed relationship. The following is an example of what the measure could look like:

```
SampleMeasure=CALCULATE
(SUM('Orders'[Sales]),
USERELATIONSHIP('Date'[Date], 'Orders'[ShipDate]))
```

Another example of a model-modifying function is CROSSFILTER, which changes the direction of a relationship.

Row Context

Now that we have introduced the filter context, let's reintroduce the row context. You may recall that I mentioned the row context in the previous chapter, when explaining calculated columns. But the row context is broader than just a calculated column. Let's use the same example we used in the last chapter: calculating sales (not including discount value). We can create two calculated columns called [Subtotal] and [LineTotal] using these expressions:

```
Subtotal=
'Orders Details'[Quantity]* 'Orders Details'[Unit Price]
LineTotal =
'Orders Details'[Subtotal]-'Orders Details'[DiscountValue]
```

But remember, we want to avoid creating calculated columns if we have an alternative. We can create a subtotal measure using an iterator function—SUMX:

```
LineTotalAsMeasure =
SUMX (
'Orders Details',
('Orders Details'[Quantity] * 'Orders Details'[UnitPrice]) - 'Orders
Details'[Discountvalue]
)
```

Iterator functions have an X at the end of them: SUMX, AVERAGEX, MAXX, MINX, and COUNTAX are examples. (Not every function has an iterator equivalent.) An iterator function evaluates an expression, row by row. In our model, we have three different methods to calculate the sales total:

- A calculated column called [LineTotal] and using it in a visual

- A measure called LineTotalAsMeasure

- A measure called All_Sales

In Figure 7-13 you can see all three methods used in the same visual.

CompanyName	All_Sales	LineTotal	LineTotalAsMeasure
Alfreds Futterkiste	$4,273.00	$4,273.00	$4,273.00
Ana Trujillo Emparedados y helados	$1,402.95	$1,402.95	$1,402.95
Antonio Moreno Taquería	$7,023.98	$7,023.98	$7,023.98
Around the Horn	$13,390.65	$13,390.65	$13,390.65
Berglunds snabbköp	$24,927.58	$24,927.58	$24,927.58
Blauer See Delikatessen	$3,239.80	$3,239.80	$3,239.80
Blondel père et fils	$18,534.08	$18,534.08	$18,534.08
Bólido Comidas preparadas	$4,232.85	$4,232.85	$4,232.85
Bon app'	$21,963.25	$21,963.25	$21,963.25
Bottom-Dollar Markets	$20,801.60	$20,801.60	$20,801.60
B's Beverages	$6,089.90	$6,089.90	$6,089.90
Cactus Comidas para llevar	$1,814.80	$1,814.80	$1,814.80
Centro comercial Moctezuma	$100.80	$100.80	$100.80
Chop-suey Chinese	$12,348.88	$12,348.88	$12,348.88
Comércio Mineiro	$3,810.75	$3,810.75	$3,810.75
Consolidated Holdings	$1,719.10	$1,719.10	$1,719.10
Die Wandernde Kuh	$9,588.43	$9,588.43	$9,588.43
Drachenblut Delikatessen	$3,		$3,763.21
Du monde entier	$1,	Three different methods produce the same results	$1,615.90
Eastern Connection	$14,		$14,761.04
Total	**$1,265,793.04**	**$1,265,793.04**	**$1,265,793.04**

Figure 7-13. *Three different methods to calculate the same results*

When should you create a calculated column and when should you use a measure with an iterator function? The answer is one we have already talked about: create a calculated column when you need to use the resulting values in a slicer or filter, as shown in Figure 7-14. *You can't use a measure in a slicer or a filter.*

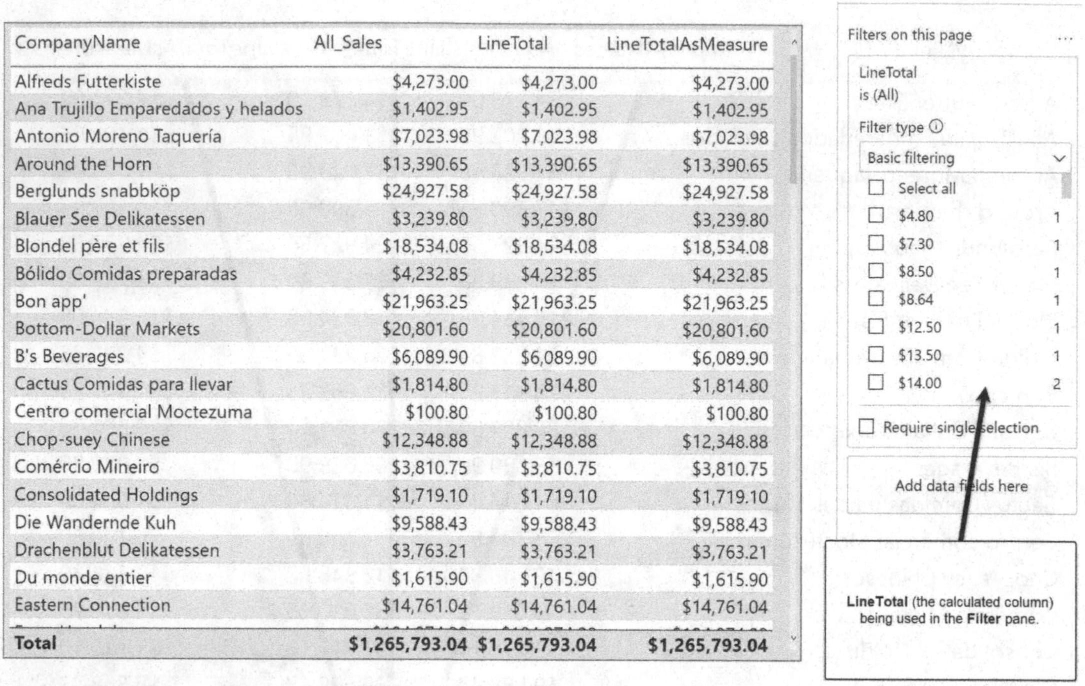

CompanyName	All_Sales	LineTotal	LineTotalAsMeasure
Alfreds Futterkiste	$4,273.00	$4,273.00	$4,273.00
Ana Trujillo Emparedados y helados	$1,402.95	$1,402.95	$1,402.95
Antonio Moreno Taquería	$7,023.98	$7,023.98	$7,023.98
Around the Horn	$13,390.65	$13,390.65	$13,390.65
Berglunds snabbköp	$24,927.58	$24,927.58	$24,927.58
Blauer See Delikatessen	$3,239.80	$3,239.80	$3,239.80
Blondel père et fils	$18,534.08	$18,534.08	$18,534.08
Bólido Comidas preparadas	$4,232.85	$4,232.85	$4,232.85
Bon app'	$21,963.25	$21,963.25	$21,963.25
Bottom-Dollar Markets	$20,801.60	$20,801.60	$20,801.60
B's Beverages	$6,089.90	$6,089.90	$6,089.90
Cactus Comidas para llevar	$1,814.80	$1,814.80	$1,814.80
Centro comercial Moctezuma	$100.80	$100.80	$100.80
Chop-suey Chinese	$12,348.88	$12,348.88	$12,348.88
Comércio Mineiro	$3,810.75	$3,810.75	$3,810.75
Consolidated Holdings	$1,719.10	$1,719.10	$1,719.10
Die Wandernde Kuh	$9,588.43	$9,588.43	$9,588.43
Drachenblut Delikatessen	$3,763.21	$3,763.21	$3,763.21
Du monde entier	$1,615.90	$1,615.90	$1,615.90
Eastern Connection	$14,761.04	$14,761.04	$14,761.04
Total	$1,265,793.04	$1,265,793.04	$1,265,793.04

Filters on this page ...
LineTotal is (All)
Filter type ⓘ
Basic filtering ⌄
☐ Select all
☐ $4.80 — 1
☐ $7.30 — 1
☐ $8.50 — 1
☐ $8.64 — 1
☐ $12.50 — 1
☐ $13.50 — 1
☐ $14.00 — 2
☐ Require single selection
Add data fields here

LineTotal (the calculated column) being used in the **Filter** pane.

Figure 7-14. Using a calculated column in a filter on the Filters pane

Implicit and Explicit Measures

In Figure 7-14, when we used the calculated column 'Orders Details'[LineTotal] in the visual, we created what is called an implicit measure. Implicit measures are convenient, but not the ideal way to perform a calculation because the default summarization behavior can be readily changed as you can see in Figure 7-15. (There are other disadvantages to implicit measures as well.)

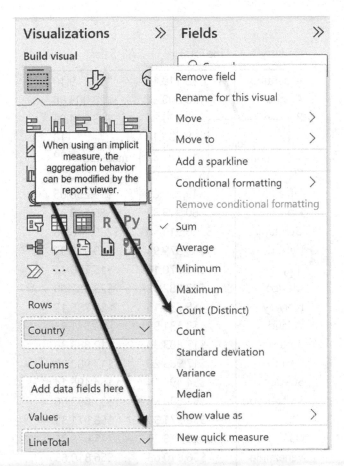

Figure 7-15. *Changing the summarization of an implicit measure*

Default summarization behavior is covered in Chapter 6, where I also mentioned that removing the default summarization isn't critical. Here's why: instead of using an implicit measure, you should create explicit measures for any (and all, if possible) calculations that a report viewer will need. In Figure 7-16, the [All_Sales] measure is used in the visual. This is an example of an explicit measure. Notice that the results of the implicit and explicit measures are the same, as you can see in Figure 7-16.

Country	LineTotal	All_Sales
Argentina	$8,119.10	$8,119.10
Austria	$128,003.84	$128,003.84
Belgium	$33,824.86	$33,824.86
Brazil	$108,789.18	$108,789.18
Canada	$50,196.29	$50,196.29
Denmark	$32,661.02	$32,661.02
Finland	$19,250.05	$19,250.05
France	$80,918.32	$80,918.32
Germany	$226,916.58	$226,916.58
Ireland	$49,979.91	$49,979.91
Italy	$15,770.16	$15,770.16
Mexico	$23,582.08	$23,582.08
Norway	$5,735.15	$5,735.15
Poland	$3,531.95	$3,531.95
Portugal	$12,883.36	$12,883.36
Spain	$17,983.20	$17,983.20
Sweden	$54,495.14	$54,495.14
Switzerland	$31,692.66	$31,692.66
UK	$58,971.31	$58,971.31
USA	$245,678.26	$245,678.26
Venezuela	$56,810.63	$56,810.63
Total	**$1,265,793.04**	**$1,265,793.04**

(Callout labels: "Implicit measure" pointing to LineTotal column; "Explicit measure" pointing to All_Sales column)

Figure 7-16. *The results of an implicit and explicit measure side by side*

An explicit measure is "locked down"—the summarization behavior cannot be modified as shown in Figure 7-17.

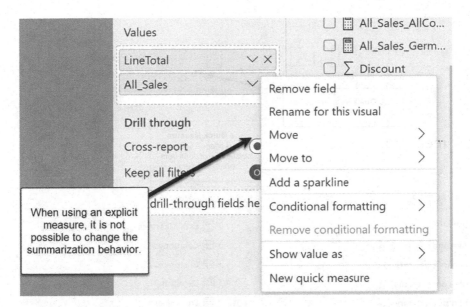

Figure 7-17. *The summarization of an explicit measure cannot be modified*

Once all the necessary explicit measures have been created, the "base" field can be hidden. As I stated in Chapter 6, the hidden column is not hidden from the report developer in the Power BI Desktop. Rather, hiding a base column (or any field) streamlines the model once the report is published.

Tip   It would not be unusual to hide all the fields in the fact table. Doing so ensures that report creators would have to use the dimension table fields to create a visual, which is almost always preferable.

Quick Measures

Learning to write DAX is a nontrivial effort. There is a way to jump-start your learning: use the Quick measure feature. In Figure 7-18, you can see the Quick measure menu.

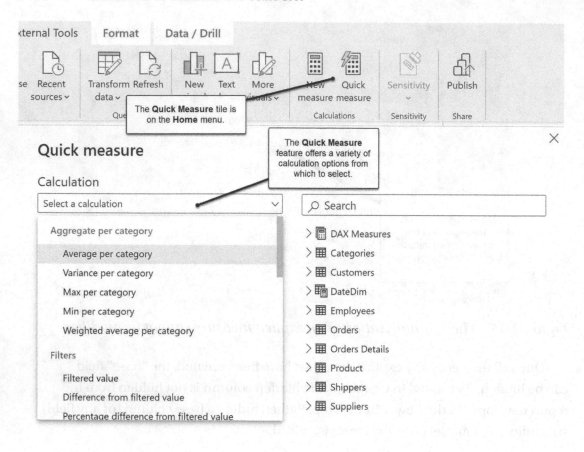

Figure 7-18. *There are built-in calculations in the Quick measure dialogue box*

To create a quick measure, drag fields from the list on the right-hand side to the appropriate field well on the left-hand side of the dialogue box. Let's create a measure that calculates the average value for the orders of each product, as shown in Figure 7-19.

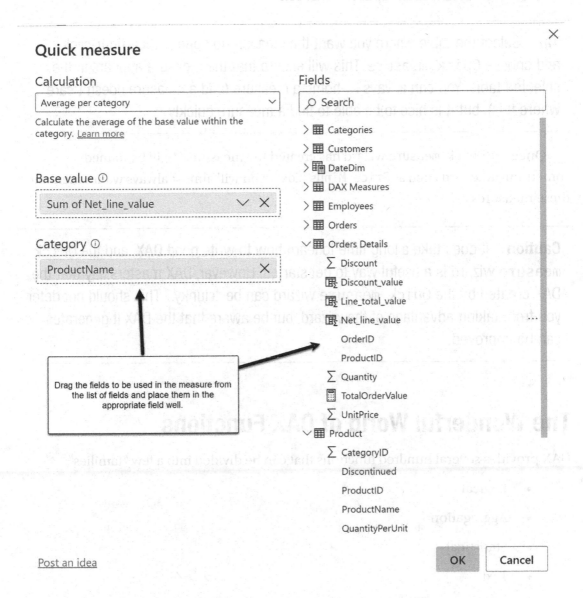

Figure 7-19. *Creating a quick measure*

The Quick measure wizard writes the DAX for you, which you can see once the measure is created.

Tip   Select the table where you want the measure to appear, then right-click, and choose `Quick measure`. This will ensure that the measure appears in the selected table. You can always re-home a measure (and a measure doesn't care where it is), but it is nice to be able to find a measure quickly.

Once the `Quick measure` wizard has created the measure, it will be named something awkward such as `Price Minus Cost`. You will almost always want to rename these measures.

Caution   It does take a long time to learn how to write good DAX, and the `Quick measure` wizard is a useful way to get started. However, DAX masters say that the DAX created by the `Quick measure` wizard can be "clunky." This should not deter you from taking advantage of the wizard, but be aware that the DAX it generates can be improved.

The Wonderful World of DAX Functions

DAX provides several hundred functions that can be divided into a few "families":

- Logical

- Aggregation

- Statistical

- Text

- Time intelligence

- Mathematical/trigonometric

- Date/time

- Filter

- Table manipulation

- Financial

Time Intelligence Functions

Once you get the hang of the most common functions, for example, SUM, AVERAGE, COUNT, and CALCULATE, the next functions most people want to master are the time intelligence functions. Time intelligence functions allow us to perform calculations that are commonly required in most reporting. Examples of these functions include

- TOTALYTD

- SAMEPERIODLASTYEAR

- PARALLELPERIOD

It's unnecessary for me to list all the time intelligence functions as that information is easily found with a simple web search. Rather, I want to use this space to share some tips and tricks for using this group of functions:

1. Time intelligence functions *require* a marked date table to work (covered in Chapter 5) because they operate on the premise that there is one row for every day between the earliest date and the latest date.

2. Time intelligence functions work best if you include a field from the date table on the visual. Otherwise, you will have a number that is opaque. Let's look at some examples. First, here's a simple time intelligence function that calculates sales year-to-date. You can see the results of the measure in Figure 7-20:

```
YTD Sales =
    TOTALYTD(
    SUM('Orders Details'[LineTotal]),
    'DateDim'[Date])
```

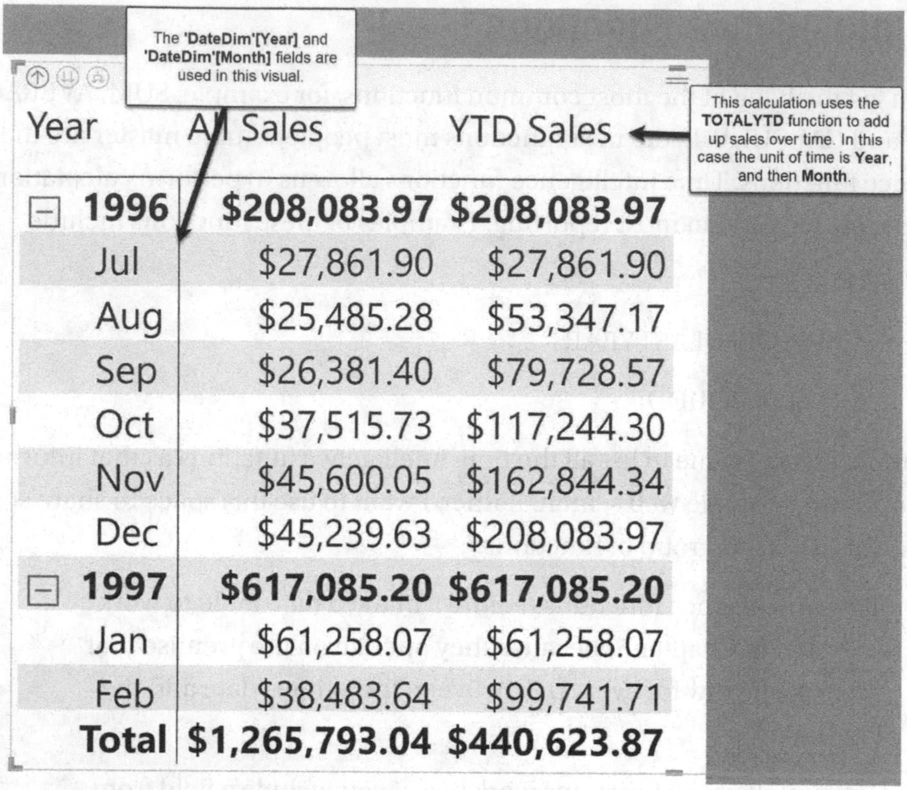

The 'DateDim'[Year] and 'DateDim'[Month] fields are used in this visual.

This calculation uses the **TOTALYTD** function to add up sales over time. In this case the unit of time is **Year**, and then **Month**.

Year	All Sales	YTD Sales
1996	**$208,083.97**	**$208,083.97**
Jul	$27,861.90	$27,861.90
Aug	$25,485.28	$53,347.17
Sep	$26,381.40	$79,728.57
Oct	$37,515.73	$117,244.30
Nov	$45,600.05	$162,844.34
Dec	$45,239.63	$208,083.97
1997	**$617,085.20**	**$617,085.20**
Jan	$61,258.07	$61,258.07
Feb	$38,483.64	$99,741.71
Total	**$1,265,793.04**	**$440,623.87**

Figure 7-20. *Using YTD in a visual*

If we use the YTD Sales measure in a visual *without* a date field, the result is opaque, as you can see in Figure 7-21.

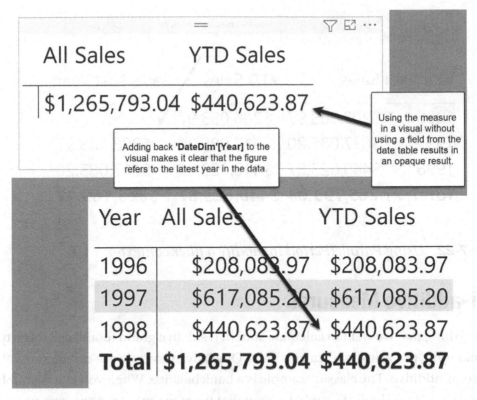

Figure 7-21. *Using a time intelligence function without a date field can be ambiguous*

3. Time intelligence functions can be used to modify the filter context. For example, what if we want to calculate the sales for the same period last year?

```
Sales_Last_Year =
 CALCULATE([All Sales],
PARALLELPERIOD('DateDim'[Date],-12,MONTH)
)
```

There is a function called PARALLELPERIOD, which allows you to set the clock back (or forward) to compare two time periods. In Figure 7-22, you can see the results of this measure.

Using **ParallelPeriod** to modify the filter context to compare two time periods.

Year	All Sales	YTD Sales	Sales Last Year
1996	$208,083.97	$208,083.97	
1997	$617,085.20	$617,085.20	$208,083.97
1998	$440,623.87	$440,623.87	$617,085.20
Total	**$1,265,793.04**	**$440,623.87**	**$825,169.17**

Figure 7-22. *Using ParallelPeriod to modify a filter context*

Semi-additive Measures

Not everything that we want to calculate should result in a grand total. I call these types of calculations "point-in-time" calculations. Officially, these types of calculations are called semi-additive. The classic example is a bank balance. When you check your bank balance, it is a "snapshot" of your balance at that point in time. Another example is inventory balances. If you are calculating inventory, you don't want to see a total of the inventory over the month; you want to see the inventory at that point in time.

Once again, DAX to the rescue! There are multiple functions that can be used to make these calculations. Examples include

- OPENINGBALANCEYEAR

- CLOSINGBALANCEYEAR

- ENDOFMONTH

- STARTOFMONTH

Once again, I am not going to list all the semi-additive measures. A great place to research these functions is `www.sqlbi.com`. They have posted in-depth articles on how these functions work.

Instead, I want to use the space to talk about semi-additive calculations that do not have dedicated functions. What if you want to total all the sales in each category, but each category is managed by a separate division and therefore adding them up is not meaningful? I call these non-totaling calculations. You can see an example in Figure 7-23.

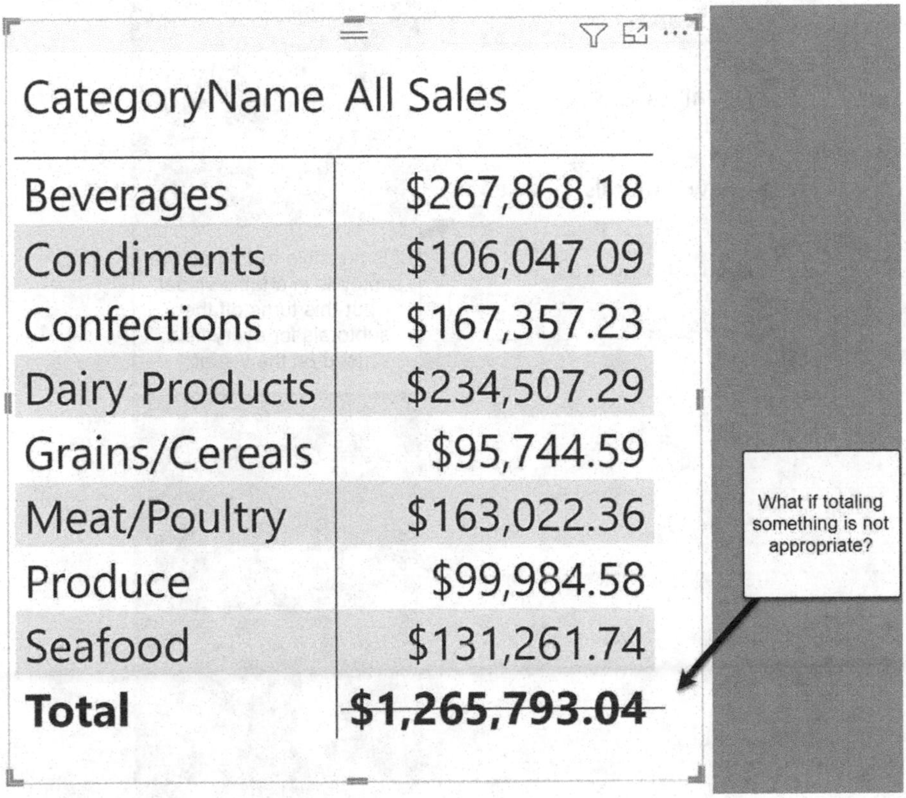

Figure 7-23. A non-totaling measure

Your first thought might be to change the visual in some way. Tables and matrices have a formatting setting where you can turn off subtotals, as shown in Figure 7-24.

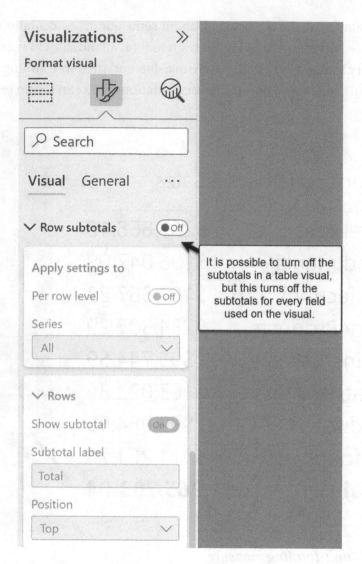

Figure 7-24. Turning off subtotals

But this is not a solution because any other field you add to the visual will also not be totaled. But there are functions that allow you to turn off the total value without resorting to clumsy formatting:

- HASONEVALUE

- HASONEFILTER

- ISINSCOPE

These are functions that test for a condition and, if the condition is true, perform the expression and, if it is false, leave a blank. Here's an example:

```
Non-Total All_Sales =
IF(
HASONEVALUE('Categories'[CategoryName]),
[All Sales]
)
```

All these functions use the IF function to perform the logical test. In the preceding measure, the logical test is whether, *in the current filter context*, the 'Categories'[CategoryName] field has one value. If the test returns true, then the [All Sales] measure is calculated. If the test returns a false, then the measure returns a blank (because the false argument is not included) as shown in Figure 7-25.

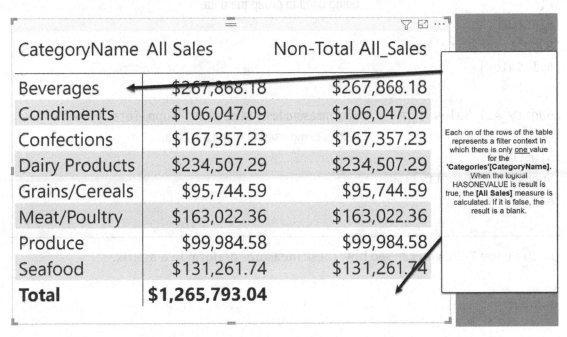

Figure 7-25. *Using HASONEVALUE to turn off the totaling for one column*

A variant of the HASONEVALUE is ISINSCOPE. At first glance, they seem to do the same thing and can, to some degree, be used interchangeably. However, there are differences. ISINSCOPE checks to see if the visual is using the field to group the data.

The easiest way to see this is in a matrix. To create this matrix, I first created a hierarchy in the data model, but the example works without a formal hierarchy as well. Then I created three measures using ISINSCOPE:

DAX Expression	Explanation
Address_All_Sales = IF(ISINSCOPE('Suppliers'[Address]), [All Sales])	This measure tests whether the 'Suppliers'[Address] field is being used to group the data.
City_All_Sales = IF(ISINSCOPE('Suppliers'[City]), [All Sales])	This measure tests whether the 'Suppliers'[City] field is being used to group the data.
Country_All_Sales = IF(ISINSCOPE('Suppliers'[Country]), [All Sales])	This measure tests whether the 'Suppliers'[Country] field is being used to group the data.

In Figure 7-26, you can see how these measures perform in a matrix.

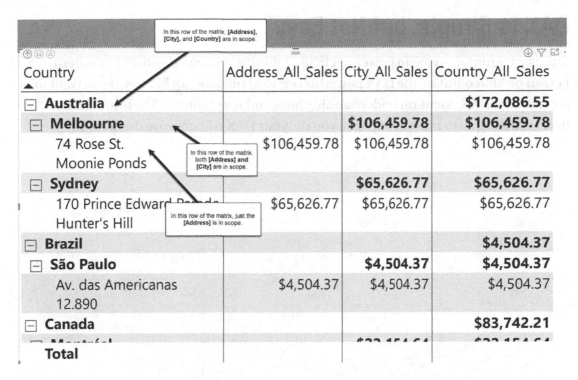

Country	Address_All_Sales	City_All_Sales	Country_All_Sales
⊟ **Australia**			**$172,086.55**
⊟ **Melbourne**		**$106,459.78**	**$106,459.78**
74 Rose St. Moonie Ponds	$106,459.78	$106,459.78	$106,459.78
⊟ **Sydney**		**$65,626.77**	**$65,626.77**
170 Prince Edward Parade Hunter's Hill	$65,626.77	$65,626.77	$65,626.77
⊟ **Brazil**			**$4,504.37**
⊟ **São Paulo**		**$4,504.37**	**$4,504.37**
Av. das Americanas 12.890	$4,504.37	$4,504.37	$4,504.37
⊟ **Canada**			**$83,742.21**
Total			

Figure 7-26. Anything lower in the hierarchy is in scope

In the `Address_All_Sales` column, the measure tests for the presence of the `'Suppliers'[Address]` in the current filter context. Because the test returns TRUE, the `All_Sales` measure is calculated. The next column, `City_All_Sales`, tests for the presence of `'Suppliers'[City]`. The test returns true for both the row with the city name and for the row with the address. Anything that is *lower* in the hierarchy is considered in scope.

In the preceding example, I used the formal hierarchy that I created. If I were to use the base fields, the result would be the same.

Statistical Functions

In the exam prep items for PL-300, there is a specific entry for the DAX statistical functions. I am going to be candid here and state that I really don't know why this subset of DAX functions was mentioned specifically. Statistical functions work the same way as other DAX functions. My guess is that while most of us can intuitively understand a logic or mathematical function, we may not be as familiar with basic statistics. I recommend that you familiarize yourself with some basic statistical principles, such as median, average, and standard deviation.

DAX Is Simple, but Not Easy

This is a common saying in Power BI circles. I think it originated with either Alberto Ferrari or Marco Russo, the DAX powerhouses who run www.SQLBI.com. If you want to get better at DAX, focus on understanding filter and row contexts. These are the two hardest concepts to master, but once you do, your DAX will improve dramatically.

CHAPTER 8

Optimize Model Performance

When you first start writing DAX, you are bound to write some "ugly baby" DAX—DAX only an author can love! And that is okay—at the beginning. There's an expression "Perfect is the enemy of done," which means don't let the quest for perfect DAX get in the way of writing DAX. Good DAX takes practice and some tools, one of which is built into the Power BI Desktop.

Measuring Report Performance

The first concept to grasp is that every visual creates a DAX expression. Even if you never write a line of DAX, your report is still using it. Any DAX that you write (for measures or tables or calculated columns) is another layer that can affect your report's performance. To see the DAX, navigate to the View tab, and then choose the Performance analyzer, as shown in Figure 8-1.

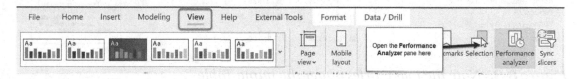

Figure 8-1. *On the View tab, click Performance analyzer*

The Performance analyzer will open. To use the Performance analyzer, click Start recording, as shown in Figure 8-2.

© Jessica Jolly 2023
J. Jolly, *Microsoft Power BI Data Analyst Certification Companion*, Certification Study Companion Series,
https://doi.org/10.1007/978-1-4842-9013-2_8

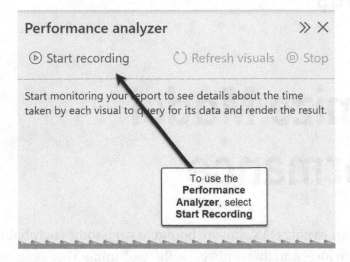

Figure 8-2. *The Performance analyzer will record your selections*

Once you have started recording, begin interacting with your report page. In the following example, I sorted the CompanyName column as shown in Figure 8-3.

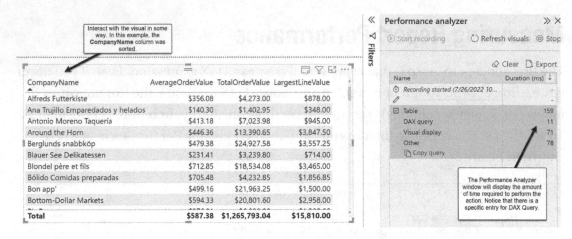

Figure 8-3. *Note the four entries under the name Table*

Examining DAX Query Performance

Earlier, I said that each visual constitutes a DAX query. To see that DAX query, on the Performance analyzer window, select Copy query and then paste the query into a text editor or DAX Studio (which we will cover in Chapter 14). Here is the DAX query from the preceding example:

```
// DAX Query
DEFINE
  VAR __DSOCore =
    SUMMARIZECOLUMNS(
      ROLLUPADDISSUBTOTAL('Customers'[CompanyName],
      "IsGrandTotalRowTotal"),
      "TotalOrderValue", 'DAX Measures'[TotalOrderValue],
      "LargestLineValue", 'DAX Measures'[LargestLineValue],
      "AverageOrderValue", 'DAX Measures'[AverageOrderValue]
    )
  VAR __DSOPrimaryWindowed =
    TOPN(502, __DSOCore, [IsGrandTotalRowTotal], 0,
    'Customers'[CompanyName], 1)
EVALUATE
  __DSOPrimaryWindowed
ORDER BY
  [IsGrandTotalRowTotal] DESC, 'Customers'[CompanyName]
```

Tip   A great way to start improving your DAX is to copy the queries from the visuals you create. You may not understand everything in the query, but you can start to get a "feel" for the syntax and logic of DAX.

Cumulatively, the number of separate DAX queries on a page can slow page responsiveness. If this starts to happen, open the Performance analyzer and interact with each visual in turn. Identify the slowest elements of the visual. If the DAX query component is slow, and if your visual uses measures or calculated columns, you can optimize those elements by rewriting the DAX. You *cannot* modify the DAX on which the visual is based.

Checking Number of Visuals per Page

There is no set number of visuals for a page, but the rule of thumb is to aim for between five and seven visuals. Of course, it very much depends on the cumulative impact of everything that is on the page, which is why it can be useful to use the Performance analyzer to see how long a page takes to refresh. To do so, first choose Clear and then Refresh visuals, as shown in Figure 8-4.

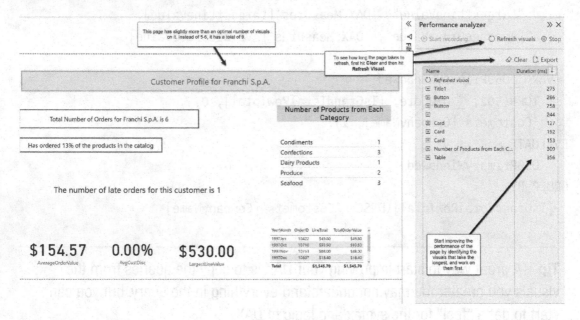

Figure 8-4. *Refreshing a page to measure the overall responsiveness*

Considering Other Performance Factors

Other factors that can affect your report's performance, with suggested remediation methods, are as follows:

Source	Remediation
Unnecessary (unused) columns	Remove those columns in the Power Query Editor.
Columns with high cardinality	Remove these columns in the Power Query Editor or reduce their cardinality by simplifying them. For example, if the column has both date and time, separate these into two columns, date and time.
Many-to-many relationships	Build bridge tables between two tables that currently have a many-to-many relationship.
Bidirectional relationships	Use DAX to reverse a relationship (e.g., build a measure using CROSSFILTER).
Using nonoptimized DAX	Many DAX functions can be replaced by one that is faster. Test various versions of a measure.
Calculated columns	Replace with a measure or add the column in the source or using the Power Query Editor.
Aggregate large tables	Create aggregated tables in the Power Query Editor or in the source.
Filter and slicer selections	Preset filter and slicer to the most commonly selected items. Close the Filters pane.
Excessive tooltips	Tooltips generate a query. Avoid using too many fields in a tooltip. If a tooltip is unnecessary, disable tooltips for that visual on the `Format visual` panel.
Reduce interactions	If a visual does not need to interact with other visuals, you can disable interactions on the `Edit interactions` panel.

As you can see, report performance is dependent on many factors, many of which should be addressed before creating the first visual.

PART IV

Visualize and Analyze the Data

CHAPTER 9

Create Reports

When I teach, I notice that many students use the terms "report" and "dashboard" interchangeably. Understandably so, because from a user perspective, the function of a report is to serve as a dashboard, as defined by the Oxford Dictionary:

> *A graphical summary of various pieces of important information, typically used to give an overview of a business.*

In the Power BI ecosystem, reports and dashboards are two different elements that can be created. Let's compare reports and dashboards, side by side.

Reports	Dashboards
Can be created in the Power BI Desktop or the Power BI Service	Can only be created in the Power BI Service
Multiple pages	One virtual page
Must be underpinned by a data model	Uses visuals from published reports
Can be shared via apps	Can be shared via apps
Cannot contain streaming content	Can contain streaming content

In this chapter, we will explore reports in depth. In Chapter 13, we will address dashboards.

The Canvas

When you launch the Power BI Desktop, it will open in the Report view. When you are new to Power BI, this canvas can be a little daunting. Where to start? A good place is to set up the overall parameters for your report. In Figure 9-1, you can see all of the formatting options available for the report and page.

© Jessica Jolly 2023
J. Jolly, *Microsoft Power BI Data Analyst Certification Companion*, Certification Study Companion Series,
https://doi.org/10.1007/978-1-4842-9013-2_9

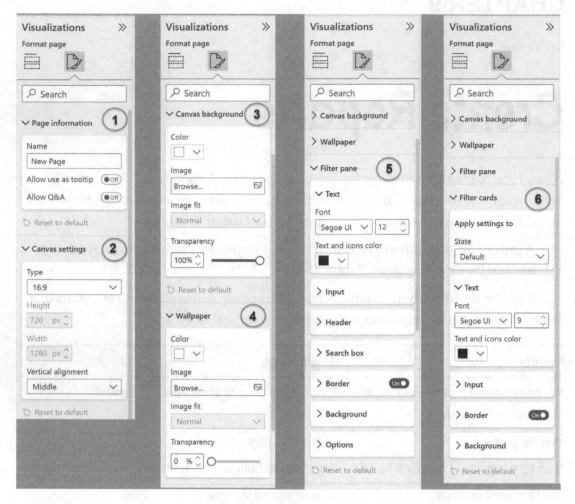

Figure 9-1. *The page- and report-level settings*

Starting from a blank page (or after selecting the white area of your page) in the Format page menu, there are a lot of formatting options. Going by the numbers in the preceding screenshot, here is a brief description of each formatting card:

1. *Page information*: If this is going to be a tooltip page, you need to enable it here. You can also re-name a page here.

2. *Canvas settings*: This controls the overall size of your canvas. Notice that the default option is an aspect ratio rather than the familiar paper sizes (letter, legal, etc.).

3. *Canvas background*: This setting allows you to place colors or a picture within the canvas (as indicated by the dotted lines).

4. *Wallpaper*: This setting allows you to place colors or a picture across the entire report area (working and nonworking). By adjusting the transparency, the background and wallpaper colors can be interactive, as shown in Figure 9-2.

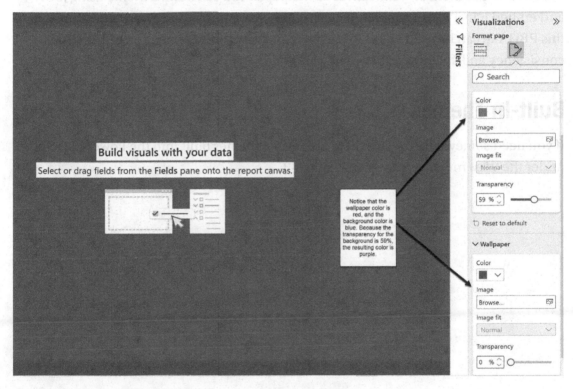

Figure 9-2. *Combining the background and wallpaper colors*

5. *Filter pane*: You can set up a background color of your Filters panel.

6. *Filter cards*: You can change the look and feel of the individual filter cards.

Just Because You Can…

…doesn't mean you should. It is easy to fall down a design rabbit hole in the Power BI Desktop. It's far better to standardize on the colors, fonts, page sizes, and images that you are going to use in your report. A great starting point is the PowerPoint template that your company probably has. You can capture your PowerPoint template slides as images and use them on your canvas or wallpaper. You can build a theme using JSON and embed it in a PBIT (template) file. Just like your company's PowerPoint template, this PBIT file can be used as a starting point for every PBIX file, thus ensuring visual consistency and accurately "branded" reports.

Built-In Themes

If you need somewhere to start, there are several themes built into the Power BI Desktop, under the View menu, as shown in Figure 9-3.

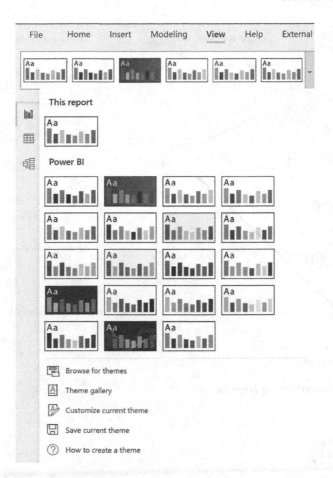

Figure 9-3. Available standardized themes

Just as in PowerPoint, the chosen theme determines the color palette used in the visuals. Be careful, though, to not overwhelm your report readers with different color schemes in reports and dashboards.

Once a theme is selected, it is possible to customize the theme at a very detailed level as shown in Figure 9-4.

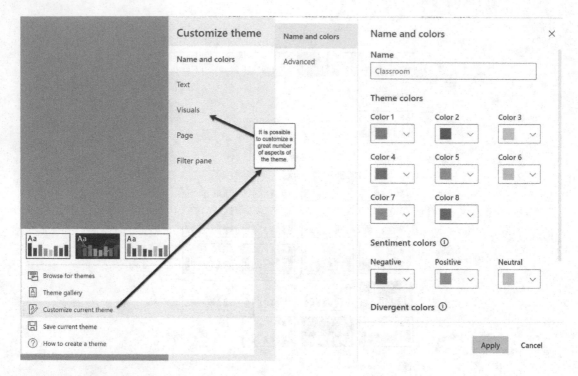

Figure 9-4. *Customizing a theme*

Accessibility

Making reports readable by everyone should be a priority for anyone designing a report. Doing so, however, is a nontrivial exercise. I am not qualified to write a comprehensive guide to accessibility, but I can point out some key techniques:

- Make sure your color scheme has sufficient contrast particularly when used in highlighting on a visual.

- Font sizes, for all text on a visual, should be at least 15 points.

- There are fonts that are preferred for accessibility. Make sure that your report uses these fonts.

- All visuals should have alternative text provided, describing the visual in detail. Avoid the use of "see" (and related words) in the description.

- Every report should be tested with a screen reader, to ensure that all
  the accessibility settings are present.

Because ensuring a report is fully accessible is time consuming, ideally your
company's Power BI theme adheres to all the design principles of accessibility.

Visualizations

At the heart of every report are the visualizations. The visualization is the materialization
of all the hard work of transforming and modeling the data. Because 80% of the work
to create a report lies in transformation and modeling, choosing, populating, and
formatting the visuals should take far less time. Despite this reality, when first getting
started with Power BI, the visualization component looms large.

Standard Visuals

Power BI offers a standard list of visualization types, which periodically expands to
include a new visualization. As of this writing, there are 37 standard visuals available as
you can see in Figure 9-5.

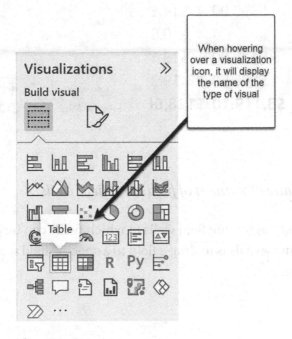

Figure 9-5. *The Visualizations menu*

To select one, simply click once the icon. To change the visualization, select the visualization on the canvas, and then click the icon for the new visualization. It is possible to drag a field directly onto the canvas, which will create a table visual. It is also possible to drag a field onto the "placeholder" for the visual. When you use this technique, the Desktop will automatically pick a field well in which to place this field. If you have ever created a pivot table in Excel, you are familiar with this behavior as shown in Figure 9-6.

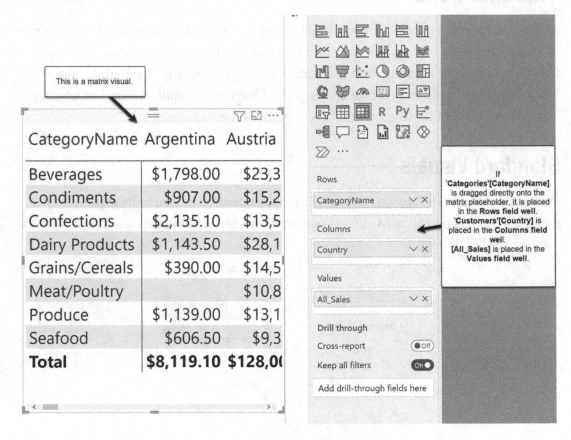

Figure 9-6. Automatic placement of fields into field wells

Every visualization has unique field wells in which fields can be placed. My preferred method for building my visuals is to drag a field to a specific field well, but of course, this is personal preference.

Custom Visuals

If the standard visual menu doesn't offer the type of visualization you are looking for, there is a large "aftermarket" of custom visuals, created by developers. You access the menu by clicking the ellipsis in the Visualizations menu, as shown in Figure 9-7.

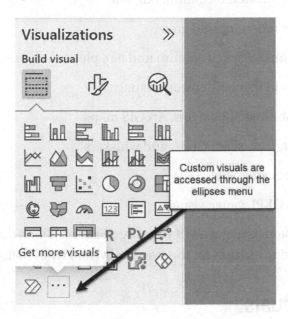

Figure 9-7. Accessing custom visuals

Many companies limit access to custom visuals, considering them security risks. There are custom visuals that have been certified by Microsoft, and many organizations consider that sufficient risk mitigation. Some custom visuals do require an additional purchase.

For Future Reference: Build Your Own Visual

Among the standard and custom visual menus, there will probably be a visual type that will meet the requirements for your data. If, however, there are specific requirements that cannot be addressed, there are tools that allow you to create a custom visual, such as Deneb and Charticulator. (This is not an endorsement of either tool set.)

Selecting the Right Visual Type

There are several categories of visuals. The type of the data should drive the type of visual used[1]:

- *Comparison*: Clustered column, bar, line

- *Change over time*: Line and area

- *Parts of a whole*: Stacked column and bar, pie, donut, treemap

- *Flow*: Area and specialty custom visuals

- *Spatial*: Globe and filled maps, ArcGIS maps

- *Distribution*: Line, scatter, box, and whiskers

- *Correlation*: Scatter, line

- *Single*: Cards, KPI, gauge visuals

Before using a custom visual type (if your organization allows them), be sure to explore all the formatting features for the standard visual types that suit the data.

Formatting Visuals

Every visual type has formatting features common to all visuals and formatting features unique to that visual type. Access these features by choosing the Format visual menu, as shown in Figure 9-8.

---

[1] I would like to credit SQLBI for these visualization categories. For an excellent one-page reference, go to www.SQLBI.com for a downloadable PDF.

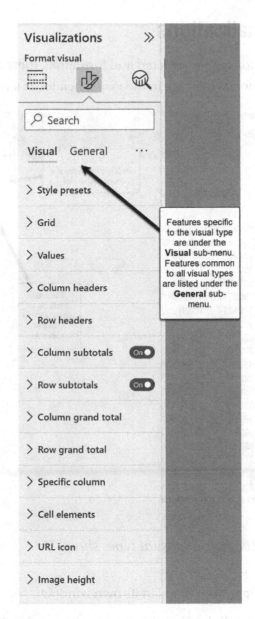

Features specific
to the visual type
are under the
Visual sub-menu.
Features common
to all visual types
are listed under the
General sub-
menu.

Figure 9-8. *The Format visual menu*

Tip   When using a visualization for the first time, always make the time to explore
all the features specific to the visual type.

Configuring Visualizations

Once the right visualization type is selected and formatted, there are some controls that every visual has in common, which are in the visual header as shown in Figure 9-9.

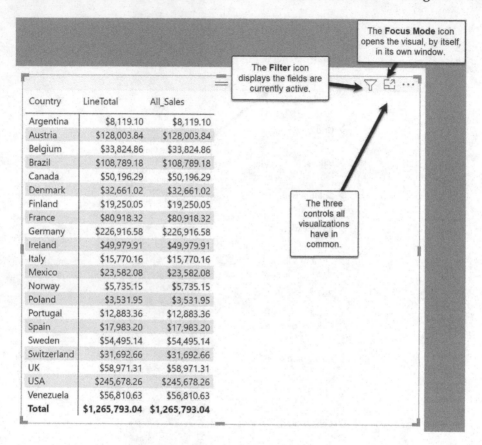

Figure 9-9. *The three controls all visual types share*

- *Focus mode*: Opens the visual in its own window

- *Filter*: Displays all the filters currently active on the visual

- *Ellipsis*: (As shown in Figure 9-10) Contains the following controls:

    - *Export data*: Export the data used in this visual to Excel.

    - *Show as a table*: Instead of exporting the data to Excel, showing the data in a table format can be sufficient.

- *Remove*: Usually selecting a visual and choosing `Delete` is sufficient to remove a visual from the canvas. However, if this doesn't work, choosing `Remove` from the `ellipsis` menu works.

- *Spotlight*: Fades back any other visuals on the report page.

- *Sort ascending, Sort descending, Sort by*: This option is only available if there are multiple fields used in the visual.

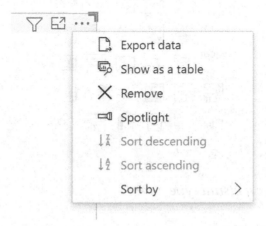

Figure 9-10. *The ellipsis menu*

Slicing and Filtering

Interactions are one way of filtering visuals. But there are several other more direct ways to filter visuals: by using slicers and/or the Filters panel. (Yes, you can use both of them together!)

Slicers

A slicer is a form of visual. You can have multiple slicers on a page, and you can have slicers that control several pages. Setting up slicers is easy, and users intuitively understand what to do with a slicer. Select a slicer the same way you would any other visual, as shown in Figure 9-11.

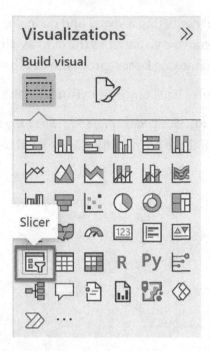

Figure 9-11. *Slicers are a visual type*

Slicers are easy to populate:

1. Drag the field directly onto the slicer placeholder.

2. Check the box next to the field to use in the slicer.

3. Drag the field into the field well.

Tip Any visual can be populated using one of these three ways, but if the visual has more than one field well, Power BI may put the field in an unexpected field well.

Slicers have different configuration options based on the data type of the field used. These options are underneath a caret in the upper-right corner, as shown in Figure 9-12.

Note In the most recent version of Power BI Desktop (as of this writing), these settings have moved to the Format Visuals menu.

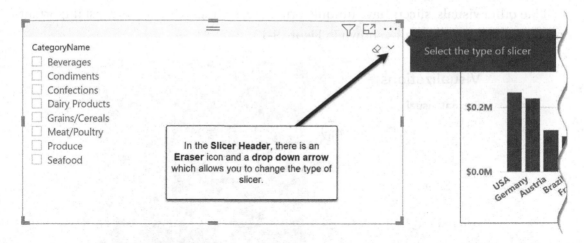

Figure 9-12. You can change the type of slicer in the slicer header

If the data type of the field is text, there are two options for the slicer format:

- List

- Drop-down

If the data type is a number, there are five options for the slicer format:

- List

- Drop-down

- Between

- Less than or equal to

- Greater than or equal to

If the data type is a date, there are seven different options for the slicer format:

- Between

- Before

- After

- List

- Drop-down

- Relative date

- Relative time

209

Like other visuals, slicers have unique formatting settings. One of the most important ones is the Slicer settings, as shown in Figure 9-13.

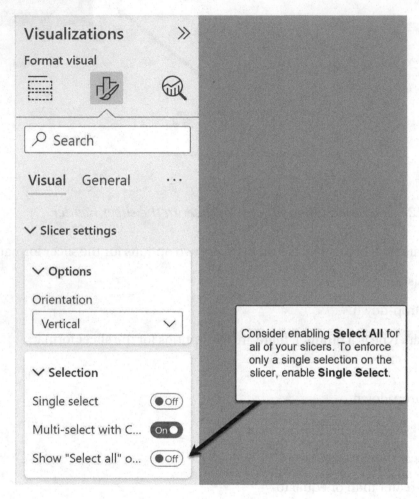

Figure 9-13. *Consider always turning Select all on*

There are custom slicers available as well, but as always, investigate all the formatting settings for the standard slicer before resorting to a custom slicer.

Copying Slicers, Syncing Slicers

If you have performed a lot of formatting on a slicer, you might want to have another slicer with the same formatting settings. Doing so is easy—simply copy the slicer you want to replicate. Select the slicer, right-click, and choose Copy, as you can see in Figure 9-14. Or use the standard keyboard shortcut Ctrl+C.

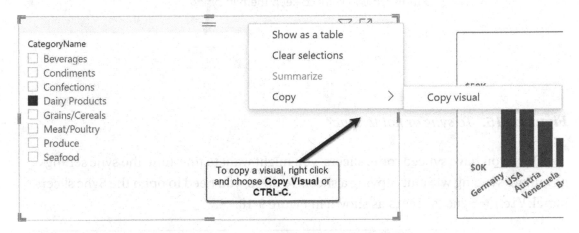

Figure 9-14. *Two different methods for copying a visual*

Use Ctrl+V to paste the slicer in a new location.

Tip   Any visual element can be copied. However, as of this writing, when copying a button, you will not be able to right-click a button and choose Copy visual. Simply select the button and Ctrl+C.

When copying a slicer, Power BI will ask if you want to sync the copy of the slicer with the original as shown in Figure 9-15. If two slicers are synced, a selection made on one slicer will be reflected on the synced slicer(s), even if on different pages.

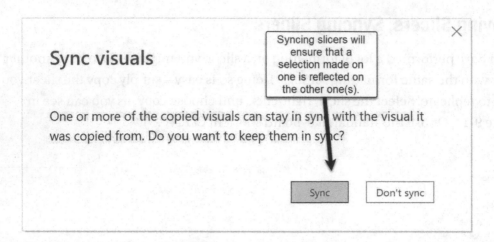

Figure 9-15. *To sync or not to sync?*

Once you have synced some slicers, you might want to fine-tune the sync settings or initiate syncing without copying a slicer. To do so, you need to open the Sync slicers panel: View ➤ Sync slicers as shown in Figure 9-16.

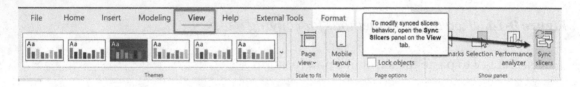

Figure 9-16. *Opening the Sync slicers panel*

Once you have the Sync slicers panel open, make sure you select one of the slicers you want to sync or to adjust. The Sync slicers panel has two columns: one for syncing the slicers and one for rendering the slicers visible (or not). You can see the Sync slicers panel in Figure 9-17.

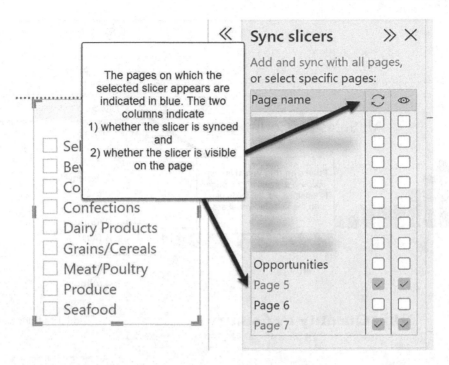

Figure 9-17. Synced slicers settings

Tip   Even though you can have "invisible" slicers on a page, use this feature cautiously. It could be very confusing to a report user to have a page filtered without any visible indicator.

The Filters Pane

Slicers are wonderful tools for filtering a report page (or several pages), but they have limitations. They are simple to set up, but that also means that they have a limited set of features. They also take real estate on the report page, something that is in limited supply. It's a good thing we have another option: the Filters pane.

The Filters pane has three areas as shown in Figure 9-18:

- Filters on this visual, (only visible when a visual is selected)

- Filters on this page

- Filters on all pages

Figure 9-18. *The Filters pane has three parts*

If you have ever created a pivot table, you are familiar with how to populate the
Filters pane—drag the field you want to use on the Filters pane directly onto it as
shown in Figure 9-19.

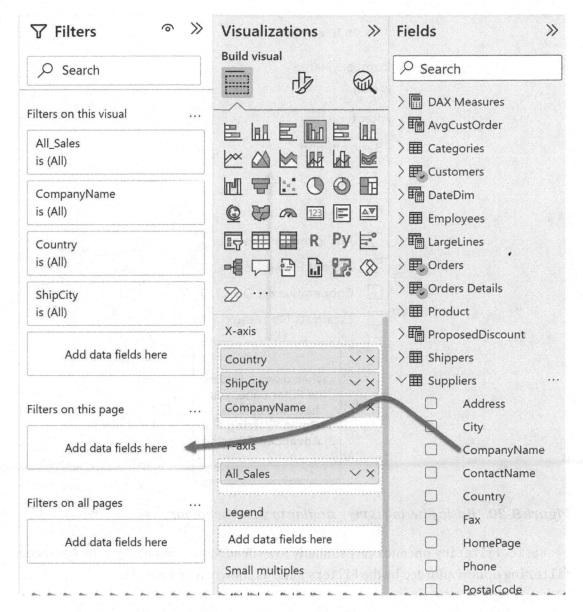

Figure 9-19. *Dragging a field onto the Filters pane*

You can drag multiple fields into the same area of the Filters pane. Using a field on the Filters pane provides two and sometimes three options for filtering as shown in Figure 9-20:

- Basic filtering

- Advanced filtering

- Top N filtering (available only for Filters on this visual)

215

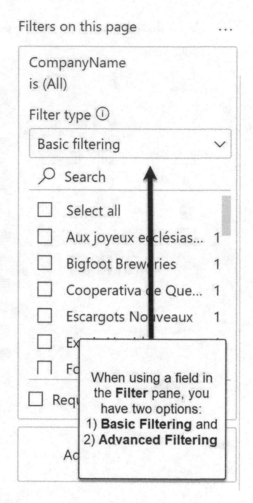

Figure 9-20. *Basic filtering is very similar to slicer behavior*

Basic filtering operates very similarly to a slicer. More compelling is the Advanced filtering option afforded by the Filters pane as shown in Figure 9-21.

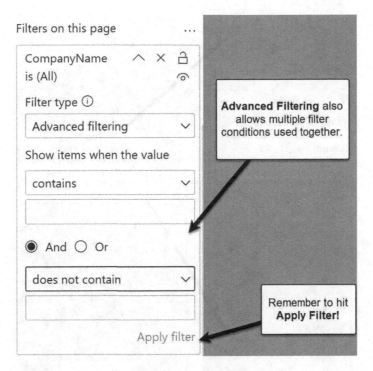

Figure 9-21. *Advanced filtering offers the opportunity to combine filter conditions*

The third type of filtering, Top N, is available for Filters on this visual, as you can see in Figure 9-22.

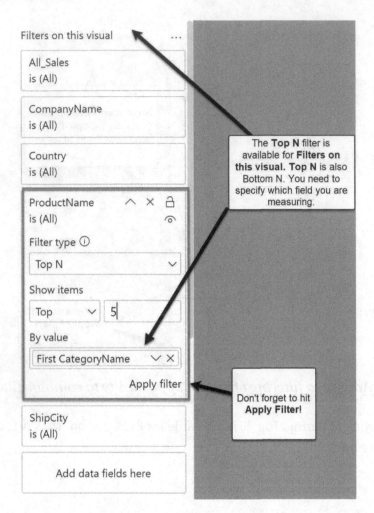

Figure 9-22. *The Top N filtering is available for Filters on this visual*

You, as the report developer, decide how much control the report user will have on the `Filters` pane. If the report user should not be able to change the filter pane settings, you can lock individual filter cards. Similarly, if the user should not even see the filter card, you can hide that card. Remember, by hovering over the `Filters` icon on a particular visual, the user can see the filters impacting an individual visual.

For Future Reference: Controlling the Performance Impact of Filtering

Every selection made on the `Filters` pane generates a query back to the engine. The overall performance of the page is dependent on a lot of variables, but the more of those variables you can control, the better your report's response. If you know that most report readers are only interested in a specific set of data, you can preselect this data on the `Filters` pane and then close the pane. Once you publish the report, most of the users will be able to see the data they are interested in, without paying a performance hit. Users who are interested in different data can open the `Filters` pane and change the filters.

Formatting the Filters Pane

At the beginning of this chapter, we covered formatting the entire canvas. In those menus, there were two that pertained to the `Filters` pane. They are numbers 5 and 6, as shown in Figure 9-23.

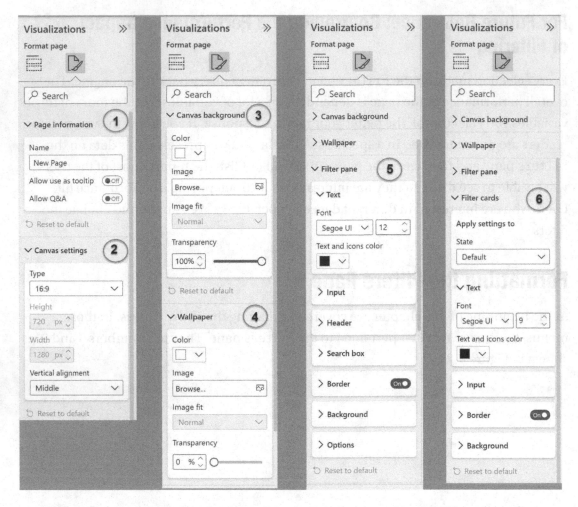

Figure 9-23. *Numbers 5 and 6 have formatting features for the Filters pane*

If you want the Filters pane to appear continuous with the report page, you can do so by using the same color scheme as your canvas and/or background.

Drill-Through

In addition to synced slicers, there is another way to transmit a filter from one page to another: the drill-through feature. When you use a field as a drill-through field on a particular page, you can navigate directly to that page from another page and visual where that field appears. Sounds confusing? Don't worry—it's easy once you have set one up. The first step is to drag the selected field to the Drill through area of the Visualizations pane on the *destination* page for the drill through, as shown in Figure 9-24.

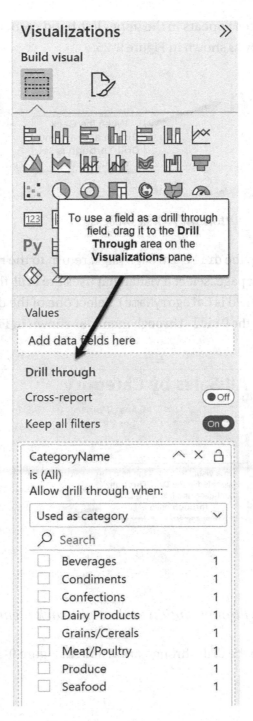

Figure 9-24. *The Drill through area*

When the back button appears in the upper left-hand corner, you have set up the drill-through successfully as shown in Figure 9-25.

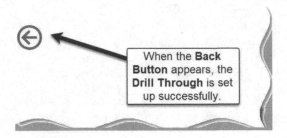

When the **Back Button** appears, the **Drill Through** is set up successfully.

Figure 9-25. *The back button indicates success*

Once you have set up the drill-through page, return to the report page *from* which you want to drill. On that page, select a visual that uses the drill-through field (in the preceding example, the field is CategoryName). Select one of the data points and right-click. From there, follow the Drill through menu, as shown in Figure 9-26.

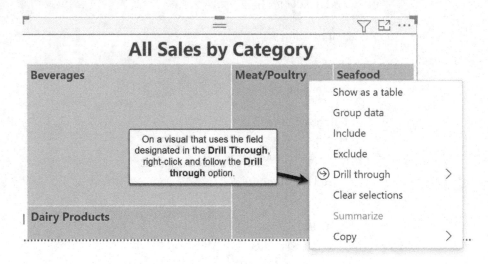

On a visual that uses the field designated in the **Drill Through**, right-click and follow the **Drill through** option.

Figure 9-26. *The Drill through option in the right-click menu*

The results following the drill-through are visible in Figure 9-27.

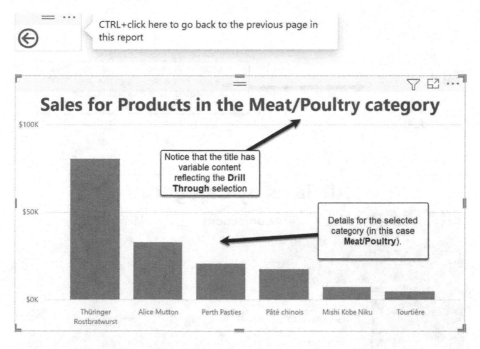

CTRL+click here to go back to the previous page in this report

Sales for Products in the Meat/Poultry category

Notice that the title has variable content reflecting the **Drill Through** selection

Details for the selected category (in this case **Meat/Poultry**).

$100K

$50K

$0K

Thüringer Rostbratwurst · Alice Mutton · Perth Pasties · Pâté chinois · Mishi Kobe Niku · Tourtière

Figure 9-27. *The drill-through page showing the filtered result*

The purpose of the drill-through is to be able to make a selection on one page and have it "carry through" to another page in the report. A side benefit is that any other filter on the originating page will also be carried through to the drill-through page. As shown in Figure 9-28, if you have a slicer on the originating page, any selection made on that slicer will be reflected on the drill-through page. You can prevent other filters carrying over to the drill through destination page by toggling the Keep All Filters setting to "off".

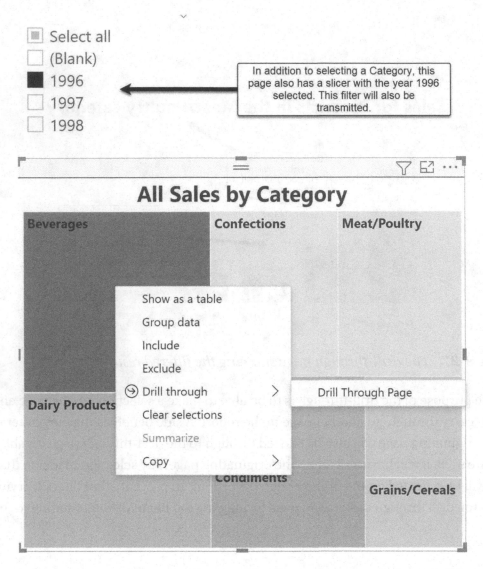

Figure 9-28. *The selected value on a slicer will also be "carried through" to the drill-through page*

For Future Reference: Drill Through from One Report to Another

The good news is that the same functionality allows you to create a drill-through from one report to another!

Conditional Formatting

Some Power BI visuals (specifically tables and matrices) have conditional formatting
built into them. The `Conditional formatting` in Power BI works very similarly to that
in Excel. As shown in Figure 9-29, access the `Conditional formatting` menu by clicking
the down arrow next to the field you want to format.

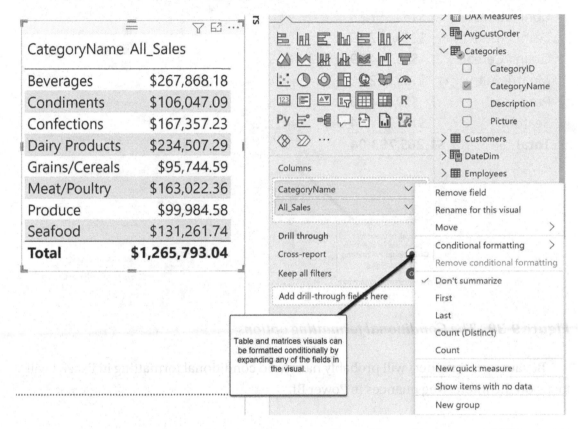

Figure 9-29. Accessing Conditional formatting for tables or matrices

As shown in Figure 9-30, the features in `Conditional formatting` include

- Background color

- Font color

- Icons

- Web URL

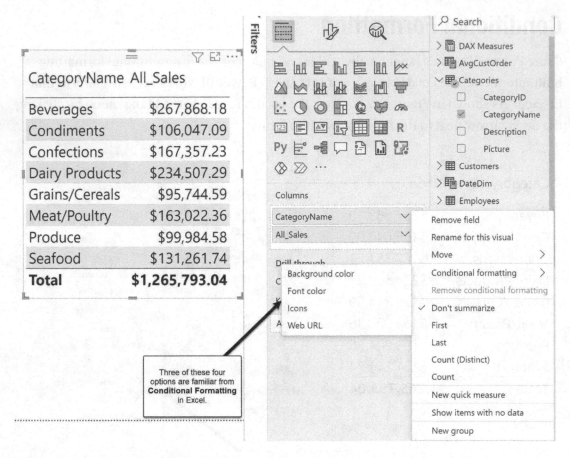

Figure 9-30. *The Conditional formatting options*

Because most readers will probably have used conditional formatting in Excel, I will focus on the interesting nuances in Power BI.

Web URL

If you have data that is readily viewed on the Internet, you might want to make it easy for your report reader to easily access the appropriate page. But first, you must create a connection between the field you want to format and the web URL address. Figure 9-31 shows a simple example.

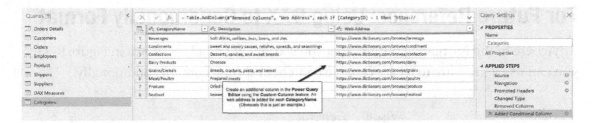

Figure 9-31. *Adding a custom column for conditional formatting as a web URL*

Once the web address is present in the data model (and related to the field you want to format with it), you can set up the conditional formatting:

1) Select `Conditional formatting` ➤ `Web URL`.

2) Set the format to be based on the value in the `Web Address` field, as shown in Figure 9-32.

Figure 9-32. *Base the conditional formatting on the content of the Web Address field*

Tip   This technique (basing conditional formatting on the value of a field) works for other formatting, such as background or font color. To turn the background of a cell a specific color, make sure you have a column with the hexadecimal color corresponding to the value you want to use in the format present in the table.

For Future Reference: Using DAX to Conditionally Format

Anywhere in the formatting settings that you see an Fx symbol, as shown in Figure 9-33, you can use a measure to create variable content or format content conditionally.

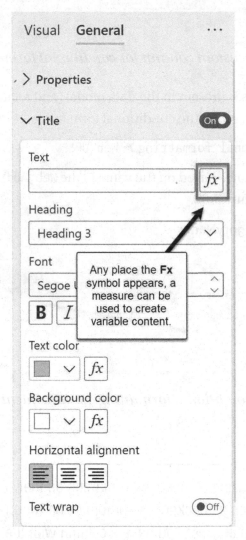

Figure 9-33. *The Fx symbol indicates an opportunity to provide variable content*

An easy example to demonstrate this capability is to create a title that will vary based on a particular value that is selected. The measure is

```
Title=
"All Sales by Country for "
& SELECTEDVALUE('Suppliers'[CompanyName])
```

Once you have created the measure (using the same methodology to create any measure), you can "point" the Title field to the measure. Eliminate any title content that already exists for the visual as shown in Figure 9-34.

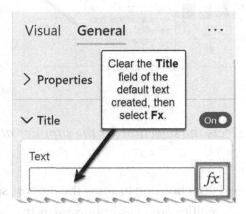

Figure 9-34. *Clear the default title text*

Point the title text to the measure that you created as shown in Figure 9-35.

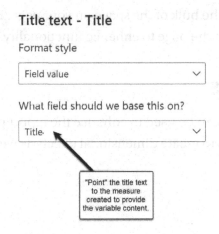

Figure 9-35. *Using a measure to create a variable title*

Because of the DAX function used in the measure (SELECTEDVALUE), the title will reflect a value chosen for the name of the supplier as you can see in Figure 9-36.

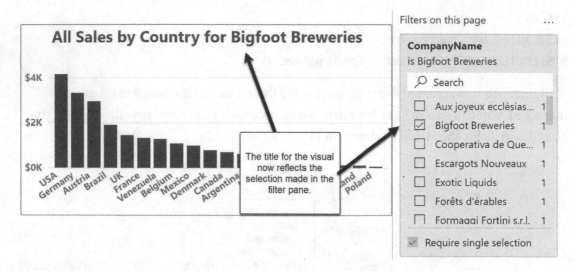

Figure 9-36. *The title reflects the selection for the supplier name made on the Filters pane*

This is just one example. I am choosing to show the process so that the idea isn't completely theoretical. The specifics aren't as important as the overall concept.

Other Page Elements

Visuals are going to take up the bulk of the space on your page. But there are other elements that you can use on the page to enhance functionality.

Images and Shapes

Both JPEG and PNG images can be used to enhance the report page. Shapes can also be placed on the report page to create dimensional effects as well as create other composite shapes.

Text Boxes

You can also place text boxes on the page to provide instruction or further details. Note that the text box contains static text. To create variable text, you need to use either the card visual type or buttons (see in the following).

Buttons

Buttons have (relatively) recently received an upgrade in features. The new capabilities now make buttons a great option to use instead of the single-value cards because they have more formatting options. When you add a button to your page, it will always appear in the upper left-hand corner of the page. There are several types of buttons:

- Left and right arrows

- Reset

- Back

- Information

- Help

- Q&A

- Bookmark

- Blank

- Navigator

Most of these button settings are self-evident, or will be with a little experimentation, which I encourage you to do. Here, we will delve into the Blank and Navigator button types. As shown in Figure 9-37, access the Buttons menu through the Insert tab.

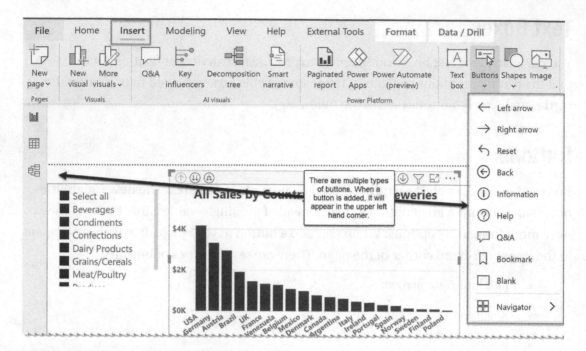

Figure 9-37.   *The Insert ➤ Buttons menu*

After inserting a button, the Format ➤ Button pane will appear. Of all the features a button has, the Action feature (shown in Figure 9-38) is the most important. Without an action, a button is a fancy text box.

Figure 9-38. *Action feature of buttons*

Assigning an action to a button enables the button to add functionality to a page. Most of the actions have an equivalent preprogrammed button option, but there are several actions that only appear in the Action menu:

- Drill through

- Web URL

What if you are not sure that your users will be savvy enough to right-click to drill through to another page? Placing a button on the page can make the process more transparent to the user. The first thing to do is to Insert ➤ Buttons ➤ Blank.

Once the button is on the page (remember, it will show up in the upper left-hand corner), you can move it to an appropriate place on the page. Once the button is placed, select it, and configure the Action to Drill through, as shown in Figure 9-39.

233

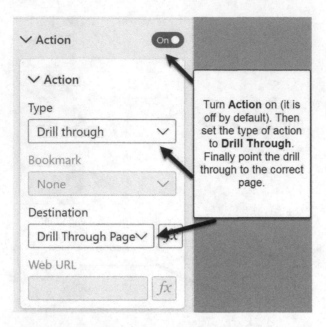

Figure 9-39. *Setting up a Drill through action on a button*

Once the button action is set up, add instructional text to tell your report user how to use the button, as shown in Figure 9-40. To do so, go to Format ➤ Visual ➤ Style ➤ Text.

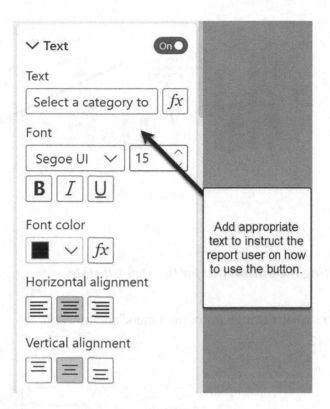

Figure 9-40. *Adding instructional text to a button*

Button States

Not only do buttons have lots of format options; they also can be formatted differently based on their "state." A button offers four states:

- Default

- On hover

- On select

- Disabled

You can add text or another formatting that is appropriate to that particular state. In this example, I am choosing to put the following text for two different states:

Default: "Select a category to get more details," as shown in Figure 9-41.

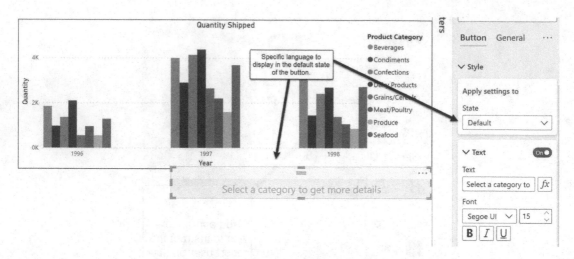

Figure 9-41. *Setting the button text for the Default state*

On hover: "Drill through for more details," as shown in Figure 9-42.

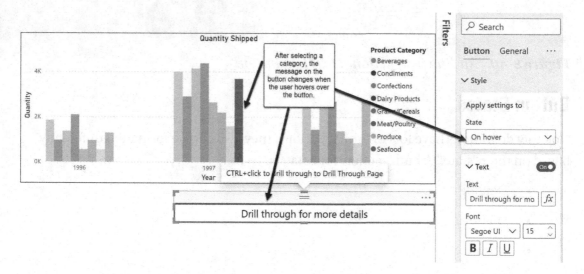

Figure 9-42. *Setting the button text for the On hover state*

Now, all the report user must do is click the button to drill through. Leveraging the states of a button allows you to design in layers of functionality and instruction on the same page.

Using the Navigation Button

One very common use for buttons is to set up convenient page navigation. In December 2021, the Power BI team made this much easier by adding a button specifically for page navigation. You can add a navigation button that includes all the pages of the report, as shown in Figure 9-43. This navigation button can be copied from one page to another and automatically adjusts to highlight the page it is on.

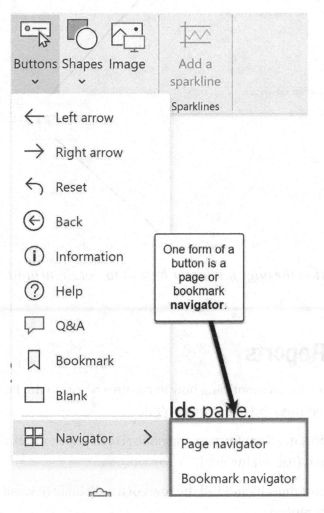

Figure 9-43. *Including a page navigator*

Once you have added the Page navigator button to a report page, you can configure it in multiple ways. Two of the most important configurations are the ability to show (or hide) hidden or tooltip pages as shown in Figure 9-44. Using the Page navigator button *greatly* simplifies page navigation and management.

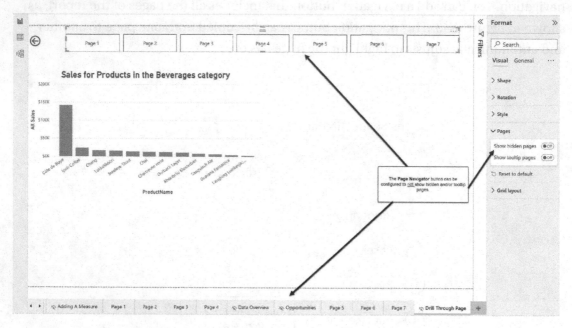

Figure 9-44. *Setting the page navigator button to not show hidden or tooltip pages*

Paginated Reports

After spending many pages describing how to create a report in the Power BI Desktop, there *are* times when this kind of report won't do:

- If the report must conform to a specific size of paper, usually because it is printed (e.g., an invoice)

- If the report must include all the rows of a long table (e.g., an inventory report)

- If all the elements must be aligned perfectly on a printed page (e.g., a report printed on pre-printed stationary or forms)

In these instances, a paginated report is required. Downloading the Power BI Report Builder is free, and you can use that to build a paginated report.

Tip   There is a paginated report visual that enables you to embed a paginated report into a standard Power BI report.

Once the report is created, you can publish it into the Service if you have Admin, Member, or Contributor rights to a workspace in a Premium capacity. If those terms mean nothing to you, fear not. We will be covering the Service in upcoming chapters.

CHAPTER 10

Enhance Reports

In Chapter 9, we covered the steps and features for creating a report. In this chapter, we will delve a bit deeper into some of the features we have already covered and explore some new ones. Because in some cases we are talking about enhancements to features we covered previously, you may need to page back and forth between these two chapters.

Specifying a Sort Order

There are times when a column needs to be sorted differently than the native sorting behavior. For example, months and days of the week need to be sorted by number, not by their names. You can create a calculated column with the sort order and then set the relevant column to sort by the new sort order column, as is visible in Figure 10-1.

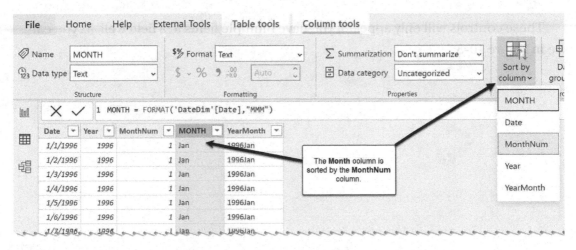

Figure 10-1. *Using the Sort by feature to sort month names*

© Jessica Jolly 2023
J. Jolly, *Microsoft Power BI Data Analyst Certification Companion*, Certification Study Companion Series,
https://doi.org/10.1007/978-1-4842-9013-2_10

Expand Down and Drill Down Controls

If you have data in a hierarchical arrangement, the controls for expanding the hierarchy to the next level and the control for drilling down will appear as shown in Figure 10-2.

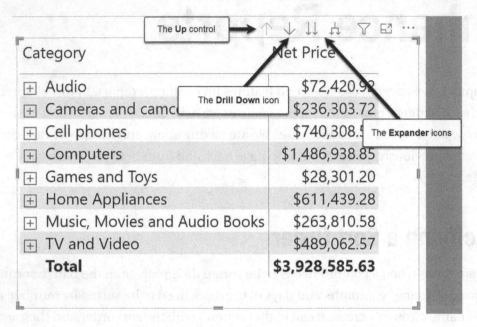

Figure 10-2. *The drill down and expand down controls*

These controls will only appear if you have multiple fields in a field well, as you can see in Figure 10-3.

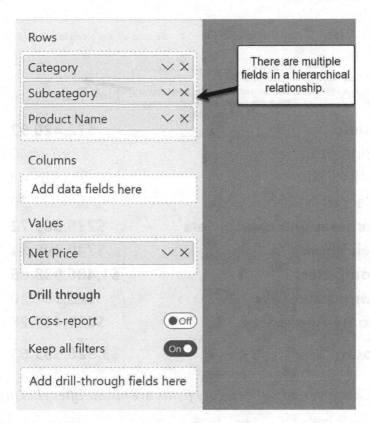

Figure 10-3. *Fields in a hierarchical arrangement*

Notice that I don't say "in a hierarchy," which is a specific structure you can set up in a data model, which was covered in Chapter 6. You *can* use a hierarchy, which will enable the drill down and expand all down controls.

When clicking the "trident" once, the next layer in the hierarchy will display as you can see in Figure 10-4.

Expand all down one level in the hierarchy

Category	Net Price
The "trident" shows the next level of the fields, while keeping the level(s) above visible.	
⊟ **Audio**	**$72,420.92**
⊞ Bluetooth Headphones	$29,794.40
⊞ MP4&MP3	$13,255.42
⊞ Recording Pen	$29,371.10
⊞ **Cameras and camcorders**	**$236,303.72**
⊞ **Cell phones**	**$740,308.51**
⊞ **Computers**	**$1,486,938.85**
⊞ **Games and Toys**	**$28,301.20**
⊞ **Home Appliances**	**$611,439.28**
Total	**$3,928,585.63**

Figure 10-4. Category and Subcategory fields are visible after clicking the "trident" once

After hitting the "trident" twice, the next field (Product Name) in the arrangement is visible, as shown in Figure 10-5.

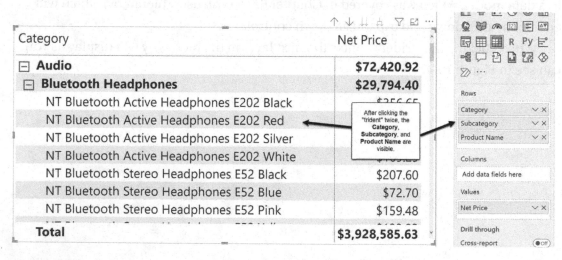

Figure 10-5. Category, Subcategory, and Product Name are all visible

The next icon, the double arrows, displays each "layer" of the data by itself, as shown in Figure 10-6.

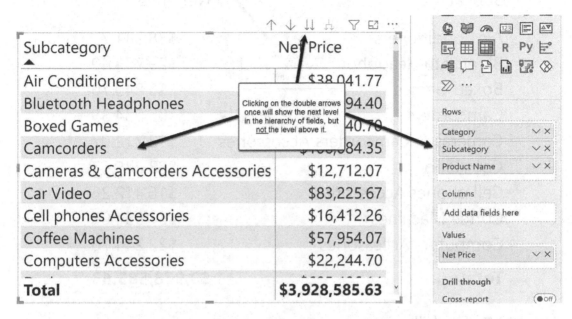

Figure 10-6. *The double arrows show the next level of the hierarchy but not the level above it*

Finally, when you are done drilling or expanding down, to go back up the hierarchy, use the `drill up` arrow, as you can see in Figure 10-7.

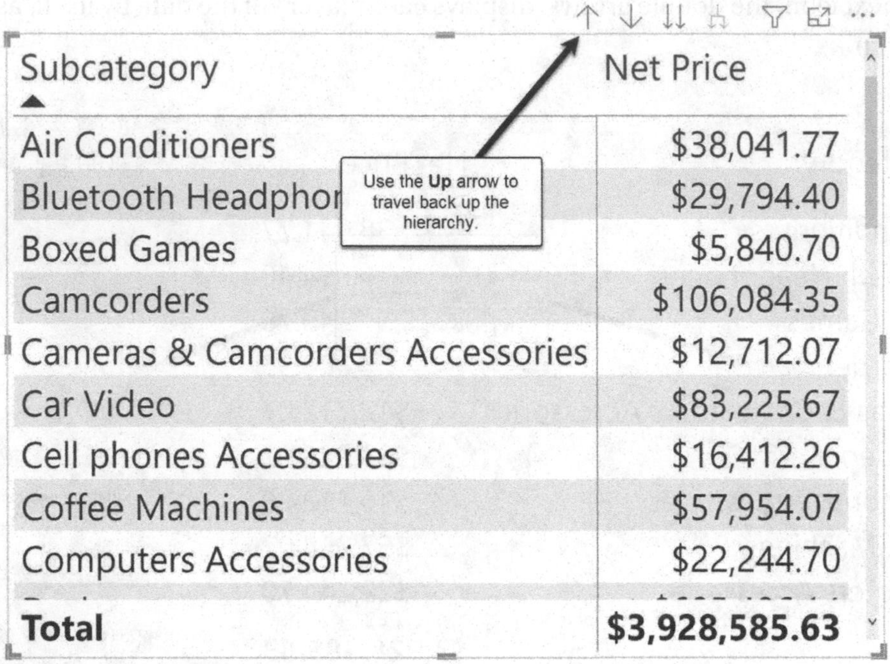

Subcategory	Net Price
Air Conditioners	$38,041.77
Bluetooth Headphor	$29,794.40
Boxed Games	$5,840.70
Camcorders	$106,084.35
Cameras & Camcorders Accessories	$12,712.07
Car Video	$83,225.67
Cell phones Accessories	$16,412.26
Coffee Machines	$57,954.07
Computers Accessories	$22,244.70
Total	**$3,928,585.63**

Use the **Up** arrow to travel back up the hierarchy.

Figure 10-7. *The drill up arrow*

Interactions Between Visuals

Visuals, once placed on a page, interact with each other by default. If you make a selection on one visual, the other visuals on the page will respond. The default interaction is highlighting: graying back the color of the data elements in order to highlight only the values that are relevant to the selection on the other visual. You can see this in Figure 10-8.

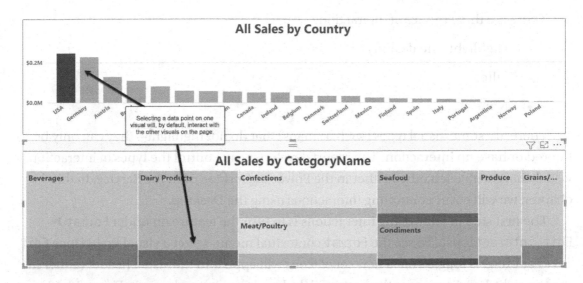

Figure 10-8. *Selecting the USA data point highlights the sales by category in just the USA*

The reverse is also true. Making a selection on the bottom visual will highlight the appropriate values on the top visual, as shown in Figure 10-9.

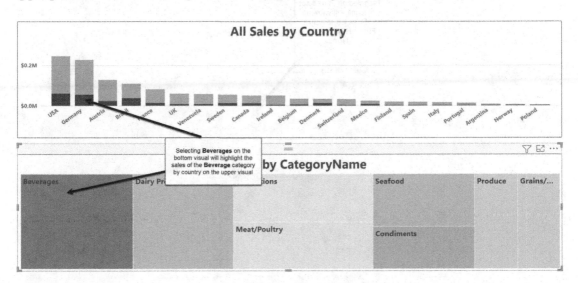

Figure 10-9. *Interactions work from any visual to any other visual*

There are three modes of interaction:

- Highlight (the default)

- Filter

- None

There are some visual types (such as maps) that do not highlight—they can only be filtered or have no interaction. The report developer can control the types of interactions visuals have with each other, either in the Power BI Desktop or in the Service. In this chapter, we will cover controlling interactions using the Desktop.

The first step in controlling interactions is to turn the feature on under Format ➤ Edit interactions. (To see the Format contextual menu, select a visual first.) Once Edit interactions is toggled on, a new set of icons will appear in the visual header (either in the top right-hand corner or the bottom right-hand corner) as shown in Figure 10-10.

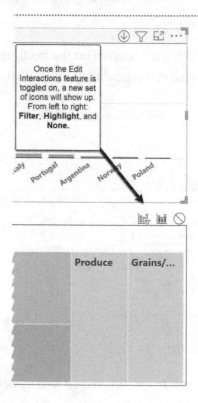

Figure 10-10. *The Edit interactions icons*

If the visual does not support highlighting, you won't see the highlight icon. Interactions are controlled from the selected visual to the other visuals on the page. In other words, to edit interactions you select the source visual *first* and then change the interactions it has with the other visuals. The current interaction mode is darker than the other options, as you can see in Figure 10-11.

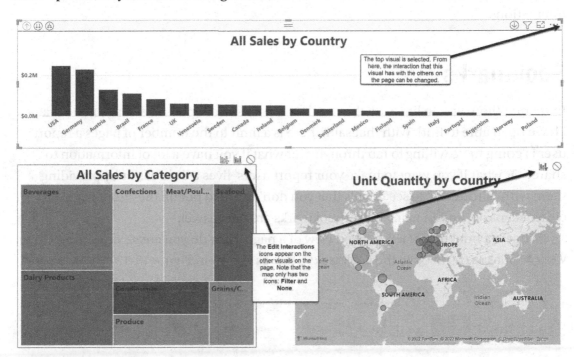

Figure 10-11. *Editing interactions from the selected visual to the others on the page*

The interaction between two types of visuals does *not* have to be reciprocal. In the preceding example, `All Sales by Country` can *highlight* `All Sales by Category`, and `All Sales by Category` can *filter* `All Sales by Country`.

Tip   When selecting colors for your theme, be sure to consider how the colors will look when highlighted. A light color will be difficult to see once it is grayed back and therefore difficult for a screen reader to "read."

For Future Reference: Interactions Impact Page Performance

Interactions can have an impact on the performance of your report. If your users are complaining about the page performance, one option is to disable some or all of the interactions.

Bookmarks

In theory, there are no limits on the number of pages in a report or, at least, none that I have been able to find. With that said, there is a limit to the number of pages a report user is going to be willing to tab through. But what if you have a lot of information to share? Or what if you want to make your report users' lives a little easier by providing them with "shortcuts" to see details that you don't want to put on the "front page"? In either scenario, and in many more, bookmarks are the answer.

What is a bookmark? It is a saved view of a page. How do you create one? Easy. Go to View ➤ Bookmarks to open the Bookmarks pane as shown in Figure 10-12.

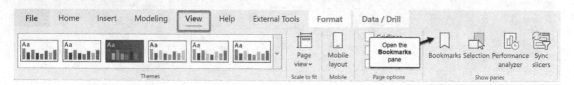

Figure 10-12. *Open the Bookmarks pane*

Once the Bookmarks pane is open, your next step is to make selections on your page to "capture." The easiest example is to set a slicer (or a filter on the Filters pane) to a particular selection. In Figure 10-13, I have set the 'Customers'[Country] field to Canada.

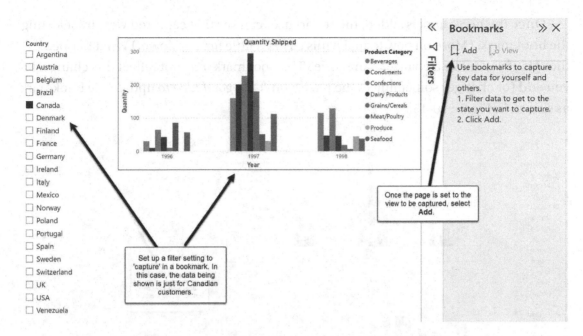

Figure 10-13. *Setting the view to be captured and adding a bookmark*

Once the bookmark is created, rename it something that will make it clear what the bookmark captures as is shown in Figure 10-14.

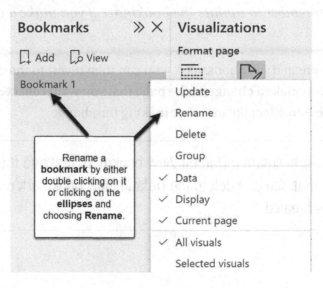

Figure 10-14. *Renaming a bookmark*

Once the bookmark is added, the report user can see that captured view by selecting the bookmark. (More on how to make this easier a little further down.) What happens, though, if you make a change to the page? The bookmark *may* not reflect this change. If you add (or change) something to the page, you *it is a good idea to* update the bookmark as shown in Figure 10-15.

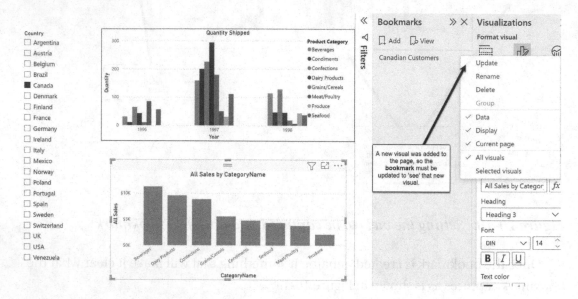

Figure 10-15. *Remember to update the bookmark if you make a change to the page*

Once you have created your bookmark, you can then revert to the default (or standard) view. If you make a change to the page that you want reflected on the bookmark, *remember* to select Update after making the change.

Tip   I find it easier to create a Default View bookmark first and then build bookmarks from that. You can delete the Default View bookmark once you have all of the bookmarks created.

Using the Bookmark Navigator Button

If you want all your bookmarks visible to your report user, you do not have to create a button for each bookmark. Rather, you can use the `bookmark navigator` button, which is very similar in functionality to the `Page navigator` button covered earlier, as you can see Figure 10-16.

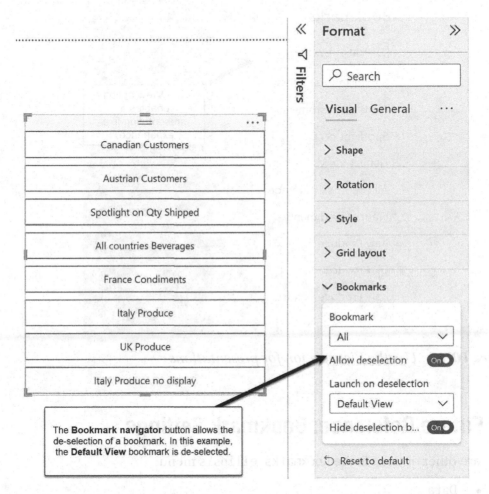

***Figure 10-16.** Selecting bookmarks to exclude in the bookmark navigator button*

And there is a bonus: both the `page` and `bookmark navigator` buttons have all of the rich formatting options available for buttons.

Viewing Your Bookmarks

When I ask students what they want to be able to do with Power BI, many say that they want to be able to present their data without having to create PowerPoint decks. One way of doing this is to use the View option on the Bookmarks panel, as shown in Figure 10-17.

Figure 10-17. *Use the View option for presentations*

For Future Reference: Bookmark Settings

There are other options in the Bookmarks ellipsis menu:

- Data
- Display
- Current page
- All visuals
- Selected visuals

Understanding the nuances of each of these settings is *not* on the PL-300 exam. However, the first time you create a bookmark, you will probably be curious about what each of these settings does. I will summarize the Data and Display options, and I encourage you to experiment with the others for yourself.

Data: Preserves the filtering and/or slicing selections you made when you *first* created (or when you update) the bookmark. In the preceding example, Data *was* checked, and my slicer selections were preserved in the bookmark. This is default behavior and without a doubt a setting you want active *most* of the time.

Display: Preserves the display settings you made when you first created (or when you update) the bookmark. If Display is unchecked, any display selections you made *before* switching to the bookmark are transferred to the bookmark. The easiest way to understand this is to see two examples as shown in Figures 10-18 and 10-19.

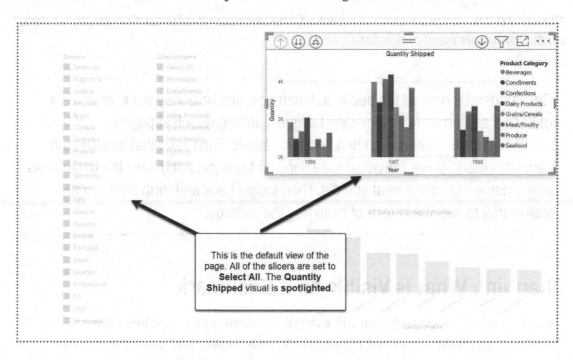

Figure 10-18. *The Default View, with Spotlight turned on for one visual*

In Figure 10-18, all the slicers are set to Select All, and a single visual is spotlighted. In Figure 10-19, the bookmark has been saved with the Display option unchecked.

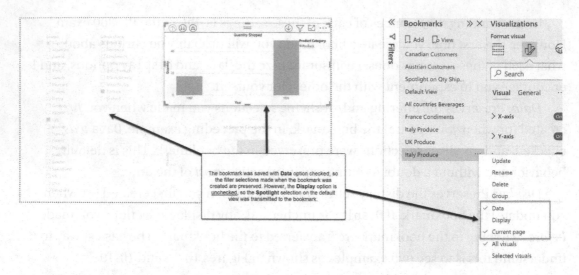

Figure 10-19. *With Display unchecked, the bookmark inherits the selections made on the previous view of the data*

Tip   Understanding all the bookmark settings, and how they work, requires a lot of trial and error (in my opinion). I suggest setting up a test page with at least two slicers (or a slicer and a filter) and two visuals. Then save that as a Default View bookmark. Make individual selections on the slicers and save the bookmarks with a name indicating what you did. Then toggle back and forth between the bookmarks to see the impact of changing the settings.

Changing What Is Visible on a Bookmark

Many times, on a bookmark, you will want some elements to show and others to be hidden. To do that, you need to open the View ➤ Selection pane as shown in Figure 10-20.

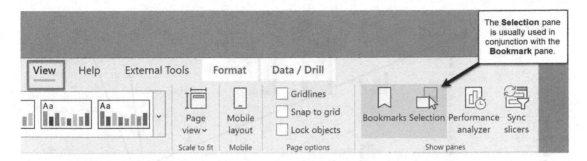

Figure 10-20. *Opening the Selection pane*

The Selection pane is easy to use. As you can see in Figure 10-21, to make something "invisible," toggle the eye icon so that it has a slash through it.

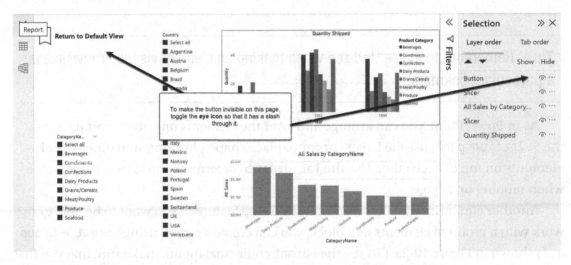

Figure 10-21. *Making an element invisible (or visible) on a page*

One of the typical uses of making an element invisible is when using a bookmark and a button. In the preceding example, the Return to Default View button is not necessary, because this is the Default View. But on other bookmarks, this button should be visible to make navigation back to the Default View easier as shown in Figure 10-22.

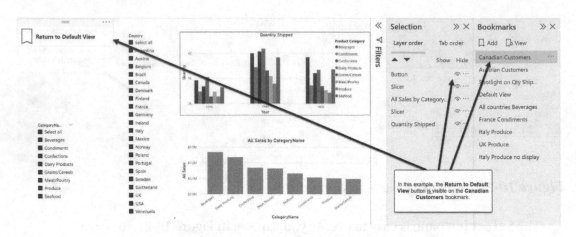

Figure 10-22. *Making an element visible using the Selection pane*

Tip   Remember to toggle `Update` when making an element visible or invisible on a particular bookmark.

As in PowerPoint, you can arrange and layer the elements on your report page. On the `Selection` pane, use the `Layer order` to place shapes, buttons, and other visual elements on top of each other. Use the `Tab order` to determine the selection sequence when tabbing on a page.

Another similarity with PowerPoint is the `Group` feature. If you want to be able to work with a group of elements as a block, you can create a group, using `Format ➤ Group` as is shown in Figure 10-23. (To see the `Format` contextual menu, make sure that you first select a visual. To activate the `Group` feature, select at least two elements on the page.)

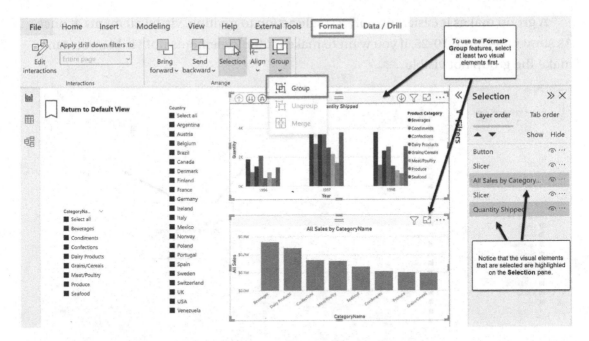

Figure 10-23. *Select at least two visual elements to see Format ➤ Group*

As soon as you create a group, it will show up as a group on the Selection pane. You can rename this group to make it easier to identify as shown in Figure 10-24.

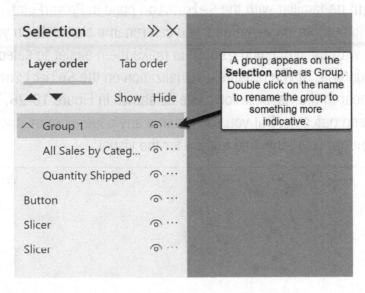

Figure 10-24. *Groups appear with their constituent elements on the Selection pane*

A group makes it easier to apply a single action to multiple visual elements at once. As shown in Figure 10-25, if you want to make multiple elements not visible, you can make the group not visible.

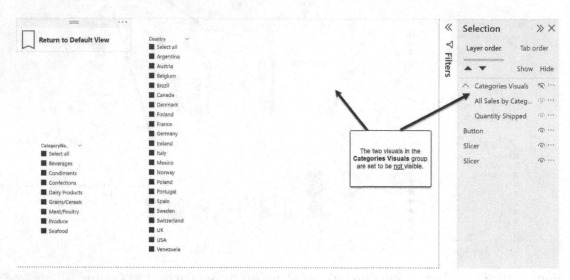

Figure 10-25. *Setting a group as not visible*

Tip   You might be familiar with the `Selection` pane in PowerPoint. (If not, it is worth checking out!) As in PowerPoint, you can rename elements on your Selection pane (as I did with the preceding `group`) to make them easier to select. However, there is one "gotcha." If you rename a visualization on the `Selection` pane, that name will appear in the visualization's title as shown in Figure 10-26. This is not usually a desired outcome. But you can rename any page element successfully, as long as you are not using the Title feature for the visual.

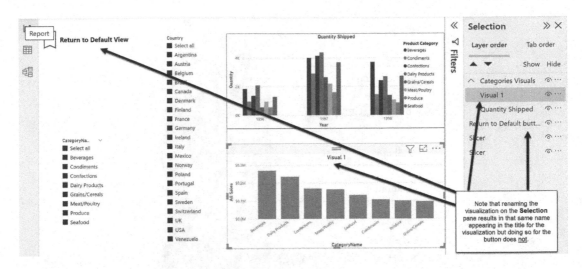

Figure 10-26. *Renaming visual elements on the Selection pane*

Combining Bookmarks and Buttons

Expecting the report user to know how to open the Bookmarks pane to view and
use bookmarks might be a big "ask." Many report developers combine buttons and
bookmarks to make it easy for report users to navigate to a bookmark. We have already
seen how to set up a button and how to set up a bookmark. All that remains is for us to
combine them together.

The first step is to create the bookmark. Once that is created, you then create
a button. After both elements are present, the button is configured to "point" to
the bookmark. You can use two different kinds of buttons to point to a bookmark. I
demonstrated the Blank button option earlier, so I will use the Bookmark button option
here. When using the Bookmark button option, all you choose is the bookmark that the
button will "point" to as shown in Figure 10-27.

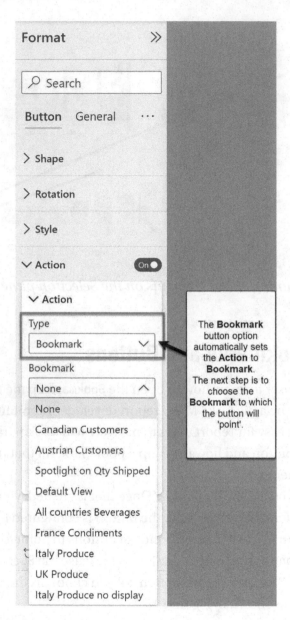

Figure 10-27. *A Bookmark button*

A `Bookmark` button will include a bookmark icon, but the icon alone will not be sufficient to tell a report user what the button does. Don't forget to add some helpful text to the button as shown in Figure 10-28.

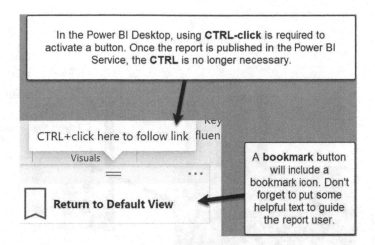

Figure 10-28. Add helpful text to your button

Tip   In an earlier chapter, I said that when you are working in the Power BI Desktop, you are in developer mode. Some features do not work without using the Ctrl key. Once the report is published into the Service, Ctrl is no longer required.

Tooltips

Perhaps you have reached saturation in the number of features you can use in a Power BI report. Take a break and stretch. Maybe take a walk outside—because we have one very rich area still to cover: `tooltips`.

If you have ever hovered your mouse over a data point on a visualization, you have seen a tooltip. Figure 10-29 shows an example of a tooltip.

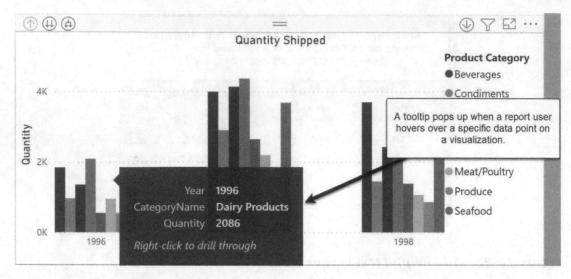

Figure 10-29. *A typical tooltip*

As useful as the default tooltip is, it can be configured to be much richer. By default, a tooltip displays the default values for each field used in the visualization. The first step to enhance a tooltip is to add a field or *a measure* to the tooltip, as shown in Figure 10-30.

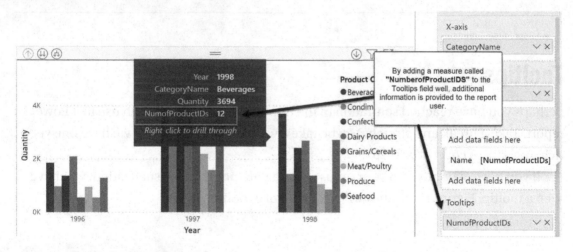

Figure 10-30. *Adding a measure to the Tooltips field well for a visual*

Be *very judicious* when adding additional measures to a visual in the Tooltips field because every measure will require additional calculation time, which can slow down the report's performance. This is true even if the report user never hovers over a data point to see the tooltip! If your report page is slow, one reason can be too many measures in the Tooltips field for one or more visualizations.

Tip Don't forget that if the field or measure has a "clunky" name, you can rename it just for the visual in question as shown in Figure 10-31.

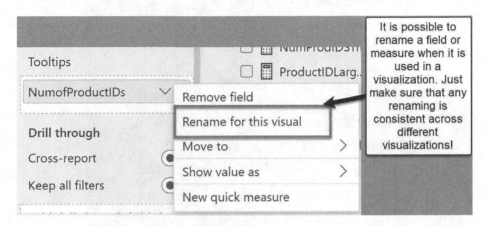

Figure 10-31. *If you rename a field or measure, be consistent across visualizations*

After renaming the measure (in this case), the tooltip is more readable. You can judge for yourself in Figure 10-32.

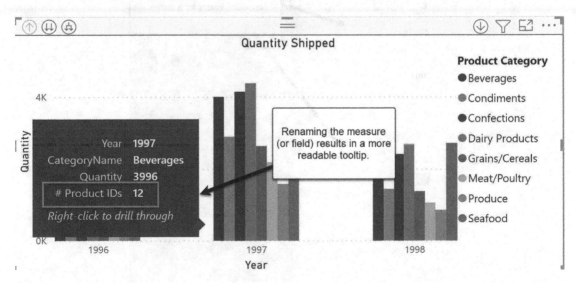

Figure 10-32. *A more readable tooltip*

But wait… There's more! As you can see in Figure 10-33, the background and text properties of a tooltip can be adjusted as well, under `Format visual ➤ General`. However, before you change the tooltip for each visualization, remember you are changing it for *just that visualization*. If you want consistency in your report (which most people do), *you will have to perform these formatting changes for all your visualizations.*

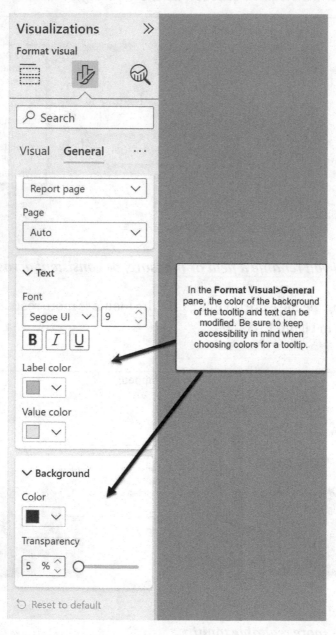

Figure 10-33. Formatting tools for the background and text of a tooltip

Always keep accessibility in mind before changing all your tooltips.

Tooltip Pages

A tooltip page is just what it sounds like—an entire page that shows up in a tooltip! The setup for a tooltip page has several steps, but it isn't hard. The first step is to create a new page in your report and hide the page as shown in Figure 10-34. (It is rare that you will want viewers to access your tooltip page.)

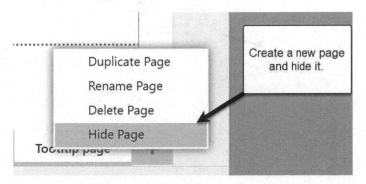

Figure 10-34. *A new tooltip page, named "Tooltip Page" for clarity*

Before adding anything to the report page, navigate to Format page ➤ Page information and set the page as a tooltip page as shown in Figure 10-35. If you skip this step, you cannot set up a tooltip page.

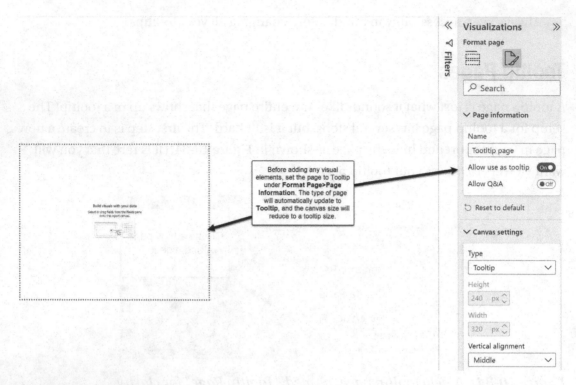

Figure 10-35. *Setting the page as a tooltip page*

If you want the tooltip to be smaller than the default tooltip canvas size, you can set
the Canvas settings to Custom and change the pixel size as shown in Figure 10-36.

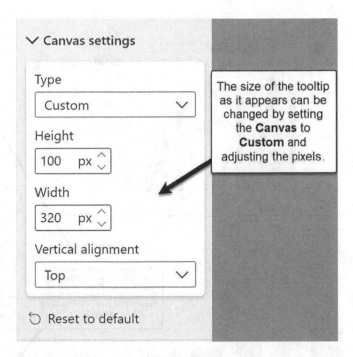

Figure 10-36. *Adjusting the tooltip display size*

Now you can add your visualizations. Keep in mind that you are designing for a tooltip, so be judicious about adding multiple visual elements. In Figure 10-37, I have added a single-value card visual to display the largest order value and formatted the visual for more impact.

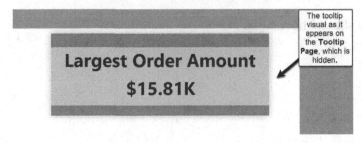

Figure 10-37. *The tooltip page, formatted*

Once you have the tooltip page set up, navigate back to the page and visualization where you want this tooltip to appear. (In Figure 10-38, I have named the page "Tooltip Page," but this is not necessary; the page can be named anything.)

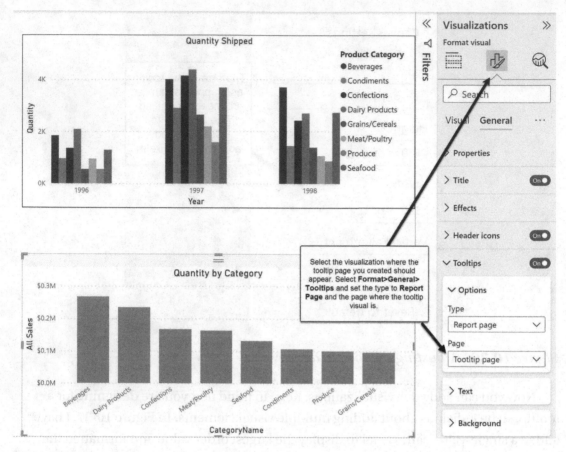

Figure 10-38. *Setting up the visualization to display the tooltip page*

Figure 10-39 shows the results.

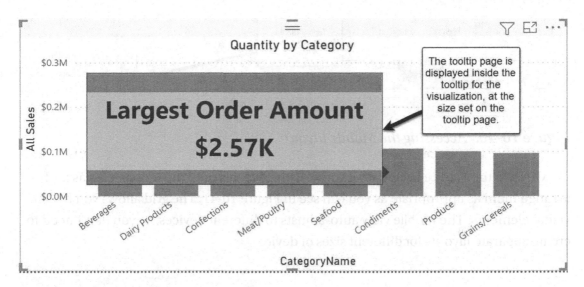

Figure 10-39. Displaying the entire tooltip page

Not only are tooltip pages a cool concept, but they can also help improve the performance of your report page. Unlike a garden variety tooltip, *a measure used in a tooltip page is not evaluated* unless the report user hovers over the data point.

Tip   For a tooltip to work, the fields (or measures) used in the visualization and tooltip must be related in the data model.

Designing for Mobility

The formatting that we have discussed thus far is for Power BI reports viewed on a monitor or on a laptop. If you know that some of your users are going to be viewing your report on their tablets or phones, you can design your report so that it fits nicely on mobile devices. As shown in Figure 10-40, to start designing the mobile version of your report, go to View ➤ Mobile layout.

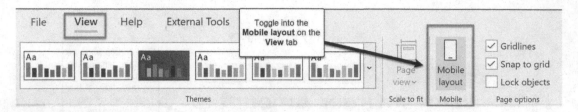

Figure 10-40. *Accessing the Mobile layout*

Once in the Mobile layout, drag your existing visuals onto the mobile canvas and arrange them as appropriate as you can see in Figure 10-41. The grid allows you to lock visual elements. The mobile view auto-adjusts to different devices, so you don't need to create separate layouts for different sizes of device.

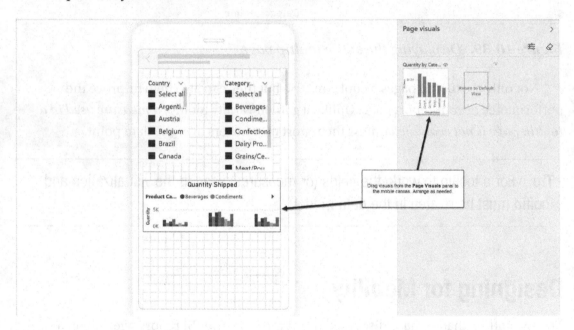

Figure 10-41. *Drag, drop, and arrange selected visuals on the mobile canvas*

Once the visuals are laid out, you can adjust formatting features as needed as you can see in Figure 10-42.

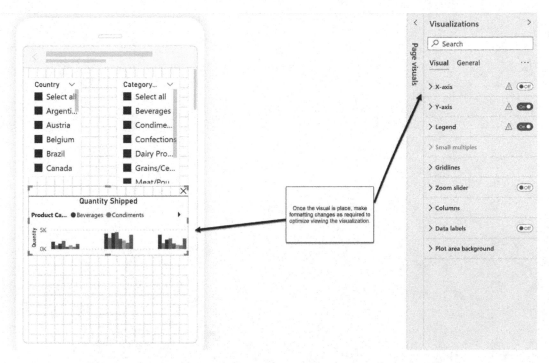

Figure 10-42. *Adjust the formatting of visualizations for optimized viewing*

CHAPTER 11

Identify Patterns and Trends

Power BI's purpose is to allow you to visualize your data and thereby facilitate analysis of that data. In this chapter, I will explore several features and visualization types that are available to make analysis both easy and comprehensive. Let's start with the `Analytics` feature.

The Analytics Pane

Power BI has a lot of visualizations that we readily recognize: column, bar, the much maligned pie, and, of course, line charts. Some of these visualization types have an additional feature available: `Analytics`.

Let's start our exploration of the `Analytics` pane using a `line` chart. When a visualization type supports analytics, these options will appear on the `Analytics` pane. The full range of the `Analytics` feature is present in the `line` visualization, as shown in Figure 11-1. Other visualizations will have some (or none) of these features.

© Jessica Jolly 2023
J. Jolly, *Microsoft Power BI Data Analyst Certification Companion*, Certification Study Companion Series, https://doi.org/10.1007/978-1-4842-9013-2_11

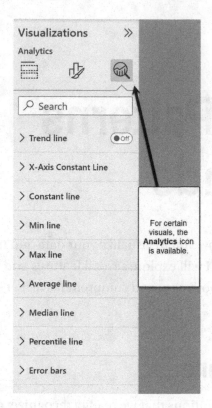

Figure 11-1. *The Analytics pane for a line chart*

In Figure 11-2, I have added a `Trend line`.

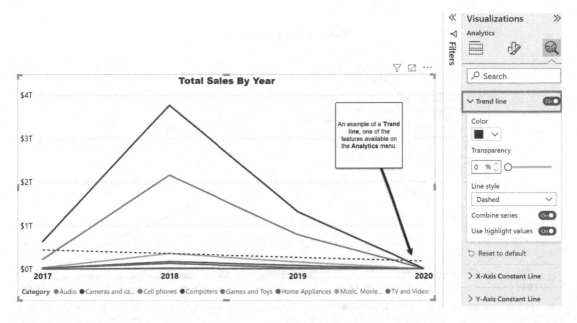

Figure 11-2. Adding a Trend line to a line visualization

In the "Identifying Outliers" section, there is another example of using an Average line to a visualization.

If the type of data you are working with supports it, the Analytics pane will display an option for Forecasting. For the PL-300 exam, be sure to understand the components that go into creating a forecast in case you are asked to create a forecast line. There are many excellent blog posts that walk through the steps, using data that supports forecasting.

Using the Analyze Feature

When looking at data, there may be dramatic increases or decreases. Power BI has an Analyze feature that can be activated to explain the change. The Analyze feature processes the entire data model, looking for relationships between different data points. To activate the Analyze feature, select a data point, right-click, and choose Analyze ➤ Explain the increase (or decrease) as shown in Figure 11-3.

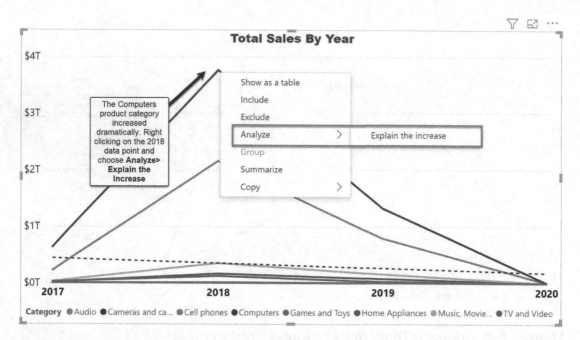

Figure 11-3. *Right-click a data point and choose Analyze ➤ Explain....*

The benefit of the `Analyze` feature is that it looks at all the data and the relationships in the data model. It will surface insights that may (or may not) be useful. If you like one of the visuals it creates, you can click the + sign in the upper right-hand corner, and the visualization will be added to your report page as shown in Figure 11-4.

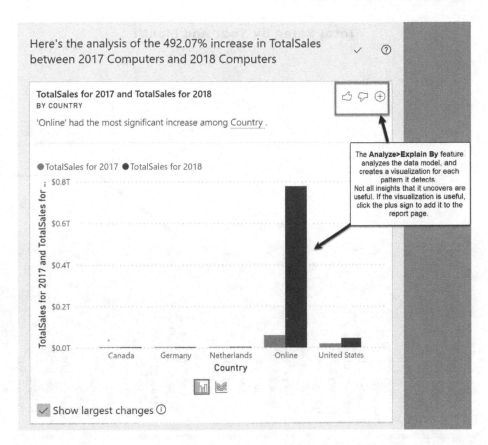

Figure 11-4. *One of the visualizations produced by the Analyze feature*

Identifying Outliers

When analyzing data, we often want to find data points that don't fit the dominant pattern because that data may reveal insights about the rest of the data. The scatter plot visualization is a very useful tool for discovering outliers. In the following example, the data points cluster between 0.1 and 0.2 trillion dollars each month, with a few months clearly well above the average. Depending on how narrowly the band is defined, there will be fewer or more outliers as you can see in Figure 11-5.

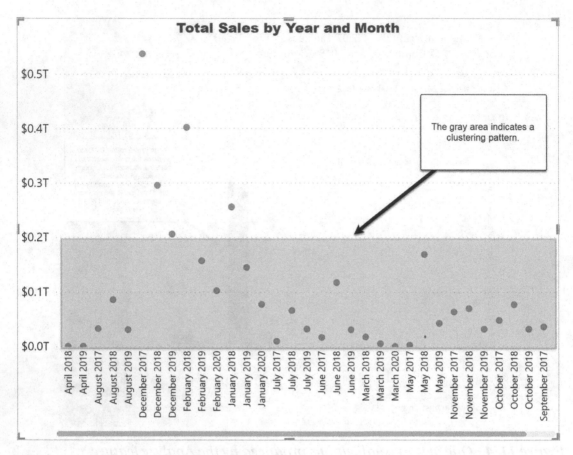

Figure 11-5. The gray band indicates a pattern

The scatter plot makes it easy to see clustering because you can add average, median, or trend lines to make the pattern clear. On the Analytics pane, choose the type of line you want to add to the scatter plot. In Figure 11-6, I have added an Average line.

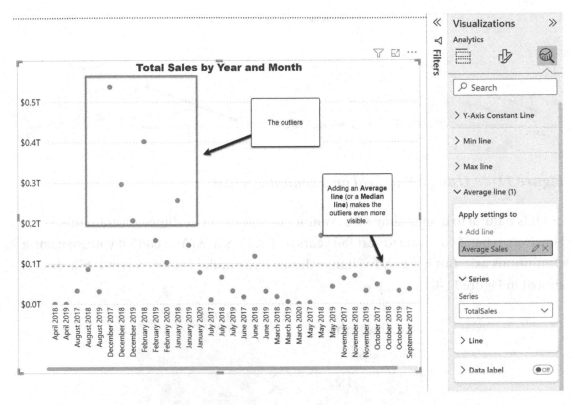

Figure 11-6. *An average line makes the clustering clear*

Categorical vs. Continuous Axes

What is categorical data? What is continuous data? It turns out that you know the answer
to this question intuitively. Categorical data is data that has discrete points. For example,
in a product table, you can have different categories (e.g., computers, electronics, toys,
etc.). In a customer table, there may be an education column that has high school, some
college, BA, MA, or PhD. These are examples of data that is categorical. This data is best
displayed using visuals that can show the data in distinct elements, such as a bar or
column chart. Continuous data is data that is not readily divided into groups. Time is the
classic example of continuous data, even though time can also be divided into groups
(years, months, days). In the two visuals (Figures 11-7 and 11-9), I show the same data,
one using a continuous axis and one using a categorical axis.

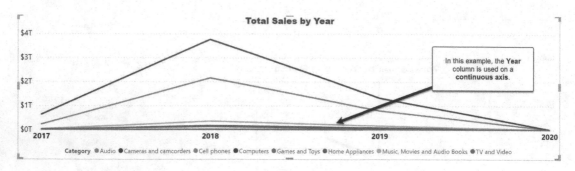

Figure 11-7. *Using a Year field on a continuous axis*

It is natural to display time on a continuous axis because...time is continuous. However, what if you want to sort the years by Total Sales? You can't if you are using a continuous axis. But it is easy to change the axis type under Format visual ➤ X-axis as shown in Figure 11-8.

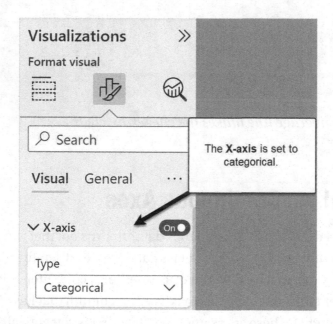

Figure 11-8. *Setting the X-axis to Categorical*

Once the type of axis is changed, the visualization will change, and you will be able to sort the years by other fields on the visual as shown in Figure 11-9.

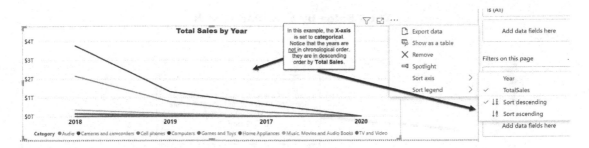

Figure 11-9. *Using a Year field on a categorical axis*

Most data will naturally fall definitively in one of the two types. But if you are working with data that can be either continuous or categorical, experiment with the different types of axes to see if one suits your analysis better than the other.

Groupings, Binnings, and Clustering

Sometimes your data has a lot of values, and it would be useful to be able to organize them into larger groupings. Power BI has several useful tools to help you accomplish this.

Creating Groups

Start with a column or bar visualization and then select the data points you want to group. Select multiple data points by holding down the Shift key as you select each one and then right-click, as shown in Figure 11-10.

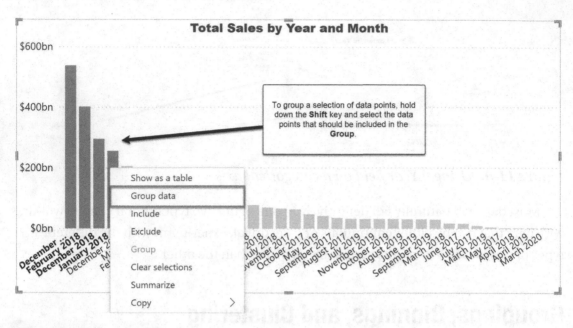

Figure 11-10. *Selecting the data points for sales over 200 billion*

Once the group has been created, it will appear on the `Fields` pane, in the same table as the base field. In Figure 11-11, the base field is `Year Month`, and the group appears in the `Date` table.

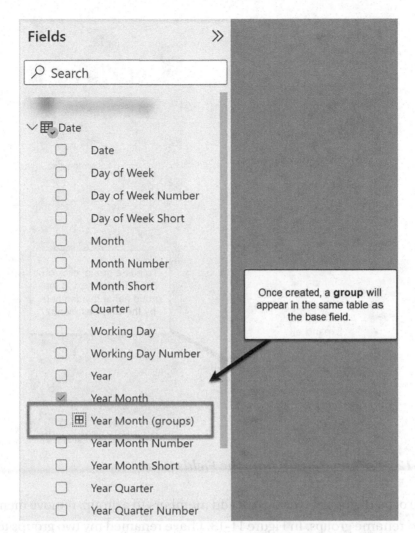

Figure 11-11. *A group appears in the same table as the base field*

Once created, a group can be edited easily, as shown in Figure 11-12. Click the
ellipsis menu next to the group name on the Fields pane. (You can also click the
drop-down arrow next to the group if you use it in a visual.)

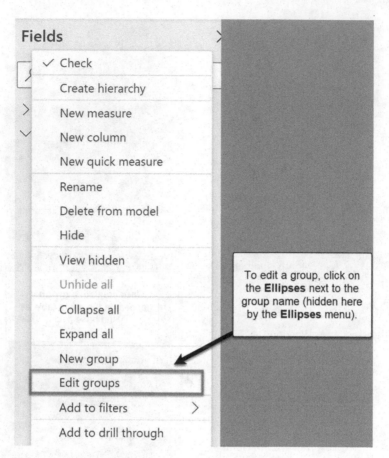

Figure 11-12. Editing a group from the Fields pane

In the Groups dialogue box, you can add members to a group, remove members from a group, and rename groups. In Figure 11-13, I have renamed my two groups to make their composition clear.

Groups

×

Name *	Field
Year Month (groups)	Year Month

Group type

List ∨

Ungrouped values

April 2017
April 2018
April 2019
April 2020
August 2017
August 2018
August 2019
August 2020
December 2020
February 2017
February 2019

Groups and members

▲ Above $200 billion
  ○ December 2019
  ○ January 2018
  ○ December 2018
  ○ February 2018
  ○ December 2017
▲ Below $200 billion (Other)
  ○ Contains all ungrouped values

Group   Ungroup

> In the **Groups** dialogue box, members can be added (or removed) from a group. It is also a place to rename a group.

☑ Include Other group ⓘ

OK   Cancel

Figure 11-13. *Editing groups*

An advantage of renaming a group is to control how it appears on a visualization. In Figure 11-14, the legend much more clearly reflects the two elements on the chart. The data colors also reflect the two groups.

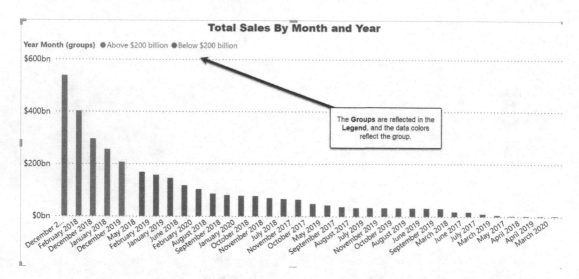

Figure 11-14. *Naming a group improves the clarity of a visualization*

But wait… There's more! You can use a group either in a `slicer` or on the `Filters` pane, making it easy to filter multiple data points at once, as shown in Figure 11-15. To use a group in a slicer, simply drag the group to the `slicer` visualization field well.

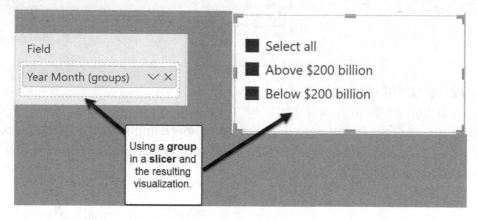

Figure 11-15. *Groups can be used in a slicer*

Groups can also be used on the `Filters` pane, with the same results. To do so, right-click the group and choose `Add to filters` and then the appropriate filter area as shown in Figure 11-16. (You can also drag the group to the `Filters` pane.)

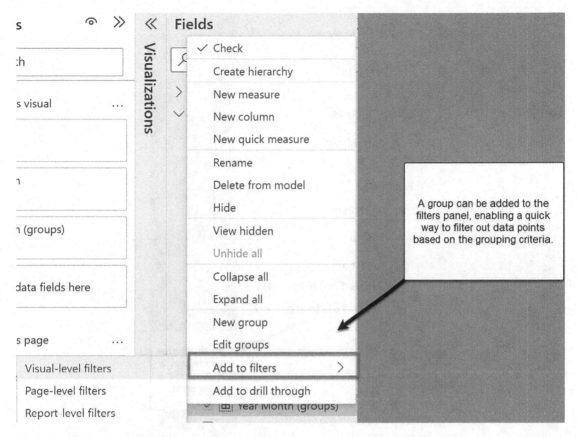

Figure 11-16. Adding a group to the Filters pane

Once the group is on the Filters pane, it behaves like any other field that is acting as a filter as shown in Figure 11-17.

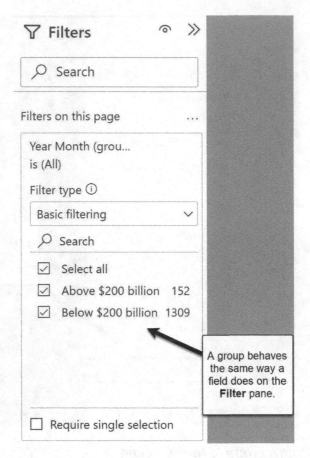

Figure 11-17. *A group on the Filters pane*

Creating Bins

Groups work well with data points created by a measure. In the preceding example, the Total Sales field is a measure that I created. What if you want to group values in a calculated column? It's just as easy as creating groups (hopefully you found that easy!). I am starting with a calculated column called Total Sales CC (to distinguish it from the Total Sales measure). Right-click the calculated column and choose New· group as shown in Figure 11-18.

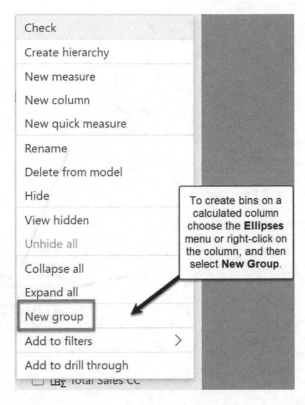

Figure 11-18. *Choose New group to create bins on a calculated column*

The Bins dialogue box will open, and you can choose whether to create bins based on the size or create bins based on a set number of bins as shown in Figures 11-19 and 11-20.

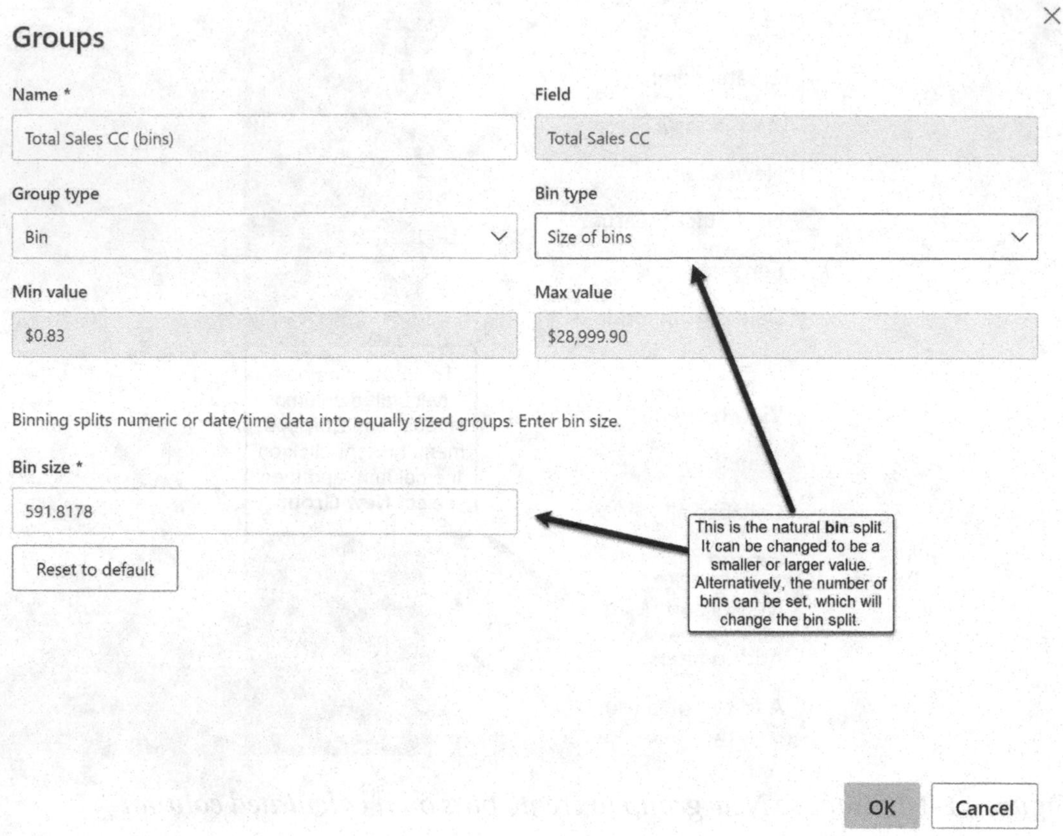

Groups

✕

Name *

| Total Sales CC (bins) |

Field

| Total Sales CC |

Group type

| Bin   ⌄ |

Bin type

| Size of bins   ⌄ |

Min value

| $0.83 |

Max value

| $28,999.90 |

Binning splits numeric or date/time data into equally sized groups. Enter bin size.

Bin size *

| 591.8178 |

Reset to default

This is the natural **bin** split. It can be changed to be a smaller or larger value. Alternatively, the number of bins can be set, which will change the bin split.

OK   Cancel

Figure 11-19. *Creating bins based on the size of each bin*

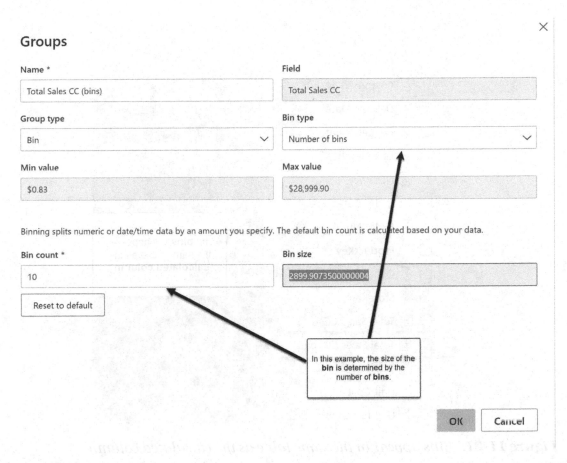

Figure 11-20. *Setting a predetermined number of bins*

Once the bins have been generated, they will appear in your Fields list in the same table as the calculated column, as you can see in Figure 11-21.

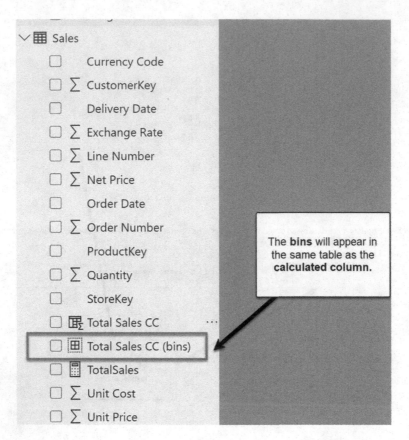

Figure 11-21. *Bins appear in the same table as the calculated column*

Now you can use bins just as you would a field. In Figures 11-22 and 11-23, I want to know how many orders are in each of the bins.

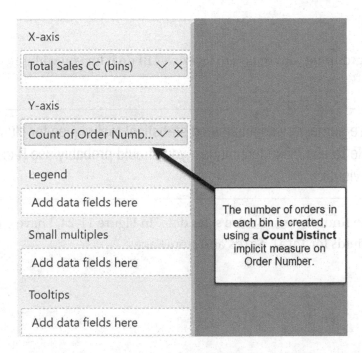

Figure 11-22. *Using a Count Distinct implicit measure with the bins*

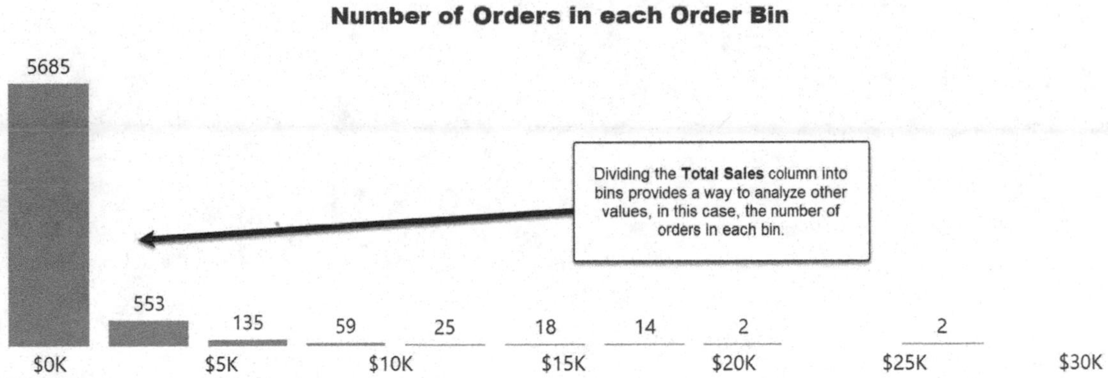

Number of Orders in each Order Bin

Figure 11-23. *The resulting visualization*

Tip If I were using the visualization shown in Figure 11-23 in a report, I would spend more time perfecting the formatting on the X-axis!

Clustering

The last way of grouping your data is to let Power BI do it for you with the clustering feature.

Tip   There are some very sophisticated statistical techniques for clustering. If you want to be able to use those techniques, you should probably use R or Python and then create a visual.

I am going to find clusters in store sales data. In Figure 11-24, I have created a table and added the fields for Total Sales and store Name.

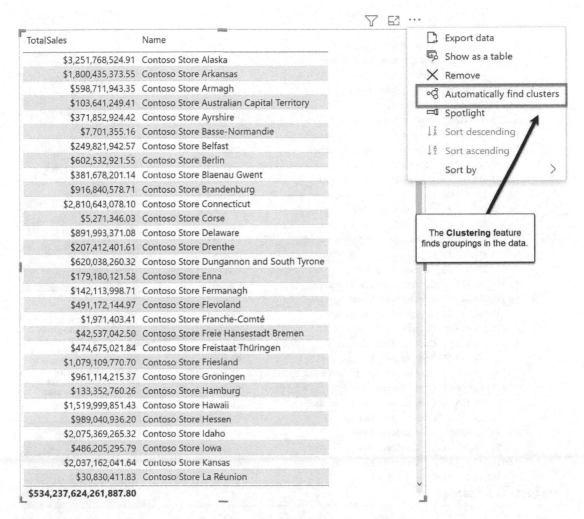

Figure 11-24. Access the clustering feature from the ellipsis menu on the visual

Once Power BI has found the clusters, it will create a new field and display it on the same visual as shown in Figure 11-25.

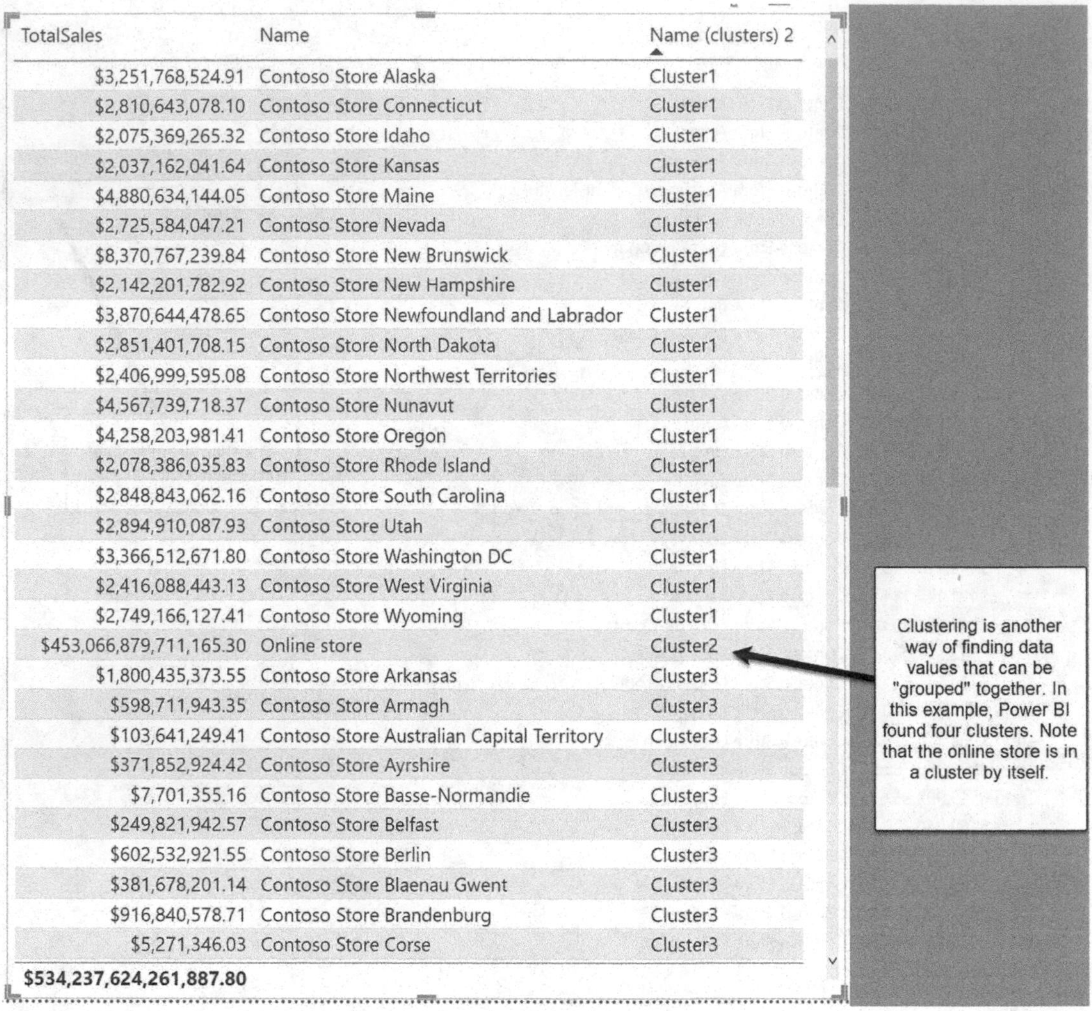

TotalSales	Name	Name (clusters) 2
$3,251,768,524.91	Contoso Store Alaska	Cluster1
$2,810,643,078.10	Contoso Store Connecticut	Cluster1
$2,075,369,265.32	Contoso Store Idaho	Cluster1
$2,037,162,041.64	Contoso Store Kansas	Cluster1
$4,880,634,144.05	Contoso Store Maine	Cluster1
$2,725,584,047.21	Contoso Store Nevada	Cluster1
$8,370,767,239.84	Contoso Store New Brunswick	Cluster1
$2,142,201,782.92	Contoso Store New Hampshire	Cluster1
$3,870,644,478.65	Contoso Store Newfoundland and Labrador	Cluster1
$2,851,401,708.15	Contoso Store North Dakota	Cluster1
$2,406,999,595.08	Contoso Store Northwest Territories	Cluster1
$4,567,739,718.37	Contoso Store Nunavut	Cluster1
$4,258,203,981.41	Contoso Store Oregon	Cluster1
$2,078,386,035.83	Contoso Store Rhode Island	Cluster1
$2,848,843,062.16	Contoso Store South Carolina	Cluster1
$2,894,910,087.93	Contoso Store Utah	Cluster1
$3,366,512,671.80	Contoso Store Washington DC	Cluster1
$2,416,088,443.13	Contoso Store West Virginia	Cluster1
$2,749,166,127.41	Contoso Store Wyoming	Cluster1
$453,066,879,711,165.30	Online store	Cluster2
$1,800,435,373.55	Contoso Store Arkansas	Cluster3
$598,711,943.35	Contoso Store Armagh	Cluster3
$103,641,249.41	Contoso Store Australian Capital Territory	Cluster3
$371,852,924.42	Contoso Store Ayrshire	Cluster3
$7,701,355.16	Contoso Store Basse-Normandie	Cluster3
$249,821,942.57	Contoso Store Belfast	Cluster3
$602,532,921.55	Contoso Store Berlin	Cluster3
$381,678,201.14	Contoso Store Blaenau Gwent	Cluster3
$916,840,578.71	Contoso Store Brandenburg	Cluster3
$5,271,346.03	Contoso Store Corse	Cluster3
$534,237,624,261,887.80		

Clustering is another way of finding data values that can be "grouped" together. In this example, Power BI found four clusters. Note that the online store is in a cluster by itself.

Figure 11-25. *Power BI found four clusters in the data*

Now the resulting field can be used in a `slicer`, on the `Filters` pane, or on another visualization.

Using AI Visuals

There are several types of visualizations that use artificial intelligence to detect patterns that may not be immediately apparent. I will cover two of these here, but I encourage you to experiment with all the visualization types before sitting the PL-300 exam.

The Key Influencer Visualization

Many times, when looking at data, we want to know what is causing the patterns we see. If we are working with millions of rows of data, finding those patterns is a herculean task. But using the AI technology embedded within Power BI, the key influencer visualization can visualize underlying patterns, if there are any, as shown in Figure 11-26. Setting up the key influencer visualization can be a little confusing. (I often experiment with the placement of fields to produce a result. Sometimes the data doesn't support any findings in the visualization.)

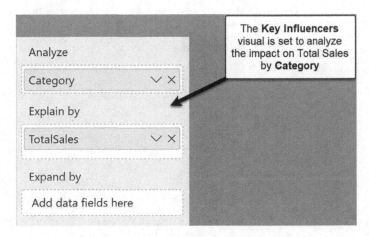

Figure 11-26. *Setting up the key influencer visualization*

Once the fields are in place, the key influencer visualization looks like Figure 11-27.

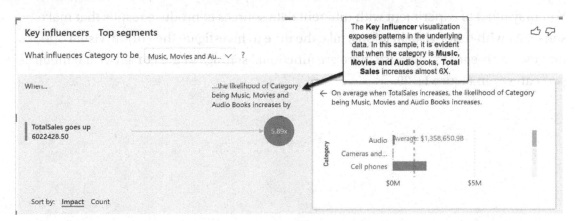

Figure 11-27. *The Music, Movies, and Audio Books drive up sales*

There is a second pane for the key influencer visualization called Top segments. On this pane, Power BI detects groupings of data and profiles those segments as you can see in Figure 11-28.

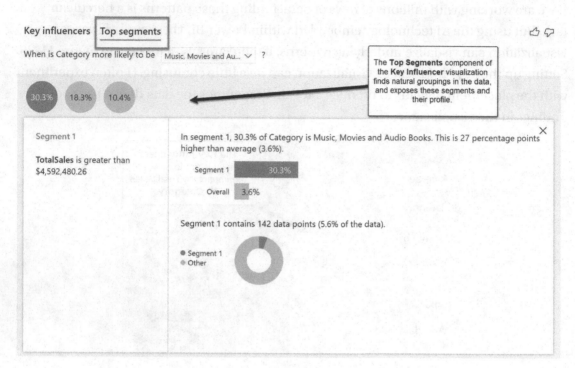

Figure 11-28. *Profiling a segment of the data*

I strongly recommend taking the time to understand the key influencer visualization because it uses some statistical concepts that you may not use regularly. You may need to experiment with different data sources to produce results that make sense. As with other visualizations, take the time to investigate the Format visual options for key influencers, because there are functional settings in the Format visual menu as you can see in Figure 11-29.

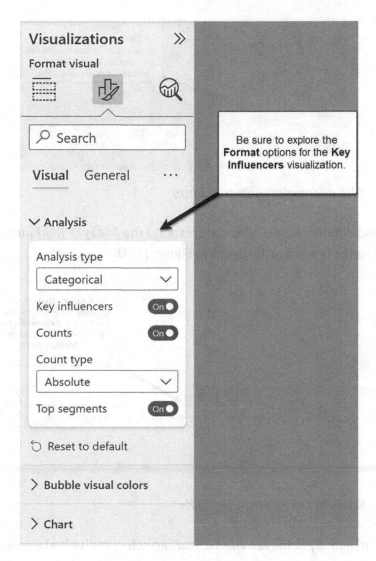

Figure 11-29. *The Format visual pane has functional features as well*

The Decomposition Tree Visualization

While the key influencer visualization is interesting, I confess that it isn't my favorite AI visualization. That title is reserved for the decomposition tree. Despite its unattractive name, the decomposition tree is elegant and simple to use.

This visualization breaks down the component parts of a field. Setting it up is identical to the setup for the key influencer visualization, as shown in Figure 11-30.

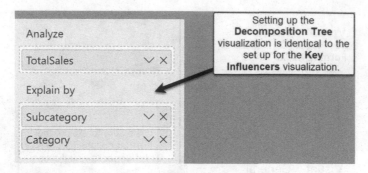

Figure 11-30. *The decomposition tree setup*

Once the visualization is set up, you can expand the Analyze field into its constituent parts by choosing the + symbol as shown in Figure 11-31.

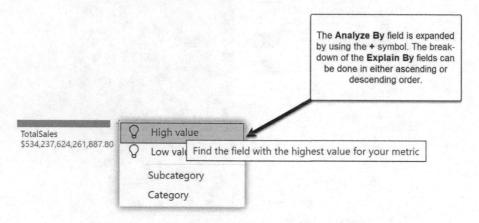

Figure 11-31. *Sorting the Explain by fields*

Once the Explain by fields are visible, you can select individual elements by selecting the appropriate bar as shown in Figure 11-32.

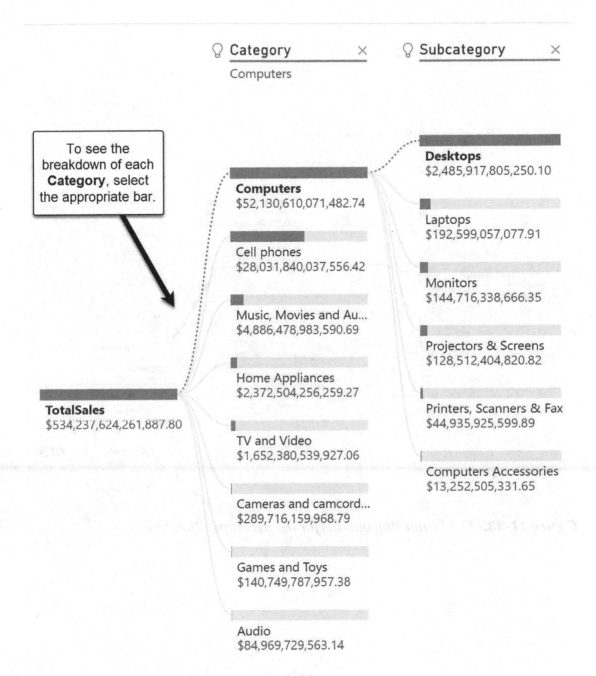

Figure 11-32. *Viewing the Explain by fields*

As befits my favorite visualization, the decomposition tree has some wonderful formatting options as you can see in Figure 11-33.

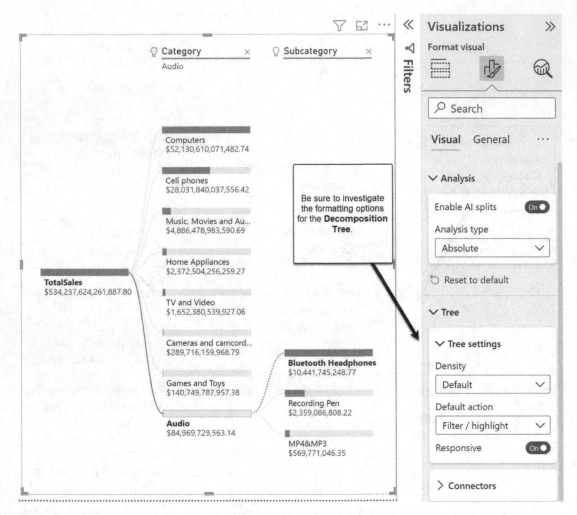

Figure 11-33. *The formatting options for the decomposition tree*

PART V

Deploy and Maintain Assets

CHAPTER 12

Manage Files and Datasets

You have created and published your report. Bravo! In Chapter 14, you will read about how to publish and update a report once it is published in the Service. In that chapter, I specifically say that updating the report does *not* include updating the data. "But wait," you say! Isn't the whole point to be able to see the latest data in the report, at any time? Yes, you are correct—having up-to-date data in the report is one of the main benefits of using Power BI. It is time to talk about refreshing the data.

Schedule a Refresh

How often you can refresh your data automatically depends on the license you have:

- *Free license*: No automated refresh, just manual refreshes
- *Pro license*: Up to eight scheduled refreshes per day
- *Premium per user*: Up to 48 refreshes a day
- *Workspace in Premium capacity*: Up to 48 refreshes a day

Once you have published a report (and its accompanying dataset) in the Service, you will need to schedule automated refreshes, license permitting. A refresh is set up on a dataset, not the report itself.

Tip   Datasets do not *have* to be in the same workspace as the report.

© Jessica Jolly 2023
J. Jolly, *Microsoft Power BI Data Analyst Certification Companion*, Certification Study Companion Series,
https://doi.org/10.1007/978-1-4842-9013-2_12

On the same line as the dataset, there are two icons that are shortcuts to the refresh menu as shown in Figure 12-1. One is a manual refresh, and the other is a scheduled refresh.

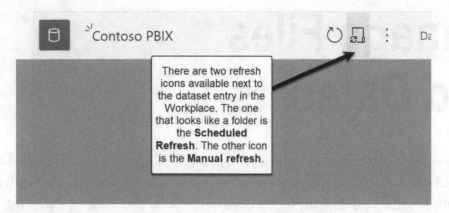

Figure 12-1. *Accessing the Scheduled refresh for a dataset*

The Scheduled refresh is a subitem in the Settings menu (in Figure 12-2), which is accessed through the ellipsis menu shown in the Figure 12-1.

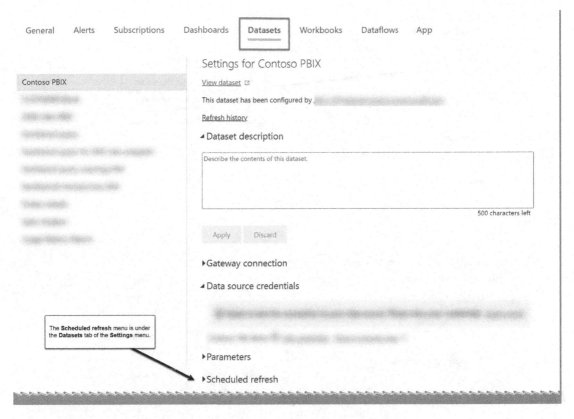

Figure 12-2. The Scheduled refresh in the Settings menu

To set up the refresh, there are several steps to complete:

1) Turn on `Scheduled refresh`. It is not on by default (shown in Figure 12-3).

2) Set the refresh frequency.

3) Set the time zone.

4) Add the times when the refresh should occur.

   Note: Microsoft does not commit to meeting these times to the minute. For example, if you set the refresh time as 2:00 p.m., the refresh may happen at 1:58 p.m. or 2:01 p.m.

5) Determine who should receive notification if the refresh fails. It is very important to make sure that someone is notified because *if a refresh fails three times, the refresh is turned off.*

Figure 12-3. *The Schedule refresh settings*

If, when you open the Scheduled refresh menu, all the items are grayed out, that means that the Power BI Service is not able to access the source data to perform the refresh.

Do You Need a Gateway?

To refresh data, Power BI has to be able to connect to the data source. If the data is stored behind a firewall, the Schedule refresh menu will be grayed out. To enable an automated refresh, you will need to set up a gateway connection. There are two types of gateway connections:

- On-premise data gateway

  - On-premise data gateway (personal mode)

- Virtual network data gateway

Unless you are in IT, you will probably only ever install an on-premise data gateway in personal mode. (These used to be called personal gateways.) If you wish to install one, you will need to download the software to do so. After installing the gateway, you can view it under the Settings ➤ Datasets menu as shown in Figure 12-4.

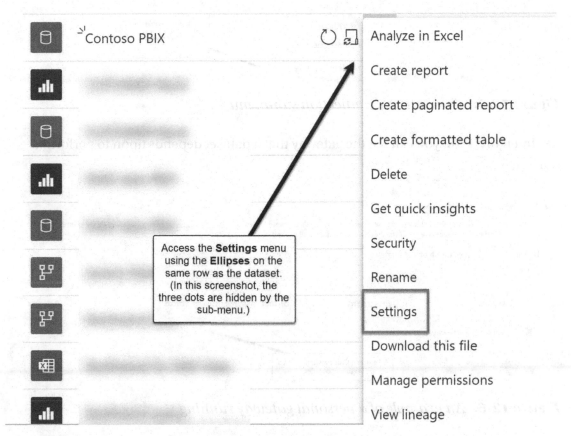

Figure 12-4. *Accessing the Settings menu for the dataset*

As you can see in Figure 12-5, under the Settings menu, open the Gateway connection menu.

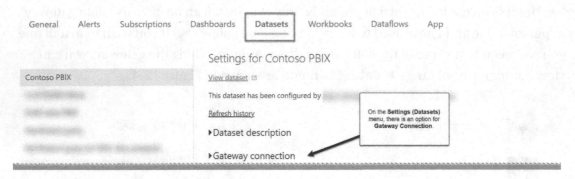

Figure 12-5. *The Gateway connection sub-menu*

In Figure 12-6, you can see the gateway that a dataset depends upon to perform a refresh.

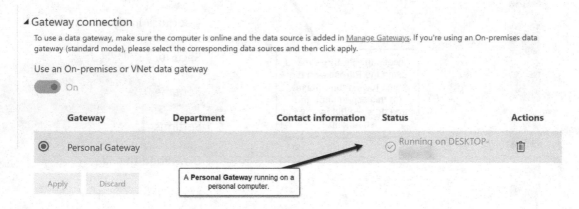

Figure 12-6. *An example of a personal gateway running*

You can access the list of gateways to which you have access through the Settings ➤ Manage gateways menu, as shown in Figure 12-7.

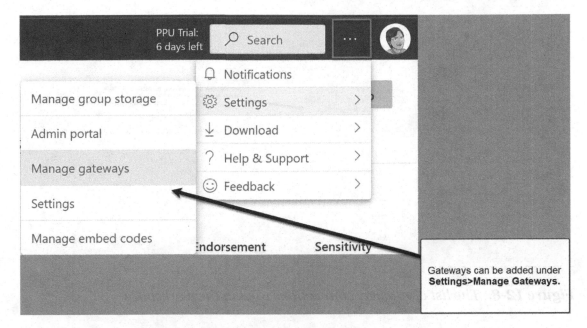

Figure 12-7. *Accessing the Manage gateways menu*

Personal gateways are typically used to connect to datasets stored on your computer. Personal gateways use your credentials to access the data source. Also, personal gateways will only be active while your device is connected to the data source. If your organization needs a gateway to enable multiple users to access data sources behind a firewall, then one of the other two types of gateways is necessary:

- On-premise data gateways

- Virtual network data gateways

Both are shown in Figure 12-8.

313

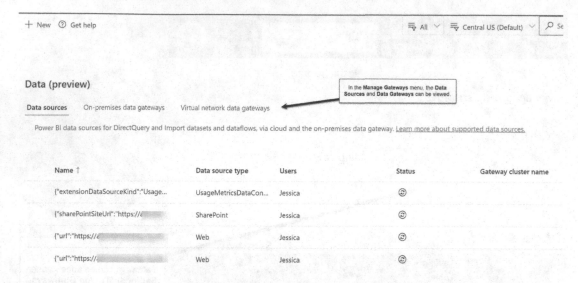

Figure 12-8. *The list of gateway connections used in the workspace*

For Future Reference: Connecting OneDrive and Power BI

Sometimes, you may want to access Excel and CSV content without having to install a gateway (personal or other). When you create a workspace, you can associate a OneDrive instance with it and then store Excel and CSV content. In this scenario, the Power BI Service can access the data sources and refresh once an hour.

Configuring Row-Level Security

In an earlier chapter, we discussed how to create the row-level security roles in the Power BI Desktop. The second half of this process must be completed once the report is published. In the row for the dataset, choose Settings ➤ Security, as shown in Figure 12-9.

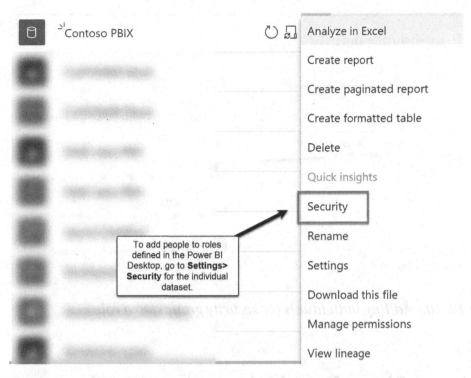

Figure 12-9. *Accessing the Settings ➤ Security menu for the dataset*

Once you are in the Security dialogue box, you will see a list of the roles that have been defined in the PBIX, as shown in Figure 12-10. Enter the names of individuals (or security groups) who should be assigned these roles.

315

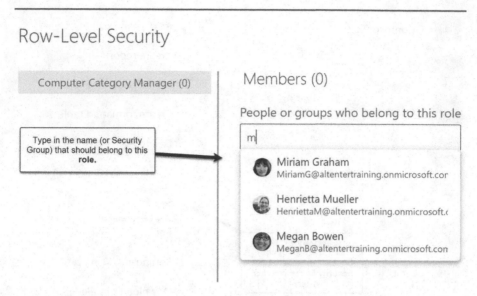

Figure 12-10. *Adding individuals (or security groups) to a role*

Build and Share Permissions

Anyone who is an Admin, Member, or Contributor in a `workspace` automatically has both `build` and `share` permissions. This means that they can create a new report using an existing published dataset (even if they didn't publish it). Admins, Members, and Contributors can also share a report (and its underlying dataset) with others who do not belong to the workspace.

Tip   Sharing with colleagues who are not members of the workspace (or subscribed to the associated app) can lead to "security sprawl." It is a good idea to have very clear governance about when sharing with non-workspace members should be allowed.

Share and build permissions are enabled on a particular dataset. To initiate the process, go to `Settings ➤ Manage permissions` on the same row as the dataset as shown in Figure 12-11.

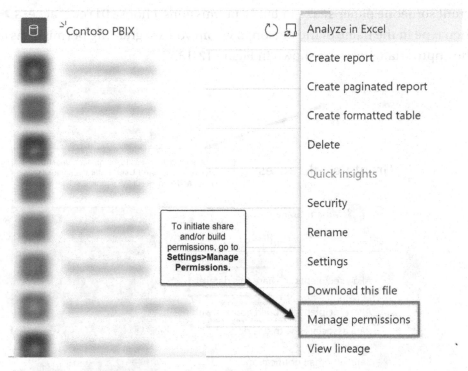

Figure 12-11. *Accessing the Manage permissions sub-menu*

In the Permissions dialogue box, there are two areas: Links and Direct access. Anyone who is an Admin, Member, or Contributor in the workspace has direct access to any dataset in the workspace, as is shown in Figure 12-12.

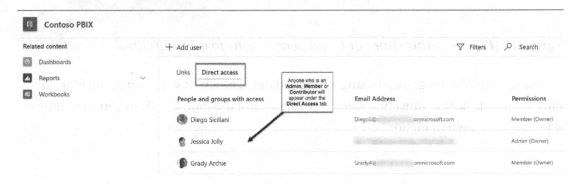

Figure 12-12. *Workspace members have share and build permissions by default*

To grant someone either `share` or `build` permissions, choose `Direct access` ➤ `Add user`. Then type in the name of the person to whom you are granting permissions and check the appropriate boxes, as shown in Figure 12-13.

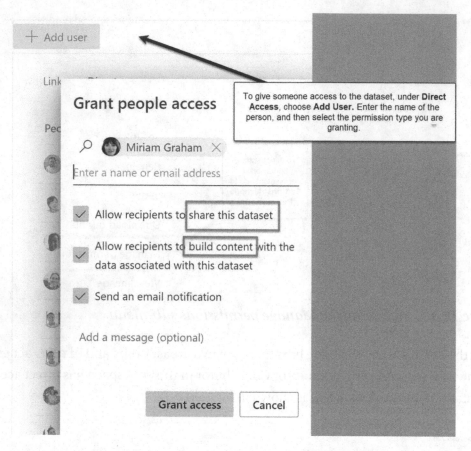

Figure 12-13. *Granting share or build permissions to an individual*

Access can also be granted using generated links, much as you do in OneDrive. To share using a link, you must first select the report, not the dataset. Then you can choose `Add link` as shown in Figure 12-14.

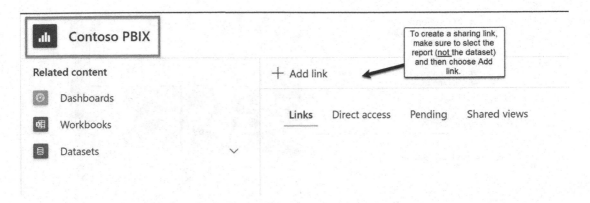

Figure 12-14. *To create a link, you must select the report*

As shown in Figure 12-15, you can adjust who can use the link and set whether the link will allow sharing of the report and/or using the underlying dataset to build new reports.

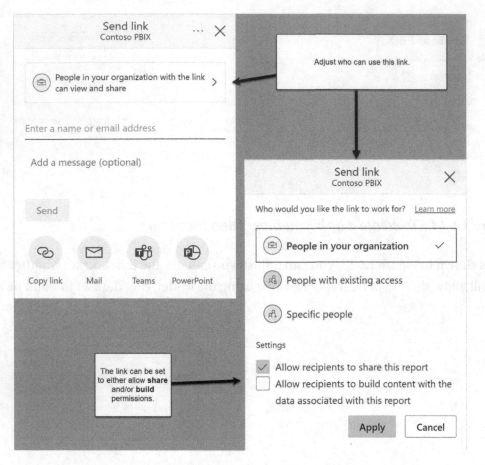

Figure 12-15. *Defining the permissions granted by the link*

Once the link is created, it will show up under Links, and it will list the permissions it grants, as you can see in Figure 12-16.

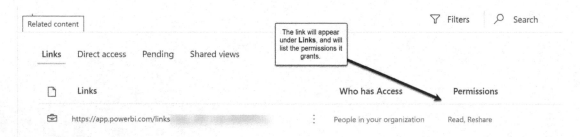

Figure 12-16. *Displaying the links*

If you need to delete the link, or adjust the associated permissions, use the `ellipsis` menu to display these options as shown in Figure 12-17.

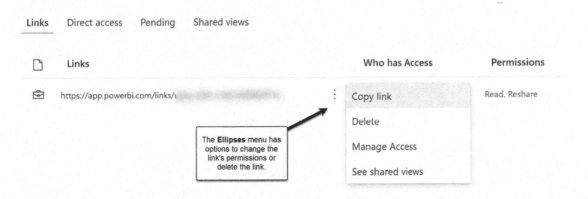

Figure 12-17. *Adjusting the links*

CHAPTER 13

Create Dashboards

When students introduce themselves in my classes, I ask them to tell me what they want to learn. Invariably, I will hear that they are using dashboards and they want to learn how to create one. When I dig a little deeper, it often turns out that they are using reports, not dashboards. Now that we are close to the end of this book, I hope that it is clear that dashboards and reports are two different things. So far, we have focused on reports. This chapter is dedicated to dashboards.

Creating a Dashboard

If reports and dashboards are different, what *is* a dashboard? A dashboard

- Is a virtual one-page document

- Can only be created in the Service

- Can contain visuals from multiple reports published in the `workspace`

- Can contain streaming content (reports cannot)

The purpose of a dashboard is different from that of a report. It is intended as a "snapshot" of the data being represented by the visualizations that are included on the dashboard. I say "snapshot" quite deliberately because, by default, the visual tiles do *not* interact with each other. This is in sharp contrast to reports, where visualizations interact with each other by default. (Remember `Edit interactions`?) There is some anecdotal evidence that organizations don't use dashboards as much as reports, perhaps because users expect dashboards to act exactly as reports do. I have a suggestion for the ideal purpose for a dashboard—feel free to use it as a jumping-off point for your imagination.

© Jessica Jolly 2023
J. Jolly, *Microsoft Power BI Data Analyst Certification Companion*, Certification Study Companion Series,
https://doi.org/10.1007/978-1-4842-9013-2_13

In a previous working life, I was a facilities manager. After the 9/11 events, I was asked to put up large TV monitors in common areas, for example, the lobby, the break rooms, and the cafeteria. (You may have noticed this in your own office.) The perfect application for a dashboard is to be displayed on these monitors. They are usually mounted high on a wall, so no one expects to interact with the dashboards. The data is being displayed for information, not investigation. Setting users' expectations appropriately can reduce their frustration with the mechanics of dashboards.

Creating a Dashboard

Setting up a dashboard is easy. Starting from a report, find a visualization you want to include on a dashboard and pin it, using the pushpin icon in the visualization's header, as you can see in Figure 13-1. (If you don't see a header above the visualization, it may be hidden by the report creator.)

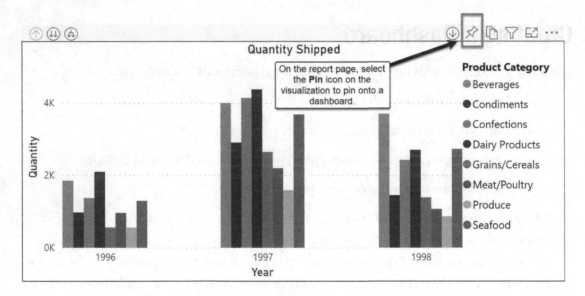

Figure 13-1. *Pin your visualization using the pushpin icon*

The Service will ask you if you want to add the visualization to an existing dashboard or create a new one, as you can see in Figure 13-2.

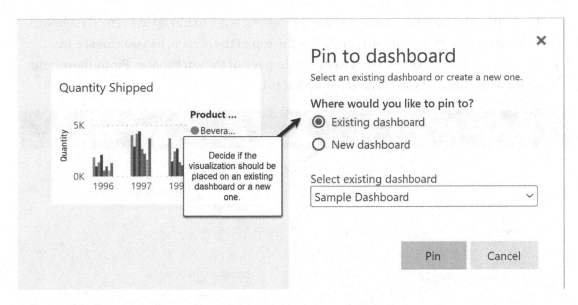

Figure 13-2. *Choose an existing or create a new dashboard*

Tip   Keep scrolling to a minimum on a dashboard by limiting the number of visualizations you pin.

Immediately after choosing the dashboard, you will see a pop-up menu (Figure 13-3) that allows you to go to the dashboard.

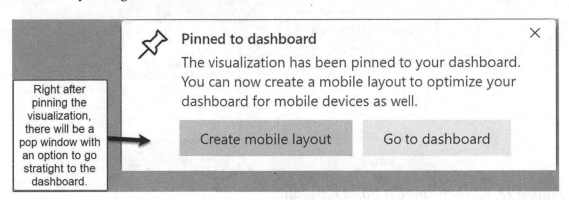

Figure 13-3. *This pop-up menu only stays up for a short time*

If you miss the pop-up window, there are several ways to navigate to the dashboard. The first way is to use the "breadcrumbs" at the top of the screen, as you can see in Figure 13-4. This will take you back to the main page of the workspace. From there, you can pick the dashboard you created (or added to).

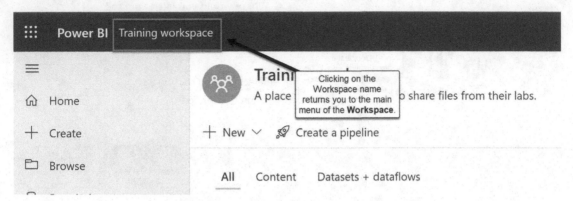

Figure 13-4. Follow the "breadcrumbs" at the top of the screen

The other way to find your dashboard, or any other content, is to use the navigation on the left side of the screen as shown in Figure 13-5. From there, you can find the content organized into groups.

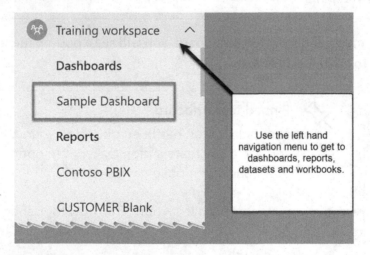

Figure 13-5. Using the left-hand navigation

Once you have navigated to the dashboard, you can see the visualizations you have pinned. A sample dashboard is shown in Figure 13-6. If you are at all familiar with the AdventureWorks data, you will notice that in Figure 13-6, there are clearly visuals from more than one report (and dataset). *Dashboards can contain content from multiple reports.*

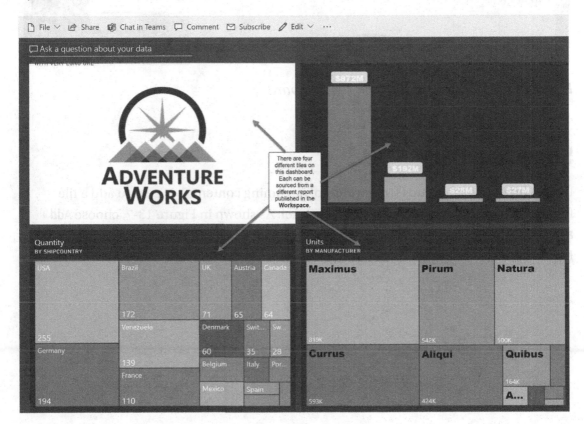

Figure 13-6. Example of a dashboard

Editing the Dashboard

In Figure 13-7, you can see that the editing options for a dashboard are limited, which in some ways is refreshing, given how many editing options there are for reports!

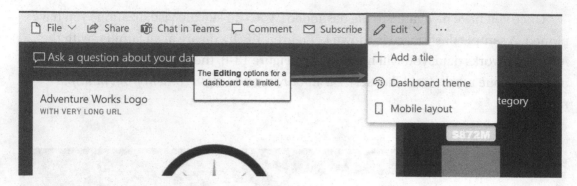

Figure 13-7. Editing options on a dashboard

Streaming Data

Unlike reports, dashboards support live or streaming content. It is easy to add a tile for streaming data or a YouTube video channel. As shown in Figure 13-7, choose Add a tile in the Edit menu. You will then see the Add a tile dialogue box, as shown in Figure 13-8.

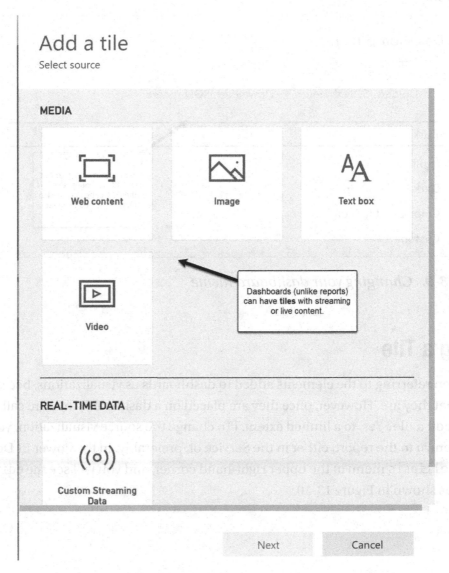

Figure 13-8. *Adding a tile with live data (or an image or a text box)*

Dashboard Themes

The built-in creative options with a dashboard are very limited. You can change the theme from light to dark or color-blind-friendly. If you need more formatting options, the best option is to upload a JSON theme you have created, as shown in Figure 13-9.

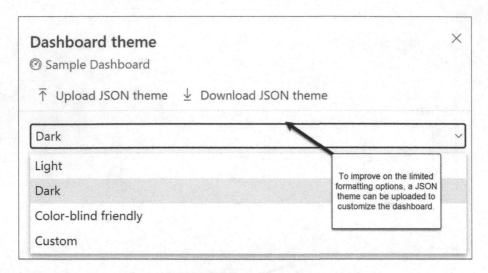

Figure 13-9. *Changing your dashboard theme*

Editing a Tile

I have been referring to the elements added to dashboards as visualizations, because that is what they are. However, once they are placed on a dashboard, they are called tiles. Can you edit a tile? Yes, to a limited extent. (To change the source visualization, you will need to return to the report, either in the Service or, preferably, in the Power BI Desktop.) Click the ellipsis menu in the upper right-hand corner, and you will see the edit options, as shown in Figure 13-10.

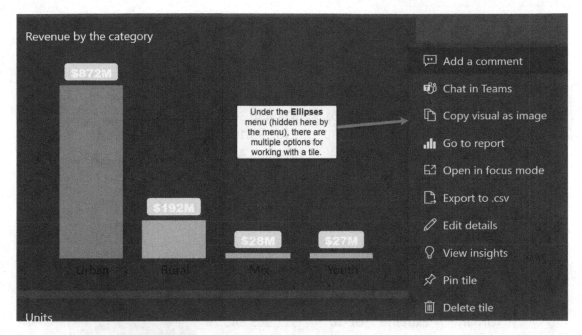

Figure 13-10. Limited editing options on a tile

Most of the options are straightforward, but there are a couple worth exploring.

Export to .csv

If you want to see the data underlying this particular tile, choose `Export to .csv`. (Unlike in the Power BI Desktop, there is no option to view the data as a table.) In Figure 13-11 you can see the result of exporting data underlying a visual to Excel.

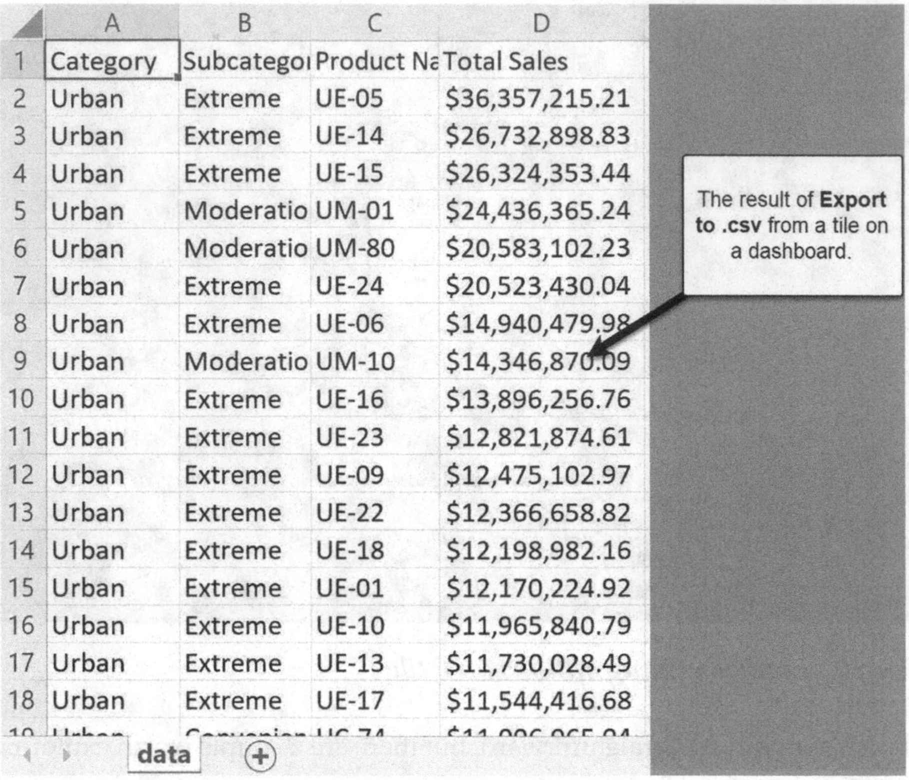

	A	B	C	D
1	Category	Subcategor	Product Na	Total Sales
2	Urban	Extreme	UE-05	$36,357,215.21
3	Urban	Extreme	UE-14	$26,732,898.83
4	Urban	Extreme	UE-15	$26,324,353.44
5	Urban	Moderatio	UM-01	$24,436,365.24
6	Urban	Moderatio	UM-80	$20,583,102.23
7	Urban	Extreme	UE-24	$20,523,430.04
8	Urban	Extreme	UE-06	$14,940,479.98
9	Urban	Moderatio	UM-10	$14,346,870.09
10	Urban	Extreme	UE-16	$13,896,256.76
11	Urban	Extreme	UE-23	$12,821,874.61
12	Urban	Extreme	UE-09	$12,475,102.97
13	Urban	Extreme	UE-22	$12,366,658.82
14	Urban	Extreme	UE-18	$12,198,982.16
15	Urban	Extreme	UE-01	$12,170,224.92
16	Urban	Extreme	UE-10	$11,965,840.79
17	Urban	Extreme	UE-13	$11,730,028.49
18	Urban	Extreme	UE-17	$11,544,416.68

The result of **Export to .csv** from a tile on a dashboard.

Figure 13-11. Export to .csv result

View Insights

In a previous chapter, we reviewed various ways that the underlying AI capabilities can be used to find relationships and patterns in the data that you may not be able to surface easily. This capability is also built into `dashboards`. If you want to generate insights from just the data underlying a specific tile, choose `View insights`. If there are any insights, Power BI will generate new visuals to represent them. If one (or more) is useful, you can pin it to your dashboard using the pushpin icon, as shown in Figure 13-12.

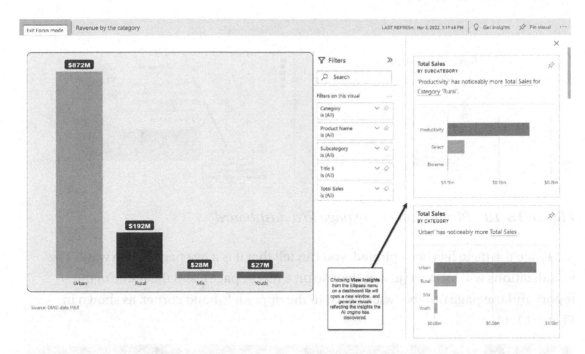

Figure 13-12.   *Visualizations generated by the AI engine using View insights*

Pin Tile

This option may seem odd—isn't this visualization already pinned? Yes, but what if you want to pin it to another dashboard? Nothing easier.

   As I mentioned at the beginning of the chapter, some users are disappointed when viewing dashboards, because the tiles do *not* interact with each other. Upon consideration, this is only to be expected, as visuals can come from multiple reports and different datasets. If you click a tile, you will return to the source report. But there is one way to achieve interactions between tiles on a dashboard: pin an entire report page.

Pinning Live Pages

To pin an entire report page, return to the report. In Read mode, select the `ellipses` ➤ `Pin to a dashboard`, as shown in Figure 13-13.

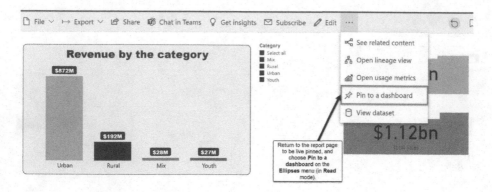

Figure 13-13. *Pinning an entire page to a dashboard*

Once the page has been pinned, you can tell that it is a live page in two ways. The visualizations will interact (just as they do on a report page), and the name of the report and the page number will appear in the upper left-hand corner, as shown in Figure 13-14.

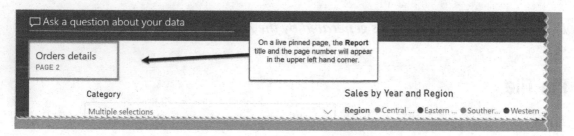

Figure 13-14. *A live page has the report name in the upper left-hand corner*

Think carefully before pinning a live page to a dashboard. Can the users benefit from simply using the source report? Dashboards and reports are not the same thing and shouldn't be used interchangeably. Can the report be simplified and shared with users via the app?

Managing Tiles on a Dashboard

We have already looked at some of the editing features built into each tile. From the `ellipsis` menu, a tile can be deleted. But in addition to the settings in the tile's `ellipsis` menu, there are other controls that can be accessed in the `File ➤ Settings` menu, as you can see in Figure 13-15.

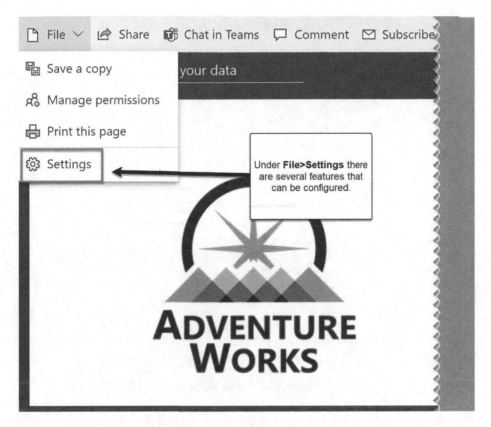

Figure 13-15. *Accessing the File ➤ Settings menu on the dashboard*

You can rename the dashboard and add a contact for the dashboard. There are additional controls in the menu, as shown in Figure 13-16.

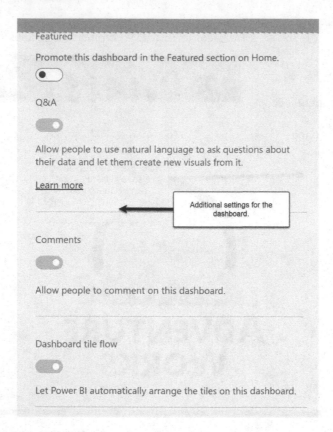

Figure 13-16. *Part of the Settings menu for a dashboard*

We will be talking about Q&A in the following. The `Dashboard` tile flow automatically rearranges the tiles if a tile is added or deleted.

Configuring the Mobile View

Setting up your dashboard to perform well on a mobile device is easy. Simply choose `Edit` ➤ `Mobile layout`. You can unpin tiles from the dashboard to make the mobile view easy to navigate.

Use the Q&A Feature

In an earlier chapter, we covered setting up the natural language feature, Q&A. There are several settings that must be enabled in the Service and in the Power BI Desktop.

Enabling Q&A in the Power BI Desktop

Back in the Power BI Desktop, choose Modeling ➤ Q&A setup, as shown in Figure 13-17.

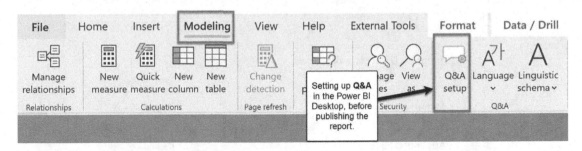

Figure 13-17. *Setting up Q&A in the Desktop*

Enabling Q&A in the Service

Once the report is published, use the Dataset ➤ Settings ➤ Q&A menu to enable Q&A, as you can see in Figure 13-18.

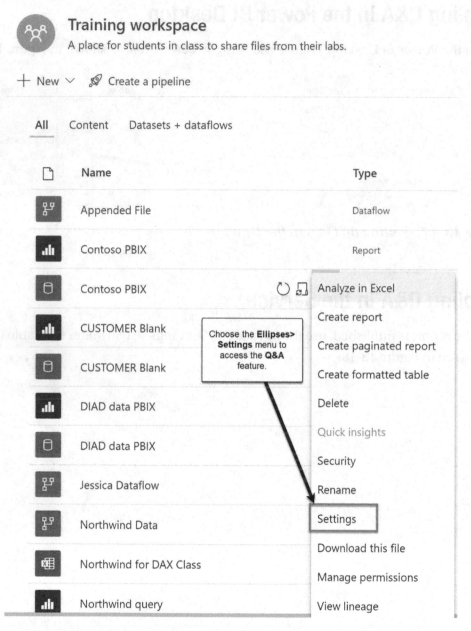

Figure 13-18. *Accessing the Settings menu for a dataset*

As you can see in Figure 13-19, in the Settings sub-menu, you will find an entry for Q&A.

Figure 13-19. Making sure Q&A is turned on for the dataset

Now that Q&A is enabled, you can take advantage of it on a dashboard and on a report.

At the top of a dashboard, there will be a line where you can type in a question using natural language as shown in Figure 13-20.

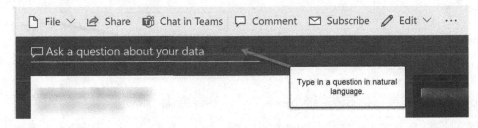

Figure 13-20. The Q&A feature at the top of a dashboard

As soon as you click into the Q&A area on the dashboard, a new window will open where you can type in your own question or choose a suggested question from those offered, shown in Figure 13-21. (You can set up suggested questions in the Power BI Desktop.)

Figure 13-21. The Q&A window

As shown in Figure 13-22, after typing in a question or choosing one of the suggested questions, Q&A will generate a visualization.

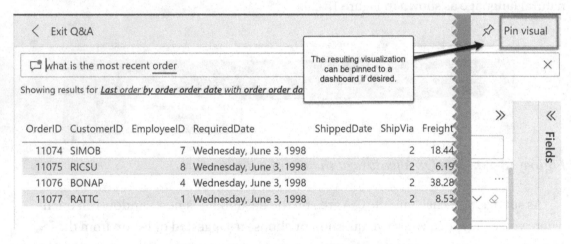

Figure 13-22. *Q&A generates a visual from a question*

If you like the visualization that Q&A produces, you can pin it to the dashboard as shown in Figure 13-23.

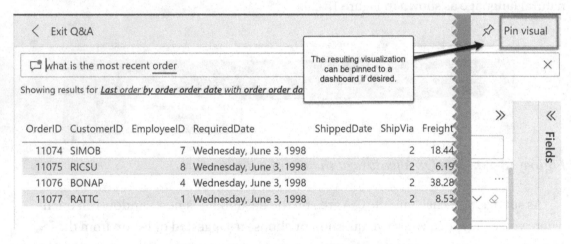

Figure 13-23. *You can pin a Q&A visual if you like it*

Refreshing a Dashboard

The data that underpins the visualizations will be updated by the refresh schedule you set up for a dataset. If the *visualizations* are changed, you will need to refresh the dashboard to reflect those changes. This is easy. Choose the refresh icon in the upper right-hand corner of the dashboard, as shown in Figure 13-24.

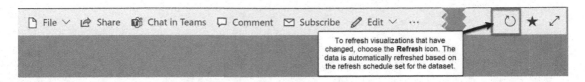

Figure 13-24. *Refreshing visualizations*

CHAPTER 14

Manage Workspaces in the Service

Your report is done, and you want to share it with colleagues and, possibly, a wider audience within your organization. It can be tempting to email your PBIX (a Power BI Desktop file), but you will quickly find this method of sharing less than optimal, to say the least. PBIX files can be very large, and many email servers will block them. Additionally, there are features of your report that will not work properly unless the report is published to the Power BI Service. So what do you do? You publish your report to a specific workspace in the Power BI Service. Not sure what that means? Read on.

Publishing Your Report

There are several steps to complete before starting the `publish` process:

1. Save your report with a unique name.

2. Log into the Power BI Service.

3. Choose the workspace where you want the report to be published.

4. Publish.

Logging Into the Power BI Service

The Power BI Service is integrated into Office 365, so you will *probably* use your Office 365 credentials to log in. (Check with your IT department.) You can log in directly from the Power BI Desktop, by going to the upper right-hand corner and hitting `Sign in`, as shown in Figure 14-1. You can also log in to the Power BI Service by using `https://app.powerbi.com`, using the credentials you used to sign up for your trial or license.

© Jessica Jolly 2023
J. Jolly, *Microsoft Power BI Data Analyst Certification Companion*, Certification Study Companion Series,
https://doi.org/10.1007/978-1-4842-9013-2_14

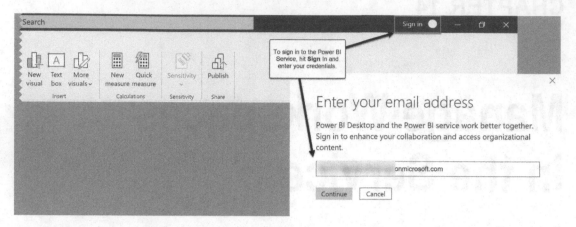

Figure 14-1. *Sign into the Power BI Service using your credentials*

When you have successfully signed in, your name will appear in the upper right-hand corner. If you need to sign out and sign in with different credentials, you can do so readily, as you can see in Figure 14-2.

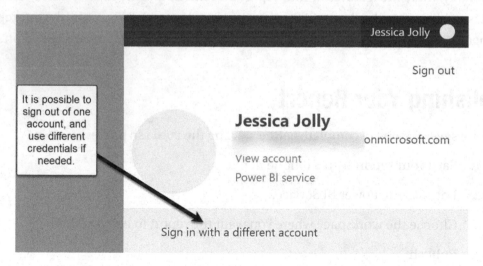

Figure 14-2. *You can sign in with different credentials if needed*

Now that you are signed in, you are ready to publish your report to a workspace in the Service.

Choosing the Workspace

After navigating to Home ➤ Publish, you will need to choose a workspace in which to publish your report. There are two types of workspaces in Power BI:

- My workspace

- Workspaces

My workspace is a personal sandbox in which you can publish a report, create dashboards, and manually refresh the data populating your report. You can use My workspace without a paid Power BI license. However, using My workspace to share reports with others in your organization is not a sustainable method for collaborating with others. Rather, the best practice is to publish to a workspace. In Figure 14-3, the name of the workspace is Training workspace. (A workspace does not have to include the word "workspace" in its name.)

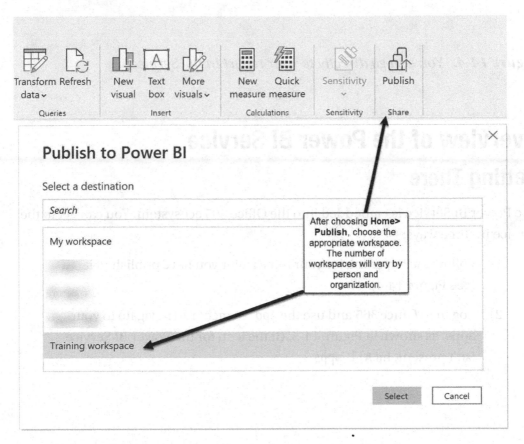

Figure 14-3. Selecting the appropriate workspace

Once the report is published, you can keep working in the Power BI Desktop or go directly to the report in the Service by following the link in the Publishing to Power BI dialogue box, as shown in Figure 14-4.

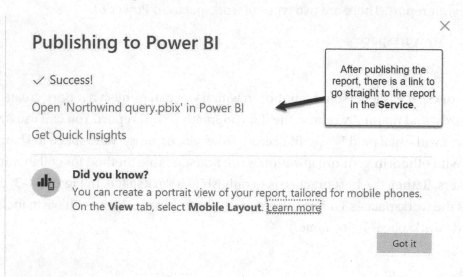

Figure 14-4. You can go directly to your report in the Service

Overview of the Power BI Service

Getting There

The Power BI Service is embedded into the Office 365 ecosystem. You can get to the Service in three ways:

1) Follow the hyperlink for your report after you have published it (see Figure 14-4).

2) Log in to Office 365 and use the App Launcher to navigate to your apps, as shown in Figure 14-5. (If the icon for the Power BI Service isn't present, hit All apps.)

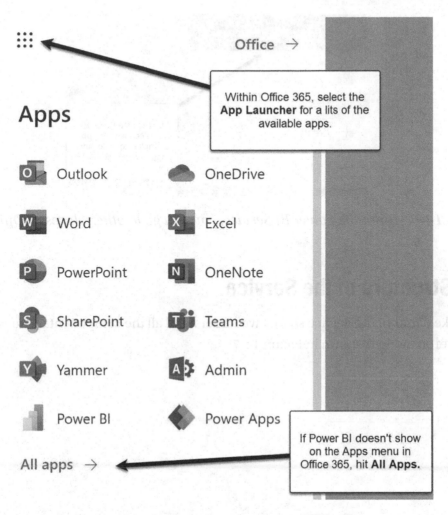

Figure 14-5. *Find Power BI in the list of your apps in Office 365*

3) Go to https://app.powerbi.com and sign in using your
   credentials.

As shown in Figure 14-6, you can tell you are there once you see the App Launcher
and Power BI in the upper left-hand corner.

347

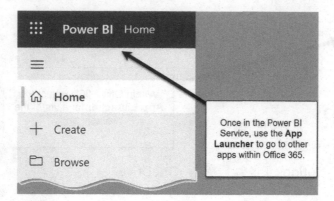

Figure 14-6. *From the Power BI Service, you can go to other places in Office 365*

The Structure of the Service

Let's take a tour of the Service so that we understand all the components. The navigation menu is shown in Figure 14-7.

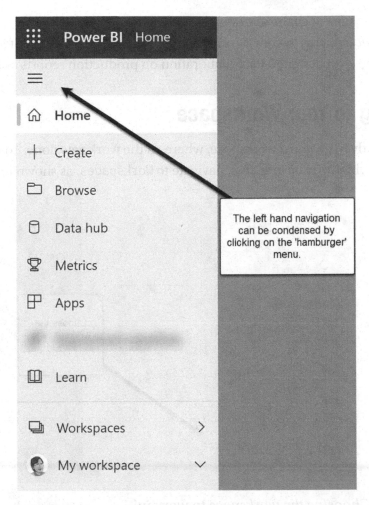

Figure 14-7. The navigation menu for the Service

Home: Frequently accessed reports and dashboards, recent files, favorited files. Everybody's Home screen will vary based on your organizational settings and your use of the Power BI Service.

Create: Initiate the creation of a report in the Service. Note that you will have to use a previously published dataset.

Browse: Browse the contents of the Service.

Data hub: Lists all the datasets published and available to you in the Service.

Apps: Where all the apps to which you have access are listed. You may have to hit Get apps to find an app initially.

Learn: One-stop shop for finding additional learning resources.

Workspaces: A list of all the workspaces to which you have access.

My workspace: Access to your My workspace, a sandbox environment ideal for experimentation. Not designed for collaboration on production reports and dashboards.

Navigating to Your Workspace

Now we are ready to go into a workspace, where all the work gets done. To find the list of workspaces to which you have access, navigate to Workspaces, as shown in Figure 14-8.

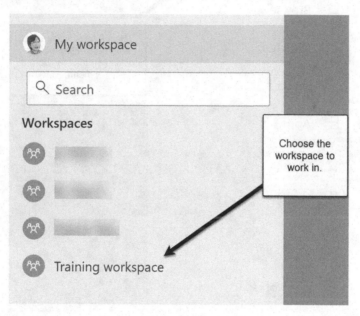

Figure 14-8. *Choosing the workspace to work in*

The Anatomy of a Workspace

Once you are in a workspace, the number of options can be daunting, so we will examine it in detail. A workspace contains five types of content, as shown in Figure 14-9:

- *Reports*: Reports can be published from the Power BI Desktop or created in the Service. If you want to create a report in the Service, you must use a dataset that has been published into the workspace or that has been shared directly with you.

- *Datasets*: A dataset accompanies every report that is published from the Power BI Desktop. It is a combination of the data model and the data.

- *Dashboards*: A dashboard is a virtual single page that can comprise visualizations from any report published in the workspace.

- *Dataflows*: A dataflow is the output of the Power Query Editor in the Service. (Yes, the Power Query Editor is available in the Service.)

- *Excel content*: Excel workbooks can also be stored in a workspace.

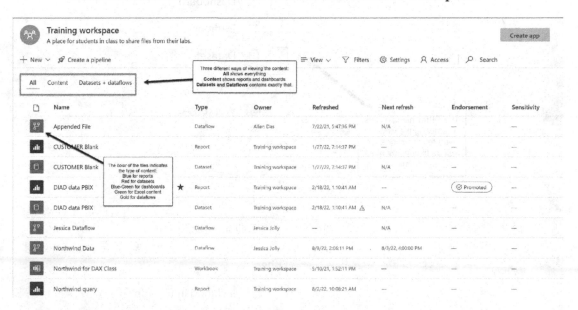

Figure 14-9. *The colors of tiles indicate the type of content*

As shown in Figure 14-10, you can also filter the view even further by using the `Filters` menu.

≡ View ∨   ▽ Filters   ⚙ Settings   👤 Access   🔍 Search

Refreshed	Next refresh
7/22/21, 5:47:36 PM	N/A
1/27/22, 7:14:37 PM	—
1/27/22, 7:14:37 PM	N/A
2/18/22, 1:10:41 AM	—
2/18/22, 1:1	
—	N/A
8/3/22, 2:06:11 PM	8/3/22, 4:00:00 P
5/10/21, 1:52:11 PM	—
8/2/22, 10:08:21 AM	—
8/2/22, 10:08:21 AM	N/A
6/23/22, 7:53:29 AM	—

Filters   ✕

𝖄 Clear all filters

Type

☐ ⦾ Dashboard

☐ 🖫 Dataflow

☐ 🗄 Dataset

☐ ᵢₗₗ Report

☐ ▦ Workbook

Owner

☐ ▓▓▓▓▓

☐ Jessica Jolly

☐ Training workspace

Other

☐ ⊞ Included in the app

☐ ⊞ Not included in the app

> The **Filter** menu allows restricting the view to even fewer options, as well as filtering by other options.

Figure 14-10. The Filters menu

Next to the Filters tab is the Access tab (Figure 14-11). This is where individuals, and/or security groups, can be added to the workspace. There are four levels of access:

- *Admin*: This is the highest level of privilege. Someone with Admin rights can delete the workspace. It is a good idea to have at least two people with Admin rights in the workspace.

- *Member*: Members can add, edit, and delete content. They can also add other people to the workspace. They can publish, edit, and unpublish the app associated with the workspace.

- *Contributor*: Contributors can add, edit, and delete content. Contributors can also be given optional rights to update the workspace's app.

- *Viewer*: Viewers can only view content. They have no other rights.

Most individuals will be added at either the Member or Contributor level.

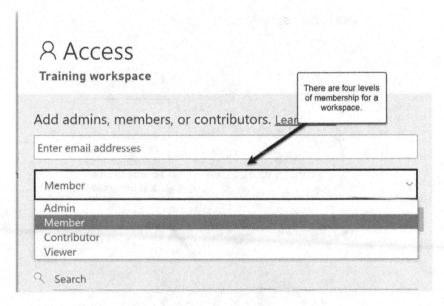

Figure 14-11. *Workspace membership levels*

Governance

Because three of the four access levels allow *the editing of any content* in the workspace, establishing governance practices is very important. Anyone with Admin, Member, or Contributor access needs to follow agreed-upon practices to ensure that unintentional changes do not occur.

Creating a Workspace

You may have the right to create a workspace if your Power BI Admin (usually someone in IT) has allowed this configuration. If you do, you will see Create a workspace, as shown in Figure 14-12.

Figure 14-12. *Creating a workspace*

Setting up a workspace is straightforward:

- *Name*: Ideally, your organization has a naming convention to avoid duplicative names. If not, name your workspace something that clearly identifies it.

- *Description*: A good description will remind participants of the purpose and audience for the workspace. An overall governance statement in the description would not be a bad idea either.

- *Contacts*: The default contacts are the workspace Admins, but it may be more appropriate to put the business owners in as contacts, particularly if IT is the only one with Admin privileges in the workspace.

- *Workspace OneDrive*: A dedicated OneDrive space can be designated for the workspace. The advantage of this is that files that support datasets can be put in OneDrive. For example, if you have Excel files that are part of a dataset, if they are stored in OneDrive associated with the workspace, the Service will be able to perform a refresh *once an hour*.

- *Template app*: A template app is one that is designed and developed for viewers external to the organization.

- *Contributors update app*: This is an optional setting.

Tip   Before creating a workspace, it is best to have a clear idea of both the purpose of the workspace and the intended audience (if any) of the reports and dashboards. This is because, as of this writing, there is only *one app allowed per workspace*. Recently, Microsoft has added the ability to define multiple audiences for a single app, which does help. Your workspace still can only have one app, but different content within the same app can be viewed by different audiences. This is a relatively new feature (as of this writing), so you may not see it implemented in your workspace yet.

Premium Capacity

There is a Premium license that allows an organization to purchase dedicated server capacity in which to house some of their workspaces. Premium capacity provides more features and functionality:

- Larger datasets (above 10 GB).

- Paginated reports.

- More frequent refreshes (48/day).

- *Viewers* do not require a Pro license.

If a workspace resides in Premium capacity, it will have a diamond icon next to it.

Creating Reports in the Service

We have discussed publishing reports from the Power BI Desktop, but that is not the only way to provide content in a workspace. You can create new reports in the Service, using datasets that have been published into the workspace. To create a new report, choose New ➤ Report in the workspace, as shown in Figure 14-13.

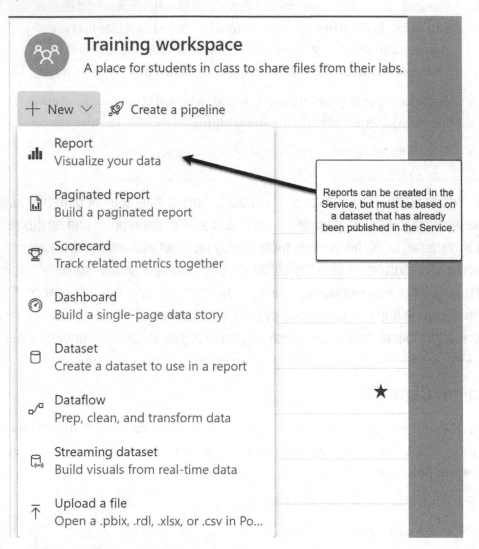

Figure 14-13. *Creating a report in the Service*

A report that is created in the Service *must* use a preexisting data model. No additional content (e.g., columns, measures) can be added to the report in the Service.

356

Adding Additional Content

You can also add additional types of content to the workspace: Excel workbooks, CSV files, and PBIX files that have been published in other workspaces (Figure 14-14).

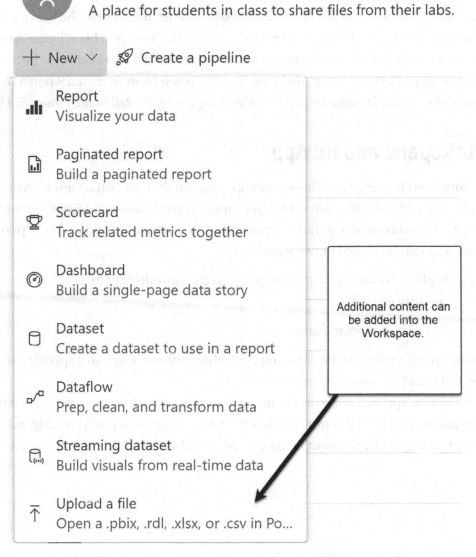

Figure 14-14. *Adding additional content to the workspace*

Updating a Report

Once a report is published, imported, or created within the Service, the question of updating will eventually arise. Not the data, of course; that is taken care of when you establish the refresh schedule. But what happens when a visual needs to be added, deleted, or changed? You *can* edit the report in the Service, but this option should be exercised with significant caution.

If a report is updated in the Power BI Desktop and republished to the Service, it will overwrite the version of the Power BI report saved in the Service. This is by design—you want to make sure that the latest version of the report is what is available in the Service. This means that if a change is made in the Service, it will be overwritten when a new version of the report is published, *unless the change is replicated in the Power BI Desktop*.

A Workspace and Its App

First things first: Power BI *does* have a mobile app, but that *isn't* what I am referring to here. The app is the distribution vehicle for reports, dashboards, and Excel content that need to be shared with others in the organization. It can then be updated on a periodic basis. An app can be shared in two ways[1]:

- With a restricted group of people (you can also share with a security group)
- To the entire organization

These are either/or conditions—you can't share the same app to a specific group of people and with the organization.

I think of an app as a magazine or newsletter. Someone decides what content is going to be included, and then the app is updated on a periodic basis (daily, weekly, monthly, quarterly). The great thing about using the app as a sharing vehicle is that app viewers

---

[1]At the time of writing, Microsoft has just released a new way of sharing apps. Because these features are not fixed in stone (yet), the PL-300 exam will probably not have questions on this new set of features. However, I strongly urge you to go to Microsoft docs and familiarize yourself with the new methods for organizing apps.

do not see the working copy of the content. If a report is published in the app (e.g., in January), viewers will only see the January version of that report until the app is updated. To designate content that should be included in the app, toggle the Include in app to Yes, as shown in Figure 14-15.

Note   Microsoft has released a newer set of features for apps, which allow for the designation of different audiences for content in the app. The screenshots below pertain to V1 Apps, not to V2 Apps.

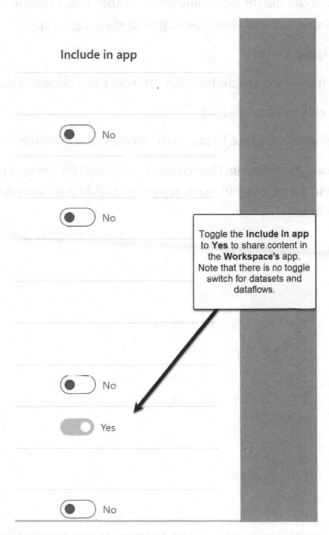

Figure 14-15. *Toggle the Include in app to Yes*

Only reports, dashboards, and Excel content can be shared in an app.

Tip   Viewing content in an app requires a Pro license unless the workspace is stored in Premium capacity (see earlier).

Creating an App

As I mentioned earlier, a workspace can only have one app, which means that it is important to think about the intended audience for the content of the workspace, *when you set up the workspace*. There are three stages for creating an app[2]:

- Setup (Figure 14-16)

  - App name (which can be different from the workspace name)

  - *Description* (mandatory)

  - *Support site*: A place to put a URL to get more information

  - *Contact information*: One contact (or group) for the app or individual contacts for each report or dashboard (this must be set individually)

---

[2] Again, I strongly encourage you to read the latest documentation provided by Microsoft, as these setup steps, and indeed the way the screens look, are changing.

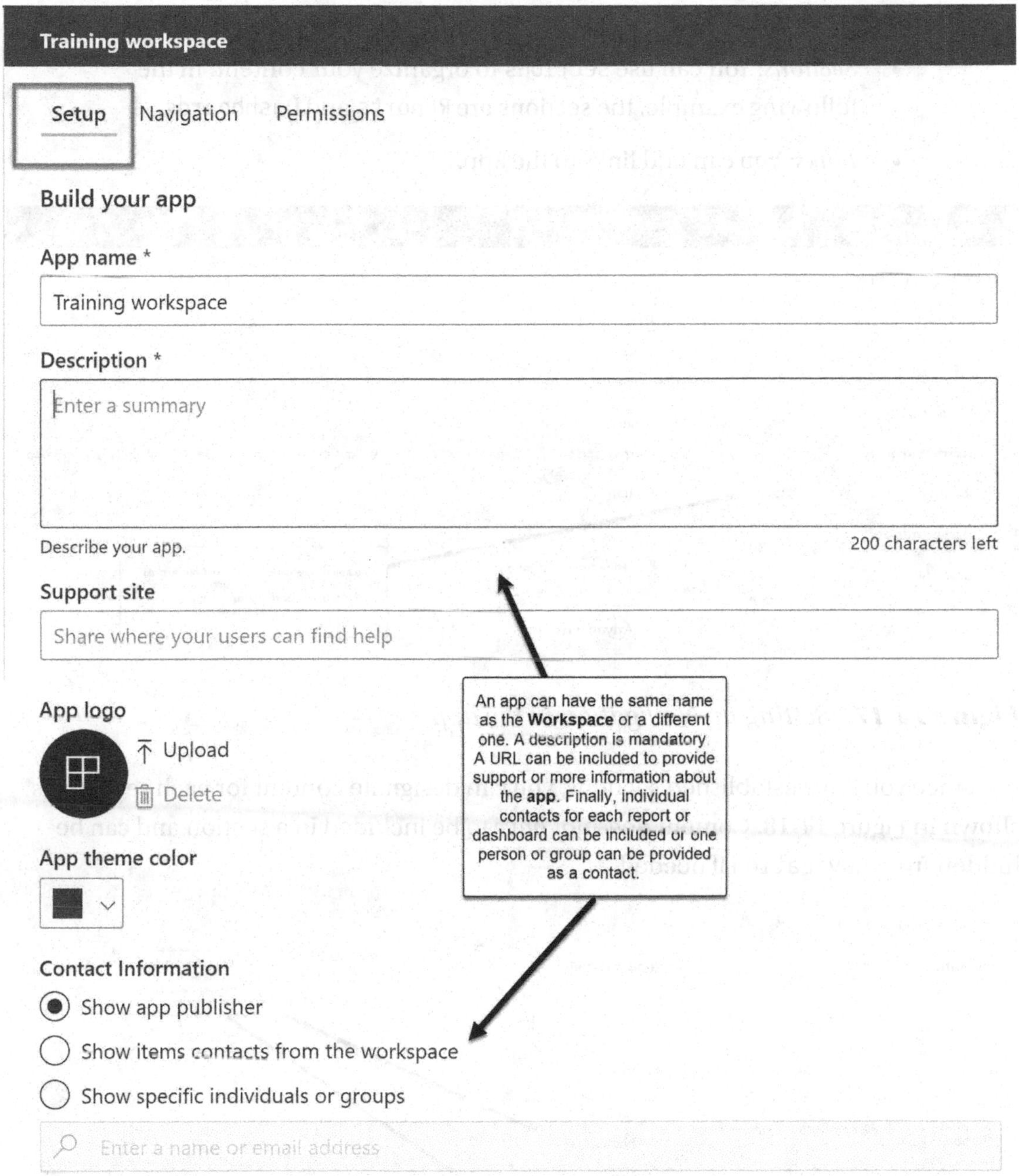

Training workspace

Setup   Navigation   Permissions

Build your app

App name *

Training workspace

Description *

Enter a summary

Describe your app.   200 characters left

Support site

Share where your users can find help

App logo

⤒ Upload

🗑 Delete

> An app can have the same name
> as the **Workspace** or a different
> one. A description is mandatory
> A URL can be included to provide
> support or more information about
> the **app**. Finally, individual
> contacts for each report or
> dashboard can be included or one
> person or group can be provided
> as a contact.

App theme color

Contact Information

⦿ Show app publisher

◯ Show items contacts from the workspace

◯ Show specific individuals or groups

🔍 Enter a name or email address

Figure 14-16. The Setup screen for an app

- Navigation (Figure 14-17)

    - *Sections*: You can use `sections` to organize your content. In the following example, the sections are `Reports` and `Dashboards`.

    - *Links*: You can add links to the app.

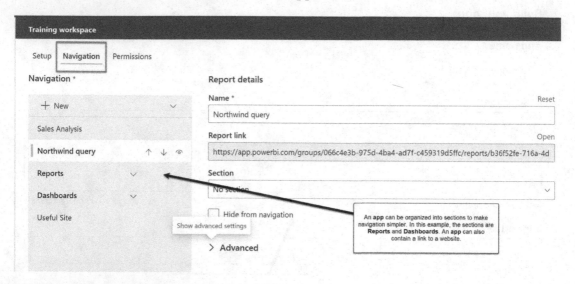

Figure 14-17. *Setting up Navigation in the app*

Once you have established sections, you can designate content for each section, as shown in Figure 14-18. Content does not *have* to be included in a section and can be hidden from `Navigation` if needed.

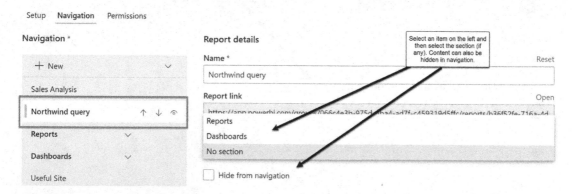

Figure 14-18. *Assigning content to a specific section*

- Permissions (Figure 14-19)

  - *Access*: This is where the audience for the app is identified. Note that it is *either* to a restricted group of people *or* the entire organization.

  - *Build permissions*: Allowing build permissions gives *anyone* who has access to the app the ability to discover the underlying dataset and build a new report off the dataset. *Think carefully before allowing build permissions in the app.*

  - *Share permissions*: Allowing share permissions gives anyone who has access to the app the ability to share the report and the underlying dataset, with accompanying build permissions. *Think carefully before allowing share permissions in the app.*

- *Pushing the app*: You can "push" the app to all authorized viewers, which saves them the step of going to Get apps and "pulling" the app.

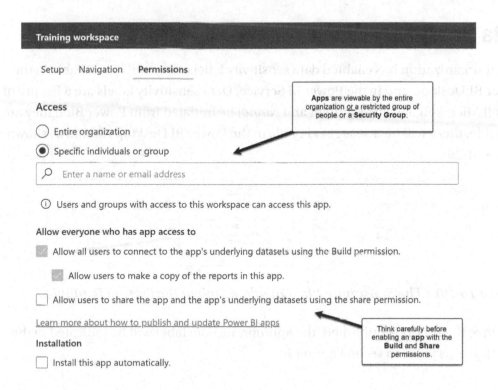

Figure 14-19. Access controls for the app

If, after creating the app, you need to change the settings, click `Update app`. The `Settings` menu will open, and you can alter settings as needed.

Deleting an App

If an app is no longer needed you can delete it, *if* you are an Admin or Member of the `workspace`.

Subscribing to a Report or Dashboard

Once a report or dashboard is published in an app, viewers can subscribe to receive notifications when the data is updated.

Other Settings in the Workspace

We have worked through a lot of settings already, but there are still more to examine.

Data Sensitivity Labels

If your organization has enabled data sensitivity labels, they will be available in the Power BI Desktop and in the Power BI Service. Data sensitivity labels are a feature of the overall Microsoft 365 environment and *cannot* be initiated from Power BI. If they are available, there will be a `Sensitivity` tile in the Power BI Desktop ribbon, as shown in Figure 14-20.

Figure 14-20.   *The Sensitivity tile is available when the feature is enabled*

Once the report is published, the appropriate data label will be indicated in the `workspace`, as you can see in Figure 14-21.

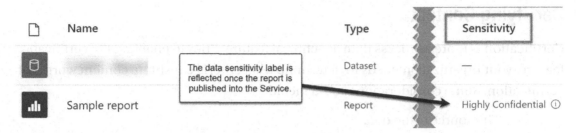

Figure 14-21. *The Sensitivity label is reflected once the report is published*

Tip   It is important to know that as a Power BI user, you do not have control over whether data sensitivity labels are available or not.

Promoting and Certifying Content

Once an organization becomes data-centric, the origin and quality of data is very important. The Power BI Service has several tools that help report and dashboard users assess the reliability of the data used.

Promoting Your Work

The first option is to promote content that you have created. Admins, Members, and Contributors can promote

- Reports

- Datasets

- Dataflows

- Apps

When you promote something, it is akin to signing your name to your work. I would suggest establishing criteria for content worthy of promotion.

Certifying Content

Certification is more a process than a technical feature. Prior to enabling the certification feature, your organization needs to determine what criteria constitute content worthy of certification. Some considerations could include

- The source of the data

- The completeness of the ETL process

- The accuracy of any measures or calculated columns

What your organization considers worthy of certification will differ from another organization's criteria. Once the criteria have been established, the policy needs to be written, and the accompanying process needs to be designed and implemented. Only after these steps are complete should the certification feature be implemented within Power BI. As a user, you don't have any control on whether the certification option is available—that is up to the Power BI Admin. Once it is, only selected individuals will be able to certify content.

PART VI

Continue Your Learning

CHAPTER 15

Where Do You Go from Here?

Congratulations! If you have made it this far in the book, my hope is that you are ready to sit the PL-300 exam. But remember what I said in the first chapter? I want you to be ready to *work* with Power BI. How can you continue your growth?

The good news is that there are a lot of resources available to you, many of them free. The bad news? There are *a lot* of resources available, but you have to discover them. In this chapter I am going to provide you with my favorite resources. Please note that

1. I am in no way affiliated with any of these resources.

2. This could never be a comprehensive list of resources. Any omissions are either unintentional or because I am unaware of them.

YouTube

Let's start with YouTube, which is where the lion's share of the resources is.

Guy in a Cube

This is the channel where I started my learning journey. Adam Saxton and Patrick LeBlanc (who both work for Microsoft) have been creating videos since 2017, so the library of videos is extensive. One of the things I love about their channel is that their content runs the gamut from beginner to complex topics. No matter the stage you are in, you will find helpful, relevant material on this channel.

© Jessica Jolly 2023
J. Jolly, *Microsoft Power BI Data Analyst Certification Companion*, Certification Study Companion Series,
https://doi.org/10.1007/978-1-4842-9013-2_15

Guy in a Cube (GIAC) provides a bonus offering: they hold a one-hour live session most Saturdays at 9:30 a.m. Eastern, which is open to anyone. Attendees are from all over the world, and, if you attend regularly, you will get to know some Power BI heavy hitters by name. Adam and Patrick take questions from participants and answer them. If you choose to join as a member, you can pre-submit questions.

Havens Consulting (Reid Havens)

I love this channel because Reid alternates between in-depth interviews with Power BI luminaries and practical videos. Reid has a design background, and many of his videos focus on enhancing both the appearance and functionality of your report. Do you have questions about buttons, bookmarks, and visualizations? Reid's channel is a must-watch. You can also support Reid's channel by becoming a member.

Ruth Curbal

Ruth's channel is wonderful because she produces videos that cover the entire Power BI spectrum. You will find videos on DAX, the Power Query Editor, and the Service. Her style is very approachable and easy to follow. She also has fun contests and events, such as the "25 Days of DAX," which she ran in December 2021. You can't go wrong following Ruth's channel.

RADACAD

Reza Rad is Power BI royalty in the Power BI community. In addition to the extensive content he produces, he also runs conferences that are affordable and well worth your time and money.

SQLBI

No list of YouTube channels (or blogs) would be complete without talking about SQLBI, run by Marco Russo and Alberto Ferrrari (colloquially known as "the Italians" in the Power BI community). There are so many good resources I don't quite know where to begin.

They have three different types of content:

- They regularly post videos about DAX functions and concepts. Some of these videos are appropriate for beginners, and some are much more advanced. Every video is accompanied by a blog post on SQLBI.com.

- They have an *Unplugged* series. In these videos they tackle a topic or challenge, but they do not edit the resulting video. I love these videos because you can follow their reasoning as they work on solving the problem. Many times, watching them solve a problem has enlightened me more than seeing the result.

- Finally, they just launched a *Whiteboard* series, which they are basing on the demonstrations they perform in class. I have attended their live DAX class and can attest to the value of seeing a concept explained using diagramming on a whiteboard.

Chris Wagner

Chris Wagner's YouTube channel is my go-to when I want to tackle some more technical concepts. He does a great job of explaining difficult concepts clearly. He has a wealth of knowledge and experience in implementing, maintaining, and governing Power BI within a large enterprise. Not to mention he has a great sense of fun!

Two Alex

For a while, Alex Powers and Alex Dupler ran a Saturday morning live stream right after Guy in a Cube. I loved this channel because they would go deep into some technical concepts. While there aren't a lot of videos on this channel, every one of them is worth watching.

Explicit Measures

Mike Carlo, Tommy Puglia, and Seth Bauer host a twice-weekly podcast called "Explicit Measures." I love this podcast because they cover real-world topics in a very approachable way. I can't recommend them enough!

Blogs

There are so many good blogs out there it is very hard to confine myself to just a few.

SQLBI

As I mentioned earlier, Marco Russo and Alberto Ferrari post articles that accompany the videos they post on YouTube. I am someone who learns by reading, so having an article to read really helps me solidify a concept. I often will watch the YouTube video, then read the article, and then rewatch the video.

I would mislead you if I said that their posts are for beginners, but it is never too early to expose yourself to DAX concepts. You will be amazed by how much you retain. And, over time, it all begins to "click."

Chris Webb

Chris' blog focuses on the Power Query Editor. I love it because he often delves into complex topics that I don't even know how to find through a search. Often his topics are above my head, but that gives me the motivation to dig deeper and learn more.

Ben Gribaudo

Are the Power Query Editor and the M language "black boxes" to you? I just took a class with Ben (see "Paid Training" in the following) because I had lots of questions about both. The class was very enlightening. But you can benefit from Ben's knowledge at no cost by reading his blog. He has a *Power Query Editor Primer* series that is a great place to start. He also regularly blogs about much more complex topics. Even if some of them are too complex for me, they inspire me to dig deeper.

Paul Turley

Paul Turley wrote one of the best blog series I have ever read: *Doing Power BI the Right Way*. If you don't explore any of the other blogs I mention, be sure to read this series. I recently met up with Paul, and, at the time of this writing, he is actively thinking about new topics for his blog page—I can't wait for his new content to drop.

Books

Sometimes it seems to me that no one uses books for learning anymore, but I love them. (Hopefully this book will be the exception to this trend!) There are several books that I rely on heavily.

The Definitive Guide to DAX by Marco Russo and Alberto Ferrari

This book is a "must" for anyone who wants to be good at DAX. I don't know a Power BI rockstar who doesn't own this book.

Collect, Combine, and Transform Data Using Power Query in Excel and Power BI by Gil Raviv

This is the book I used to "ramp up" my knowledge of the Power Query Editor. It covers the basics and then moves to crucial concepts, such as future-proofing queries. You may not be ready to put everything in this book into practice, but being aware of the concepts he explores is critical.

Master Your Data with Power Query in Excel and Power BI by Ken Puls and Miguel Escobar

This is a great companion text to Gil Raviv's book. It focuses on mechanics and techniques and is an invaluable reference.

Super Charge Power BI by Matt Allington

If you are just starting to learn DAX, Matt Allington's book is a perfect place to start. He doesn't assume any prior knowledge and includes lots of exercises.

Star Schema by Chris Adamson

Eventually, you will want to know more about data modeling generally and star schemas specifically. This is a great book to increase your understanding of what a star schema is and how to build a good one.

Paid Training

Once you are beyond the basics, there are several paid training courses that I can highly recommend.

Mastering DAX with Marco Russo and Alberto Ferrari

This is a three-day in person class that is excellent. Be warned—it isn't for beginners.

Power Query Editor and M with Ben Gribaudo

This is a 12-hour class split over three days. Take this class when you want to understand why and how the Power Query Editor does what it does.

Video Training Courses by SQLBI

Alberto Ferrari and Marco Russo have produced numerous video courses on a variety of subjects. The amount of content they pack into each course is incredible. You have several years to make your way through the content (and you will need that time!), and you can re-up your access when the initial period expires.

User Groups

The pandemic was terrible on many levels. One of the few benefits to come from it is the move to online meetings by most user groups. You can now attend a user group anywhere in the world from the comfort of your chair. Even better, most user groups record their events and make them accessible on YouTube. Some of my favorites are

- Stuttgart

- Romania

- London

- Azerbaijan/Baku

But this is by no means an inclusive list. You should explore and find your favorites.

Conferences

At the time I am writing this, conferences are back. There are a lot of different options, but they vary from year to year. Twitter is a great place to hear about them. The biggest one, "Ignite" hosted by Microsoft, has not yet returned in person but is available online. Most conferences have a virtual option now.

I love going to conferences because I get to meet Power BI folks I only talked to virtually. I also love sessions that are a stretch for me. I always make sure that I attend at least two to three of these sessions.

Tip Don't be afraid to introduce yourself to the speaker. Most of us love to meet new people, and we welcome your questions. We want to see others succeed—we wouldn't be spending our time and money speaking if we didn't!

Social Media
Twitter

By far and away, Twitter is the platform preferred by Power BI folks. Do you have a question? Do you have an insight or an opinion? Twitter is the place to post. Some good hashtags to follow are #PowerBI, #PowerQueryEditor, and #PowerBIHelp.

Reddit

There is an active Power BI subreddit where you can post questions and get help. There are some heavy hitters in that group.

LinkedIn

It is a good idea to expand your network with Power BI professionals on LinkedIn. You can start by connecting with me at `www.linkedin.com/in/jessicabjolly/`. The Power BI community is welcoming and generous. As you grow your career, you will find plenty of people who want to help you succeed.

External Tools

Once you have gained a modicum of skills in Power BI, you will want to explore some of the external tools that will make your job easier. I have listed a few of these tools in the following, but you can find a complete list at `www.sqlbi.com/tools/`. Once you have downloaded the program, the next time you open the Power BI Desktop, a new tab will appear called `External Tools`.

DAX Studio

DAX Studio enables you to write and test your DAX. You can connect it directly to your model and then evaluate different permutations of particular DAX expressions. In several places in this book, I mentioned that there are always ways to improve your DAX performance. DAX Studio helps you do this because you can measure how long a DAX expression takes to evaluate and analyze what components are taking the longest. Once you have fine-tuned the expression, you can then copy it back into the Power BI Desktop. DAX Studio is free, which is incredible given the value it adds to the development experience. And there is a bonus: Marco and Alberto have posted a free video sequence explaining how to use DAX Studio on their You Tube channel and on their website.

Bravo

Bravo is a new tool (March of 2022) that SQLBI has introduced. It can analyze your model, format your DAX, and create a date table for you. I have not had a chance to play with it, but any tool created by SQLBI is well worth exploring.

Tabular Editor

Building a data model is a nontrivial exercise. While you can do this in the Power BI Desktop, most developers are now using Tabular Editor, a tool developed by Daniel Otykier. There are two versions of Tabular Editor: the community version, which is free, and the paid version, which is approximately 350 USD/year. Please be sure to check the website (https://tabulareditor.com/) for exact pricing.

Both versions allow you to perform modeling steps more conveniently than in the Power BI Desktop. Additionally, Tabular Editor supports some features that the Power BI Desktop does not. With a free community version available, you can afford to check it out!

Other Tools

The SQLBI website maintains a comprehensive list of all the external tools available for Power BI developers (www.sqlbi.com/tools/). Be sure to check out the list as there are many other cool tools to investigate.

Conclusion

I have had a lot of fun writing this book. It has cemented some of my knowledge of topics that were a little "fuzzy," and it has caused me to think deeply about what someone *needs* to know to get started in Power BI. I wanted to give you an in-depth guide to the topics you will need to study for the PL-300, but I also wanted to get you started on the road to becoming a Power BI "ninja." I hope that I have accomplished both goals. Most importantly, I hope that this book helps you learn to love Power BI as much as I do!

Index

A

Acceptable forms of ID, 5
Access levels, 353
Advanced Editor, 53, 92–94
AdventureWorks DW, 18
AI visualization
    decomposition tree
        visualization, 301–304
    key influencer visualization, 299–301
Analysis Services source, 34
Analytics features, 275
Analytics pane, 275–277, 280
Analyze feature, 277–279
App creation
    access controls, 363
    stages
        designate content, 362
        navigation, 362
        permissions, 363
        setup, 360, 361
Append Queries
    multiple queries into new one, 78
    new query, 77, 78
Apps, 16, 17, 346, 349, 363, 365
Automated refresh, 307, 310

B

BAK file, 18, 19
Bidirectional relationship, 110–112, 123
Bins, 290–295

Blogs

Blogs
    Ben Gribaudo, 372
    Chris Webb, 372
    Paul Turley, 372
    SQLBI, 372
Bookmarks
    bookmark navigator button, 253
    Bookmarks pane, 250
    and buttons, 261–263
    Default View bookmark, 252
    elements
        Group feature, 258, 259
        invisible, 257
        visible, 257, 258
    ellipsis menu, 254
    group
        feature, 258
        not visible, 260
        renaming, 259
    PowerPoint, 258, 260
    renaming, 251
    report user, 252
    selection/capture, 250, 251
    Selection pane, 256, 257, 260
    settings
        data, 255
        default view, 255
        display, 255, 256
        nuances, 255
        test page, 256
    updation, 252

379

J. Jolly, *Microsoft Power BI Data Analyst Certification Companion*, Certification Study Companion Series,
https://doi.org/10.1007/978-1-4842-9013-2

D

Q

R

Printed in the United States
by Baker & Taylor Publisher Services

Printed in the United States
by Baker & Taylor Publisher Services